ANGEL IN BLACK

ANGEL IN BLACK

REMEMBERING DALE EARNHARDT SR.

TOM GILLISPIE

CUMBERLAND HOUSE
AN IMPRINT OF SOURCEBOOKS, INC.®

ANGEL IN BLACK
PUBLISHED BY CUMBERLAND HOUSE PUBLISHING, AN IMPRINT OF SOURCEBOOKS, INC.
P.O. Box 4410
Naperville, IL 60567-4410

Cover design: Gore Studio Inc.
Text design: John Mitchell

Library of Congress Cataloging-in-Publication Data

Gillispie, Tom.
  Angel in black : Remembering Dale Earnhardt Sr./ Tom Gillispie.
    p. cm.
  Includes bibliographical references and index.
  1. Earnhardt, Dale, 1951-2001. 2. Automobile drivers—United States—Biography.
I. Title.
  GV1032.E18G55 2007
  796.72092—dc22
  [B]

                                                              2007046057

Printed in the United States of America

RRD 10 9 8 7 6 5 4

*To the folks at Dale Earnhardt Inc.
and Richard Childress Racing,
and to all the Intimidator's friends,
coworkers, loved ones, and fans*

CONTENTS

ACKNOWLEDGMENTS

For Cumberland House's *I Remember Dale Earnhardt*, I waited until the second paragraph of acknowledgments to mention my wife, Holly. She didn't complain, but I won't make that mistake twice. Without her encouragement and suggestions, I couldn't have done the book in 2001. Without her love and patience, I probably wouldn't be here to do *Angel in Black: Remembering Dale Earnhardt Sr.*

Thanks go out to Editor John Mitchell and Publisher Ron Pitkin and his Cumberland House pit crew. They're all gems; Ron saw the wisdom of updating *I Remember Dale Earnhardt* into a better book; John has offered lots of advice and encouragement; and they've both kept me on track.

Again, I'd like to thank my friend Ed Campbell—I wouldn't have had this ride without him. He took the original call from Cumberland House in 2001 and turned the wheel over to me.

Thank you to all the people who took the time to talk to me, to busy folks such as Jim Hunter, Ken Schrader, Eddie Gossage, Ron Hornaday, Max Helton, Ken Squier, and others who were willing to play phone tag. Thanks to television personality Larry

McReynolds and former drivers David Pearson, Jerry Nadeau, Hut Stricklin, Dick Trickle, and Randy LaJoie for calling me back, and to Dave Marcis for being helpful and patient. Another former driver, Geoff Bodine, even called me back from Hawaii, where he was having a business/pleasure trip. And thanks, again, to a weary Jerry Punch, who was groggy from nearly a month at Indy in 2001.

And thanks to those trusting folks who didn't know me but dropped everything for a few minutes to talk about Dale Earnhardt. Gary Hargett, Earnhardt's car owner in Late Model Sportsman, is one of those folks. So are Dr. Joe Mattioli of Pocono Raceway, Judy Root of the Cabarrus County (North Carolina) Convention & Visitors Bureau, and Kannapolis Mayor Bob Misenheimer.

You can't race a book into production without a little networking. Humpy Wheeler, president of Lowe's Motor Speedway, led me to car owner Johnny Ray. Jim Freeman, former director of the International Motorsports Hall of Fame, suggested journalist Mike Bolton. Larry Cothren, the editor of *Stock Car Racing* magazine, led me to Gary Hargett. A security guard at Lowe's Motor Speedway gave me a brochure for the Dale Trail. That led me to Judy Root and others. Eddie Gossage of Texas Motor Speedway pointed me to Jay "the Skoal Troll" Wells. And by contacting Terri Hill of the Cabarrus Regional Chamber of Commerce in 2001, I wound up talking to Tom Dayvault and Jeff Austin, and, through them, to Doug Stackert and Steve Ellsworth.

Special thanks go to Jim Freeman and Betty Carlan of the International Motorsports Hall of Fame for use of their photos for the original book and to Judy Root for photos of the Dale Trail. And many thanks to the public relations departments at the Atlanta, Texas, Las Vegas, and Darlington tracks.

To those I interviewed in 2001 and '07, thank you for your stories, your emotion, your patience, and your help. Most of you did it for Earnhardt, and some of you did it for me. You've all earned the Goody's Headache Award.

See y'all at the races.

PREFACE

It wasn't easy writing and promoting *I Remember Dale Earnhardt* in 2001.

First, there were licensing concerns, and drivers and car owners wouldn't be quoted out of deference to Teresa Earnhardt, Dale's widow. She wasn't getting a portion of the proceeds from the book, so I got one "no" after another. In fact, I've had similar problems this year, too, in the update of the book and its transformation into *Angel in Black: Remembering Dale Earnhardt Sr.* Most race teams have not responded, and most that did respond declined interviews. Cup driver Ken Schrader and Craftsman Truck Series racer Ron Hornaday are the only current drivers who were willing to talk to me.

Second, so much came out about Dale in 2001. There were lots of books, magazines, and other merchandise about Earnhardt out there. I even contributed to the Dale rush, as I wrote a story entitled "The Next Dale Earnhardt" for a special magazine called *The Earnhardts. I Remember Dale Earnhardt* was just a snowflake in a blizzard of Dale memorabilia, and it got lost.

To compound the problem, the timing of the release was horrendous—it came out September 14, 2001, three days after 9/11. Earnhardt was still a hot topic, but he took a definite backseat to the World Trade Center, the Pentagon, terrorism, Osama bin Laden, and the stories of the valiant firefighters and policemen of New York City. The release date had been set in stone for several months, and there was nothing we could do.

The book drew a few complaints about the format, which features short lead-ins before quotes. Some people said it was easier to do a book of quotes. Personally, I find it easier just to write in the fashion that most newspaper and magazine articles are written. But I love this format, too. A reader can pick up the book, look anywhere, and find a nugget, a necklace, or a gold mine.

Now it's six years later, and there have been at least two movies about Earnhardt—the TV movie *3* in 2004 and the theatrical release *Dale* in early 2007. Earnhardt is still one of the best-selling drivers, even in death. And lots of fans say that racing is no longer fun without No. 3 out there.

Yes, physically, Earnhardt's gone, but in many important ways, he's right here. And that's why we're updating the book—he deserves it.

—————

I always said that Dale Earnhardt was determined to win races and championships, but he wasn't a shark circling the track in search of victims. He wasn't some bully who enjoyed putting guys into the wall. He wasn't even some jerk who liked to hurt sportswriters' feelings. He was just a guy from Kannapolis, North Carolina, who was determined to be one of the greatest drivers in the world—ever. True, he had his share of victims; yes, he put lots of guys into the wall (we're thinking of you, Terry Labonte); and, yes, he occasionally hurt sportswriters' feelings. Well, okay, more than occasionally. I was a victim, too.

Years ago, when I was a rookie writer on the circuit, it was a couple of hours before qualifying at Rockingham and I was trying to talk to Dale. Seeing him standing in the back of the team's transport truck, I went up and asked if I could interview him. Even though I was a newcomer as a full-time racing writer, I had already sold some magazine stories, and this, I thought, would be my best piece to date, by far. First, Dale looked at me with this silly smile that, I suppose, was meant for fans and unsuspecting writers. Apparently I didn't respond properly, so he leaned back again, crossed his arms, looked unconcerned and said, "I can't think about that right now."

I guess I stood there a little too long, because he looked a little worried. He reached down, put his hand on my shoulder, and said, "I got to think about qualifying. We'll talk about your story later." (I later learned that some drivers will talk to you anytime; others won't talk before qualifying.)

Dale didn't make first-round qualifying that day, and neither did fellow racing star Mark Martin. The next day they made a five-dollar bet on who would "win" second-round qualifying. Dale put up some tremendous speed that day, and he came into the infield media center to check on Mark.

Dale looked at me with this little-boy, "I-wish-I-hadn't-done-it" look. I spoke to him, he nodded, and he went back to helping the scorekeeping women check speeds.

It turns out that Earnhardt won the bet—his speed might have won first-round qualifying the previous day—and I didn't get to talk to him about my story. At least not that day.

Later that weekend, a couple of us reporters were waiting to talk with Earnhardt a minute. He wasn't too patient with autographs, but he had no time for reporters, at least that day. To our amazement, he said, "Gotta go," and he dove into a sea of fans. He must have spent a half-hour signing autographs—just to get away from us.

The next spring we were at Talladega, and the race was rained out on Sunday. On Monday morning, Dale was in the infield media center talking to a friend of mine, long-time journalist Bob Myers, about Earnhardt's plane and pilot. I eased over to my bag, pulled out a tape recorder and quietly taped the interview.

Afterward, Earnhardt stayed with us. The media center TV wasn't working, so Dale climbed up there and fixed it for us. Then when Chevrolet publicist Ray Cooper was playing Hangman on his computer, Dale joined us. He wasn't good at it, but he was competitive. Big surprise there.

Later, we had an impromptu press conference. Dale was asked about his goals, and I perked up. At Rockingham I had wanted to ask him about his dreams for a magazine story on drivers' dreams I was doing. I still could sell that story, I thought, and this could be the centerpiece for it. When a five-second lull came in the questions and answers, I asked him if he felt that, since he wasn't likely to catch Richard Petty's 200 career victories, would he shoot for Richard's seven championships?

Dale, who didn't feel comfortable with unknown reporters, didn't look up at me from his seated position. He said that, yes, he thought 200 wins were out of his reach, and, yes, he wanted to add three more championships and catch his hero. Then he talked a little more about his dreams, particularly about car ownership. That surprised us, because we couldn't see Dale as a car owner. But this was 1991, and what did we know?

Anyway, there had been some question that month about Dale's age. Was he thirty-nine or forty? Dale said thirty-nine; his mother, Martha, said forty. Without saying another word, Earnhardt stood up and looked me in the eye. "Last week at Martinsville, I didn't know that it was my fiftieth win, but I knowed that it was my fortieth birthday. I just wasn't saying." He smiled that wicked Earnhardt smile and clapped me on the shoulder. Apparently, I was now a member of the fraternity. He'd actually answered my questions, and he'd given me the quotes I had been pursuing at the Rock. (And, yes, it was the best magazine story I'd written up to that time, by far.)

Just then, Russell Branham, chief publicist at Darlington Raceway, strolled in. Russell had done some PR work for David Pearson in the past. Earnhardt knew Russell was a big Pearson fan, and Dale loved to pick on him. So Earnhardt lit into Branham as we watched, and Russell gave back as good as he got. In fact, he bet Dale a hundred bucks that he'd never win 105 races, Pearson's total. Earnhardt took the bet, as I recall, but, ultimately, he came up twenty-nine victories short. And Russell never got the hundred bucks.

In those kinds of situations, a driver becomes the Big Man on Campus (BMOC) to reporters. We'd give Dale our attention, and he'd happily regale us with stories. I guess, in this case, he was BMOT (Big Man on Track). One on one, he probably thought he was wasting his time. He loved being in a group, and we usually enjoyed it, too.

The next time I saw Earnhardt up close—other than at press conferences—was on the 1992 Cup Media Tour in Charlotte. We ran into each other in the doorway to the conference room in the hotel. We shook hands and exchanged pleasantries. Dale seemed to be comfortable with me now, much more comfortable than I was with him.

Later that year I was going through the Cup garage at Charlotte Motor Speedway on my way to the Busch Grand National garage. Earnhardt stepped out of his trailer, saw me, and took an angle to intercept me. We walked together to the Busch garage, and he clapped me on the arm as we parted. It was typical Earnhardt—totally unpredictable.

Earnhardt had a few reporters—like Tom Higgins and Bob Myers—that he'd talk to, but even they got the cold shoulder on occasion. At least one reporter I know simply hated Earnhardt and had nothing good to say about him. One year at Charlotte, it was announced that Earnhardt had to go to the garage with car problems, and a cheer arose in the press box. When they announced that Earnhardt had just come back, eighty-five laps down, they cheered again.

Over the ensuing years, we saw each other occasionally. Often, we'd just wave or nod. Sometimes, I'd ask a quick question and get a quicker answer. Other times, he'd spend some time just to chat with a fellow human being. He might squeeze my arm, smile wide, and walk on. Often, when we'd be in a news conference and he'd see me, he'd smile and nod, or he'd point. Other times, he'd just ignore me. You never knew with Dale.

For most of us, Earnhardt wasn't easy to interview. A female reporter once told me that Dale was solicitous of her and other reporters (I assume they were female, too). That's true, because I've seen that gallantry, but he'd sometimes make a sharp remark to most of us male reporters, even ones he liked, and walk away. It just depended on his mood.

The movie 3 bothered me for this reason. You never saw Earnhardt's surliness; he came off as a normal guy, and he wasn't. One day, I'd see Earnhardt at a press conference, and he'd wave at me; the next day, he might walk by with no acknowledgment at all.

I didn't hold Earnhardt's moodiness against him, though. Bill Elliott was at least as tough to interview, and I can safely say that Bill and I have never shared as many relaxed moments as Earnhardt and I did. Nobody wanted to do a Dale Earnhardt or a Bill Elliott story for a track program, because both drivers were tough to pin down.

Once, I was attending an International Race of Champions luncheon at a resort in Daytona Beach. I reached the double doors entering the building and looked back to see a bunch of women following. As I gentlemanly opened one door, I looked over and there was Dale, grasping the other door in both hands. He looked at me and winked. He was hunched over and had this big grin and was acting like he was pulling something on the grown-ups. Because of Earnhardt's antics, we looked like a couple of fortyish kids acting like adults.

Because of Earnhardt's personality and his six championships from 1986 to 1994, I thought of him often. And people reminded me of him often. When I worked at daily newspapers, I often was working on the sports copy desk when I wasn't at a race. Invariably, someone would call and say, "Could you tell me who's on the pole and how Earnhardt did?" Or they'd want to know the top five and how Earnhardt did.

A couple of times they asked how Earnhardt did, and I told them he was on the pole. That stunned them, since Dale won only twenty-two Cup poles (versus seventy-six victories) in 676 starts. "You mean . . . he's starting first?" they'd say with a stutter. "Oh, my." I related this to one of the people I interviewed for this book, Benny Parsons. He said, "Nobody else mattered to them."

I never became buddies with Dale. I never went fishing or hunting with him; I never rode in his plane or his truck; I didn't have his private number; and he never called me back when I, in my eternal optimism, called him. He wouldn't have picked me to write this book. In a perverse way, I was gratified as I did interviews for this book to learn that several of the older "in" reporters had the same trouble I'd had trying to connect with Earnhardt. Even my friend Bob Myers.

Still, we made a connection, tenuous as it was.

One year at Daytona, I was sitting at the end of a table nearest the door entering the Benny Kahn infield press room. Dale had just won an IROC race—I don't know if it was the one involving the double doors—but I was typing furiously on my computer.

I felt strong hands on my shoulders, so I looked straight back and there he was. I said, "Whoa!" His mustache got even wider, and he squeezed my shoulders again. He went down the line of reporters, playfully rotating fists and gently tapping each person on the shoulder. Dale was happy in the media center after winning a race, any race, and for once he was happy to see us.

One final Earnhardt story: In the late 1990s, I was walking out of a Cup garage back to the press room when I saw Dale being besieged by fans. He was frantically (but carefully) scanning the crowd for a familiar face, a savior, and he saw me and perked up. He stepped forward and stopped me in my tracks. We shook hands and pretended to chat.

The weird thing is that the fans seemed to enjoy the exchange because they were seeing Earnhardt with someone he knew (at least vaguely, in my case).

"This goes way above and beyond, you know. You realize that you owe me one?" I said nonchalantly, making it sound more like a statement than a question. We were still shaking hands, and Dale still had that Earnhardt smirk on his face.

"You're right," he said, squeezing my hand one final time, unclasping hands, smiling again, squeezing my shoulder and walking away from the teeming masses. And me.

As usual, he got away scot-free. I couldn't see it, but I imagine he was still smirking.

This book is a compilation of my memories and the memories of people I've interviewed, plus quotes from various sources. Some are from books or magazines. Others are from what they call pit notes—car manufacturers regularly send out quotes before, during, and after races. And various public relations firms provided quotes from their drivers. Of course, I got some of the quotes myself. In fact, I got all of the new quotes.

This book brings back happy and sad memories for me. I was friendly with Davey Allison—I had written a comic-book script about Davey; I had his home number, and we'd stop and chat (and mostly laugh) when we saw each other. Then he died in 1993. The following January, I called Neil Bonnett for a story, and we talked (and joked and laughed) for hours on the phone. I had known Neil before the 1990 wreck at Darlington that took his memory, and now we were getting to know each other again.

Before we hung up, Neil asked me when I'd get to Daytona. I said Tuesday. "When you get here," he said, "come to the 51 trailer. We'll get some friends and go to dinner." I was there on Tuesday, but Neil, Dale Earnhardt's best buddy and my budding friend, had died the preceding Friday in a crash in turn four at Daytona.

In *I Remember Dale Earnhardt*, you saw a Dale Earnhardt who was a little bit wild, who favored the outdoors, who loved his family and friends, who was loyal to his hometown, who was ruthless on the racetrack, and who was compassionate off it. And in *Angel in Black: Remembering Dale Earnhardt Sr.*, you'll hear frank quotes from Geoff Bodine, Larry McReynolds, Gary Hargett (Earnhardt's Late Model Sportsman car owner), Morgan Shepherd, Hut Stricklin, and others.

I knew Earnhardt a little bit and saw him often from 1990 to 1994, during which he won four titles in five years, and I still felt far removed from him. But after talking to Hargett, Bodine, McReynolds, Dick Trickle, Jay Wells, and others, I know him much better, and I think about him constantly. And, as with Davey and Neil, I miss him.

—*Tom Gillispie*
September 2007

ANGEL IN BLACK

I

THE LEGEND

"Dale Earnhardt was as good as anyone who sat in a race car."

— BUDDY BAKER

S tock-car fans learn the Dale Earnhardt legend early. Ralph Dale Earnhardt grew up in the textile mill town of Kannapolis, North Carolina, worshiping his father, Ralph Earnhardt.

Ralph—nicknamed "Ironheart" for his courage—was good enough that he would be inducted into various halls of fame. But Ralph was no Lee Petty or Ned Jarrett. While he won thirty-two Sportsman races and the 1956 national championship, he didn't win any Grand National (later called Winston Cup) races or championships.

But Ralph lived and breathed racin'. And so did Dale. The youngster followed his dad everywhere, and he dreamed of beating the best. Oh, sure, Dale played stick-and-ball sports, as most of us did. But he had little interest in them. He went to school . . . but he quit in the ninth grade in 1967.

"I wanted to race; that's all I ever wanted to do," Earnhardt said many times. "I didn't care about work or school or anything; all I wanted to do was to work on race cars and then drive race cars. It was always my dream, and I was just fortunate enough to be able to live out that dream."

Soon after quitting middle school, Earnhardt became a racer. He was rough and hard-headed, and he eventually earned the nickname "Ironhead," which was probably a play on "Ironheart." Being unpolished and uneducated probably hurt him, but he was intelligent. And many car owners saw a diamond in the rough—they just weren't too interested in polishing that jewel.

Along the way, Dale lost his mentor. Ralph died of a heart attack at age forty-five . . . naturally, he was working on a race car. The same weekend that Ralph was inducted into the National Motorsports Press Association's Hall of Fame in Darlington, South Carolina, in 1989, Dale won the Southern 500 at Darlington Raceway.

Then in the late 1990s, Ralph was inducted into the International Motorsports Hall of Fame next to Talladega Superspeedway, the site of many of Dale's greatest triumphs.

"This has been a very special time for me and for our family," Earnhardt said at the time. "I wish he could have been here to see all of this."

But Ralph wasn't there when Dale hit the big time at age twenty-nine. He didn't see Dale become the only man to be the Cup Rookie of the Year and the series champion in back-to-back seasons ('79 and '80). He didn't see Dale struggle in the early eighties, then hook up with car owner Richard Childress and win six more championships ('86, '87, '90, '91, '93, '94).

Ralph wasn't there to guide Dale through his rough years or to watch Dale eventually replace him as "Earnhardt."

In the movie *Days of Thunder*, Tom Cruise's character, Cole Trickle, and another racer named Rowdy Burns wrecked a couple of rental cars while they were feudin', tearin' up sheet metal, and bustin' glass on the streets of Daytona Beach, Florida. That was a rewriting of a true story in which staunch Southerner Earnhardt and devout Yankee Geoff Bodine were feuding, and NASCAR boss Bill France Jr. called them on the carpet. Bodine was driving a rental car, with Earnhardt riding shotgun, and they were riding behind a rental car carrying France. Earnhardt urged Geoff to "park" France's car, spin it out. Unlike the movie drivers, Bodine had some sense, and the France car went on, unscathed.

Rowdy Burns was a mixture of Earnhardt and Buddy Baker, one of Dale's friends and a mentor of sorts. Buddy, like Rowdy, was in a major crash that would end his career. And like Earnhardt (and Buddy), Rowdy was, well, rowdy.

With Earnhardt, there was always plenty of excitement.

There was the famed "Pass in the Grass" at Charlotte Motor Speedway in The Winston all-star race in 1987. It wasn't a real pass; Dale got off track while trying to hold off Bill Elliott. But Earnhardt got back onto solid pavement and collected one of his record three all-star race victories.

In the 1992 Winston all-star race, Earnhardt was leading on the last lap when he spun out in turn four. Kyle Petty and Davey Allison surged past, and Davey crashed as he edged Kyle at the line. Back in turn four, Earnhardt was smiling as he got out of the car; he'd enjoyed the racing. Then when he took off his helmet, Earnhardt haters and baiters dumped beer on his head.

Earnhardt struggled through nineteen years of failure in the Daytona 500, running out of gas in 1986 (when Geoff Bodine won) and busting a tire on the last lap in 1990 (giving the victory to upstart Derrike Cope).

Finally, there was Dale's 1998 Daytona 500 victory, with Earnhardt spinning his No. 3 Chevrolet in the Daytona logo, then driving down pit road to high-five a huge line of crewmen, crew chiefs, drivers, and even car owners.

Earnhardt got his first taste of the big time when he drove a Sportsman car for California businessman Rod Osterlund at Charlotte Motor Speedway in 1978. He finished second, so Osterlund had him drive his Cup car at Atlanta. Dale finished a lap down, but he'd held his own among the big boys, and Osterlund took note.

Legend has it that Osterlund was walking through the garage area at Ontario (California) Speedway when he ran into Cale Yarborough. Osterlund showed Yarborough his short list of possible drivers, and Cale chose the one at the bottom: "Earnhardt."

"Go with the young guy," Cale said.[1]

As trite as it sounds, the rest is history.

But then Dale struggled. He drove for Osterlund, Jim Stacy, and Richard Childress in 1981, then joined Bud Moore Engineering in 1982. In 1983, Earnhardt posted his first of twelve victories in 125-mile qualifying races at Daytona, and he won two Cup points races.

Finally, in 1984, Junior Johnson pushed Earnhardt into returning to Childress, and their long association began. They won six championships over seventeen-plus years, with all of those titles packed into a nine-year span (1986–94).

Earnhardt's legend, like all good mythologies and histories, grew a step at a time.

Joe Whitlock, Earnhardt's publicist and one of his hunting buddies, handled the account between sponsor Wrangler and Richard Childress Racing. Whitlock has been credited with coming up with the Intimidator persona, and the image became complete when Childress's team switched to GM Goodwrench Service Plus and took on the black-silver-white-and-red paint scheme.

Being a bit rough on the track didn't hurt things any. At the 1985 Cup banquet in New York, Ricky Rudd summed up his peers' feelings about Dale: "My shoes were shined when I got here, but Dale Earnhardt ran all over me when I was coming up here to get this award."[2] Ricky was smiling, but he was delivering a message.

In many fans' eyes (and perhaps drivers' as well), Earnhardt became Darth Vader, the Red Baron, and Snidely Whiplash all rolled into one. On any given Sunday, the huge Earnhardt contingent of fans would cheer, and nearly everyone else would boo.

While lots of fans ignored Richard Petty, David Pearson, and Rusty Wallace, no one ignored Earnhardt. When he stepped to the stage during pre-race introductions, the mixed roar would rock a speedway. Earnhardt, like the Oakland Raiders of the 1970s or the Dallas Cowboys of the 1990s or even Howard Cosell in his long career, was the most loved and most hated driver, all at the same time.

Along the way, Earnhardt—"Ironhead," "the Intimidator," and "the Man in Black"—became the force in NASCAR collectibles. It has been estimated that, at one point, he was selling nearly 40 percent of all NASCAR collectibles, roughly twice the Jeff Gordon products being moved.

Shortly after Earnhardt tied Petty's record of seven championships in 1994, NASCAR picked the fifty greatest drivers of all time. Naturally, racing historians and motorsports journalists started ranking the greats, and Petty and Earnhardt led the way. Some people said that Petty was the greatest—200 victories and seven Daytona 500 victories proved it.

Some people said that wasn't enough—racing historian Bob Latford, now deceased, once said that Petty should have won 250 races, considering the disparity in equipment and factory involvement. Others favored Earnhardt's hard-charging style, his almost mystic ability to surprise us.

Earnhardt's children have added to the legacy. Kerry, Kelley, and Dale Jr. all raced, and Dale Jr. shocked the racing world when he won Busch Grand National championships in 1998 and '99 and then won two Cup races and The Winston all-star race in the first half of 2000. And Kelley Earnhardt Elledge now is an executive for Dale Jr.'s Jr Motorsports.

In 1998, Earnhardt and Dale Jr. celebrated Junior's Grand National crown at Homestead, and the two raced together in the post-season exhibition race in Japan. They were even closer in 1999, as Junior participated in the IROC all-star series and drove Earnhardt's Cup cars for five races. And, again, Dale Jr. won the BGN crown.

The highlight of the 1999 IROC series, other than Earnhardt's three victories and tight points victory over Mark Martin, was the Earnhardt & Earnhardt Show at Michigan. Dale Jr. was the leader at one point in the race featuring all-stars, but, typically, he was running hard and conservative at the same time. Suddenly, Dale Sr. dove into the mix and stole the race by inches on the last lap.

Earnhardt, not the kid, showed relief, jubilation, and pride in Victory Lane. And Junior was thrilled to show Dad that he, too, could run well.

Earnhardt had his spectacular crashes and tough returns. One year he hurt his shoulder in a crash, then came back to win the pole on the road course at Watkins Glen. While everyone expected him to give up his seat at some point, he ran the whole race and finished sixth.

And Earnhardt was even a surprise as a car owner. Dale Jr. gave him his first two wins as a Cup car owner in 2000, and Steve Park won in 2000 on the road course at Watkins Glen. Then Michael Waltrip—whom Earnhardt added to Dale Earnhardt Inc. in 2001—and Dale Jr. finished one-two in the 2001 Daytona 500. While they were heading to the checkered flag, Dale was dying in a turn-four crash.

Even Earnhardt's death was spectacular. And while his 1998 Daytona 500 victory may have been the happiest moment in Cup history, his death was the saddest. While Fireball Roberts died weeks after his fiery crash at Charlotte Motor Speedway years ago, Earnhardt was just . . . gone.

It was hard to believe that Earnhardt had died at Daytona, the track where he had won a record thirty-four races. Six drivers have died during practice or in qualifying races at Daytona, but only one driver has died during the Daytona 500 or the Pepsi 400—Earnhardt.

Jim Hunter, the former president of Darlington Raceway and now NASCAR's chief publicist, told me that he was shocked with Earnhardt's death. "He seemed invincible," Hunter told me. "Everything was always on his terms. And I figured he'd be around until he got too old to drive and figured he'd then be a car owner."

For days Dale's death led sports pages and television broadcasts. Experts talked about safety, and everyone eulogized the dead champion. Earnhardt's legions of fans led the mourning, of course, but it's also fair to say that the Earnhardt haters ("Anybody But Earnhardt") were hurt and stunned, too. "The King" is still alive, but his heir to the throne is dead.

A media member later called Earnhardt a Southern martyr.

Bobby Hamilton, who had an on-track run-in with Earnhardt at Rockingham in 1996, summed up the drivers' feelings.

"I've been so mad at that man so many times because of the things he's done to me and other competitors," said Hamilton. "But the one thing I always loved about him was that he was the only true racer that I've ever known. He was there to race. It didn't make any difference what the circumstances were.

"Earnhardt is the only one I know who, if NASCAR was to call and say, 'Guys, we've got an empty grandstand this week, there's no money, and we need all of you to pay $5,000 to enter the race,' he'd be the only car that would show up. He was that kind of racer. If you looked up *racer* in the dictionary, they ought to have Earnhardt's picture and Earnhardt's picture only,"[3] said Hamilton, who died in 2006.

For years, media members, fans, and racers have argued: Who's the best ever? Was it Petty, who won seven titles, seven Daytona 500s, and 200 race victories? Was it Earnhardt, who won more than $40 million in purses, seventy-six Cup races, seven Cup titles, and three IROC championships? Or was it David Pearson, winner of 105 Cup races, three Cup titles, and the greatest Daytona 500 finish ever (beating Petty in 1976)?

Petty always says there are different eras and different champions for every era. He won't pick himself, but he won't slight himself, either. With a streak of diplomacy, Earnhardt always reminded everyone that Petty was "the King," no matter how many championships Dale won. And every time I've asked Pearson about the greatest ever, the Silver Fox has always laughed and said, "Me."

In 2001, there were a lot of discussions about Earnhardt's legacy. I was doing a radio interview promoting the book, and I told the radio guy that Earnhardt would be remembered as one of the greatest drivers of all time, that he's one of the most beloved drivers ever, and that Dale Jr. and Dale Earnhardt Inc. would fulfill his legacy. Then the guy said, "But what's his *legacy*?" I said with a laugh, "I think I already answered that. I know you want me to say that Earnhardt was the greatest driver ever. I will say that he compared favorably to Richard Petty, David Pearson and Cale Yarborough among the greatest drivers ever; that's a huge legacy."

I don't know when the program was shot, but in mid-2007 ESPN aired a program listing the top stock-car drivers of all time. When David Pearson was listed third and

Richard Petty second, I knew who No. 1 would be. It was No. 3.

Dale Jr., who entered the 2007 season with a Daytona 500 victory and seventeen career Cup victories, has since become the most popular driver in stock-car racing and the biggest force in NASCAR marketing. He'll be the biggest part of Earnhardt's remaining legacy.

Dale Jr. got a lot of Earnhardt's fans. You see tons of kids wearing the No. 8 Budweiser caps, and one has to assume that we'll see lots of people wearing Dale Jr./Hendrick Motorsports memorabilia in 2008. Some will continue to drink Bud because of Junior (even though Budweiser will sponsor Kasey Kahne in '08); they'll drink Pepsi; and they'll eat the candy (Dale Jr.'s Big Mo').

Robert Yates Racing announced in September 2007 that the organization will retire the No. 88 RYR car after the 2007 season, and **Robert Yates** requested that NASCAR give Hendrick Motorsports the 88 number for Dale Jr. Since Ralph Earnhardt drove the 88 car in 1957, the 88 would continue the family tradition and the Earnhardt legacy. Yates said this in a statement:

> Ralph Earnhardt drove the No. 88 Olds in 1957, and because of this number's history with the Earnhardt family, I felt car No. 88 should continue with Dale Earnhardt Jr. Younger fans don't realize I built cars and raced against Ralph. I also had a very close relationship with Dale Earnhardt Sr. I'm proud to transfer this number to Dale Jr. and let him know how much I appreciate the friendship and competitive racing I've always enjoyed with this family.

After Dale Earnhardt Jr. announced that he'll leave Dale Earnhardt Inc. for Hendrick Motorsports in 2008, lots of people asked me what I thought would happen. What would Dale Sr. have thought of Junior leaving? (He would have hated it, of course.) And who will drive the No. 8 Chevrolet?

*After I heard that DEI had bought Ginn Racing, I told people that **Mark Martin**, one of Ginn's drivers, might drive the No. 8 in 2008. Turns out he will, along with youngster Aric Almirola. Martin talked about upholding Earnhardt's legacy at a press conference on September 7, 2007, at Richmond International Raceway:*

I am (excited). Driving for the U.S. Army is a real special opportunity, and I think it's one of the most meaningful sponsors in the garage, so it's an honor to drive the soldiers' car, and I'm happy about it. As well as driving the No. 8 and representing Dale Earnhardt Inc. I spent a lot of years on the racetrack racing Dale Sr. and (had) a lot of battles, and I know that following that legacy is big shoes to fill. But I think he'd be really pleased with where this company is headed. I know I'm excited about it. I know that we have a good bit of work to do in front of us. We're still in the very beginning stages of merging the No. 01 with the other three DEI cars. I think he'd be very pleased with where we're headed.

Former Charlotte Observer *motorsports writer **Tom Higgins** discusses where he'd rank Earnhardt among the greats. After all, Higgins covered everybody from Lee Petty and Fireball Roberts to Earnhardt and Jeff Gordon:*

First. Even Junior Johnson says that. He could just do things with a car that didn't seem humanly possible.

*Hall of Fame driver **Ned Jarrett** says Earnhardt won't be replaced, just as other great drivers were irreplaceable:*

I've said for years that our sport is healthy as far as talent goes. When a star is gone—when Richard Petty retired—it was just coincidental that Jeff Gordon drove his first (Cup) race that day. There are always plenty of drivers waiting in the wings to come in and replace those superstars. But when you start to talk about replacing someone as the leader, that's different.

I think it's going to be harder to do in the future. I don't think we're going to see the drivers stay around as long as Richard Petty, Earnhardt, and Darrell Waltrip did. The thing that established them as the leader of the sport didn't come overnight. That's why it's going to be harder to replace an Earnhardt or a Richard Petty—they're simply not going to stay around that long. It's a different type of personality. Earnhardt's personality is a good ol' boy, American-type personality, and that's not necessarily Gordon's.

People still tend to appreciate simplicity and common sense. And those are things Earnhardt had a lot of. He had a good understanding of what needed to be done; he didn't always know how to get it done. And he stood up for it. He didn't hesitate to go to the source that could get things done, and people respected that. And the excursions he had on the racetrack made a lot of drivers mad and a lot of drivers' fans mad, and yet they all respected him.

He didn't make excuses when those things happened, and people respected that. He had a unique way of dealing with the life that he chose and the celebrity status it brought him. He could deal with it in a stern and simple way.

*Cup car owner **Bill Davis** gave Earnhardt all the respect in the world:*

To me, he was just the epitome of what we're doing here, a guy that you'd like to think of yourself as being like that, a guy who's self-made. He had nothing and wound up at the top of his career, of his sport. He was successful beyond belief, and he did everything you could do. He was a businessman, a car owner, a driver, a marketer. He was the American dream. I had as much respect for him as I possibly could have.

Obviously, he showed that he was going to be a heck of a car owner. Like you say, when that (car ownership) became his only role, who knows what he could have done? He certainly had a feel for what it took, he knew what he had to give his guys, he knew the right people, and he'd acquired a perspective on what it took to be a successful car owner.

And he trained under a similar situation. R. C. (Richard Childress) did the same thing. They were a lot alike. Certainly, Junior (Johnson) was an influence in R. C.'s life. From the way I always understand it, Junior just made Childress quit driving (and hire Earnhardt the first time).

I can't emphasize enough how much he meant to us. Dale was our leader, the one everyone looked up to, even when we were mad at him. Will we replace him? Probably not. That's a huge void in the garage that can never be filled. No one can possibly fill it, and no one would attempt to. Yeah, I think it impacted the garage—just a big, empty void. He was the leader.

Tom Higgins compared Earnhardt's death to the loss of a superstar, another North Carolinian, in another sport:

It was pretty big, very big, I think. I'd equate it to the NBA's losing Michael Jordan. There's not as much excitement about the NBA now, and look at how the attendance has dropped. I don't know if the same thing (attendance dropping) will happen at races, probably not, but he's on the minds of people.

It'll be a long time before it's as exciting as it was when Earnhardt raced. I can't count the people who have told me, "I never pulled for him, but I always watched to see where he was and what he was going to do." That was an element he brought to it. No one else mattered. If they pulled for Earnhardt, it didn't matter what anybody else did. It's not going to be the same thing for a lot of people for a long time, if ever.

Buddy Baker raced against a bunch of great drivers, and he says Earnhardt was one of the best:

Who was the best driver? I'll go way beyond that. I'll tell you this: I'll pick five drivers, and we can go from there. Fireball Roberts was the absolute best at superspeedway racing. I know Richard Petty was one of the best, David Pearson, Cale Yarborough. In my opinion, if Dale Earnhardt had been around when they ran 100-lap races, he would have won at least 200 races, in my opinion. I've raced with three generations of drivers, and, on any given Sunday, Dale Earnhardt was as good as anyone who sat in a race car.

Ken Squier did the CBS television broadcast of the 1979 Daytona 500, the first NASCAR race aired flag-to-flag. That was the first race of Earnhardt's rookie year, and Squier says Dale enlivened his broadcasts over the years:

He was a different character in a world where most of the characters assumed the same role. He allowed himself to be more than just another nice guy. Many of the others were seeking that idyllic American hero (role), and he offered something different, something that was more realistic. He didn't hide himself, and that was one of the great appealing factors. There was no public relations veneer. It was the real stuff.

If you want to talk about the legend of Earnhardt, **Squier** *can talk about legends:*

I think, to a degree, it was Beowulf. I think he was the mythical driver. If there was a driver who had to go out on his shield, it was Earnhardt. If there is one driver who has mythical proportions, real legendary stuff, it's Earnhardt. And they will be around whatever he created—overcoming those life-threatening instances, winning all of those races, being a man's man but being very gentle, having his own set of values. And he lived by them. And then his best friend (Neil Bonnett) dies seven years and seven days before him, and he loses his life in the same place (the fourth turn at Daytona). There's a lot of mythical proportions to Earnhardt.

David Green, *who has worked for various motorsports outlets, most recently the magazine* Auto World Weekly, *said Earnhardt came along at just the right time:*

I was at Charlotte for "the Pass in the Grass" in the '87 Winston and the extracurricular activities involving him and Bill Elliott and Geoffrey Bodine in '87. And I remember him dumping Sterling (Marlin) in a race at Bristol, and

Coo Coo (Sterling's dad) was mad enough to kill Earnhardt that day.

Over the years of his career, Earnhardt really polished his act. I think Earnhardt came to Winston Cup about the same time that widespread cable coverage did, and I wrote in one story that was published in *Auto World Weekly* that it was kind of like the mixture of rocket propellants. It just ignited, with the TV coverage and a larger-than-life character such as Earnhardt. That ignited the growth of the sport.

Would Earnhardt have been able to do the same thing that Richard Petty did for the sport in the sixties and seventies? I don't know. He was more of a media character, as opposed to a fan-friendly, Andy Griffith-type of character, like Richard was. Definitely a different persona from Richard. Hence the dual status of those two guys as the most compelling NASCAR figures ever.

They weren't much alike, except that they both won seven Winston Cup championships. They don't crowd each other off the stage, as far as who's the most significant figure in NASCAR's history. They can kinda share that spot, Petty because at the time he came along, he was the right man for the time. And the things he did and the attributes he had produced his own niche.

And when Earnhardt came along, I think the sport needed a little bit more of a fiery person than Richard was. I compared Richard Petty to Andy Griffith . . . maybe Dale Earnhardt was more like Jim Rockford. Or Magnum P.I. A little less aw-shucks. He was more anti-hero than Richard was.

<hr />

Richard Sowers went to school with Earnhardt, then went on to a career as a journalist, publicist, and, later, author. Sowers points out that Cup racing started growing in 1979 with the first flag-to-flag television coverage of the Daytona

500, plus the start of ESPN in September and the advent of
racing on ESPN in the early eighties. Earnhardt came along
at the right time:

In 1979 Dale Earnhardt was Rookie of the Year. In 1980 he
won his first championship. This incredible explosion of
Winston Cup racing, the growth from a regional to a
national sport, absolutely paralleled Dale Earnhardt's
career. He was the star in this era when Winston Cup racing became a national sport. He was the right guy at the
right place at the right time to help put Winston Cup racing
on the map. He was a very charismatic superstar, very controversial on the track. He had the right style for the right
time to boost the popularity of Winston Cup racing when it
was becoming a national sport.

You look at those events in 1979 and 1980—it had
everything to do with television. But hey, that was his
rookie year, and the next year was his first championship
season. It all sort of tied together very, very well.

Benny Parsons, himself a Cup champion (1973), a Daytona
500 winner (1975), and a Hall of Famer, raced with a group
of drivers that included Petty, Pearson, Bobby Allison,
Yarborough, Baker, Darrell Waltrip, and, later, Earnhardt:

Earnhardt was awfully good. Was he the best ever? I don't
know. That's so hard, because I saw Pearson and Petty back
when they were awesome.

Pearson and that 21 Wood Brothers car, they were
almost unbeatable. They probably won 30 to 40 percent of
the races they entered, which is outstanding. Richard had
200 wins, but he started 1,100 races, didn't he? In 1973, the
Wood Brothers entered eighteen races and won eleven. And
that's one reason I was able to win the championship in '73,

Dale Earnhardt's seventy-sixth and final Cup victory came at Talladega in October 2000, and Earnhardt always had something to smile about at the big track.

because Pearson, who did not run all the races, won a lot of the races, which helped me in my bid for the championship.

Later in Earnhardt's career, after he got some experience, I don't think I've seen his equal at Daytona and Talladega.

———— ❦ ————

Parsons once analyzed Earnhardt's driving style:

I can't believe he can get as close as he does and not hit them. Sometimes he does (hit them), but you don't see anyone get as close as Earnhardt does. I've never seen anyone quite like Earnhardt in that respect.

If he has a weakness, it's that he relies on his ability more than he should—if that's a weakness. He's always been able to get his chassis close, and he adjusted driving techniques. He's always able to make up for a car's deficiency. If a car's off, he's been able pick up the pace, and with the radial tires (instead of bias-ply tires) and other teams working so hard on chassis, you can't do that."

———— ❦ ————

Ed Clark, president and general manager of Atlanta Motor Speedway, knew how important Earnhardt was to promoters:

All you had to do was go into the grandstands at any racetrack and see the Earnhardt shirts and caps to see the magnitude of the effect he had on fans. You hear it in all sports. It doesn't matter what kind of response you give me, give me some kind of response. And, throughout his entire career, he was able to evoke some kind of response from fans, positive or negative. The feelings were intense.

The Dale Earnhardt fans are as loyal as any fans in motorsports. There was a special bond between Dale and the fans. The average, middle-America working person could identify with him. His dad was a racer. Ralph Earnhardt didn't ask for anything, and he taught Dale to be the same way. He came out of a mill town, and it proved to people that they could lift themselves out of situations. It encouraged others to do the same. And that created a tie with fans.

Also, people don't buy race tickets to see follow-the-leader, mundane racing. They want to see people charge into the lead, to make something happen. With Dale, you could count on him to put some excitement in racing. And I think that's why Dale was so popular with the promoters. He always made something happen.

———※———

Humpy Wheeler, president and general manager of Lowe's Motor Speedway, is famous for his pre-race Memorial Day extravaganzas. If anyone could appreciate the drama and pageantry that Earnhardt offered, it's Wheeler, the P. T. Barnum of stock-car racing:

Having him was great, because you knew there would be times when he'd produce great drama on the track, and that sells tickets. Nobody can replace Earnhardt, but we'll have exciting new stars coming along.

Will we ever see another driver like him? Probably not, just like we've never seen another Fireball Roberts or Richard Petty. They had their own unique styles and personalities.

———※———

Ned Jarrett was a two-time NASCAR champion and a longtime announcer for ESPN. He also promoted short-track races in North Carolina, and he knew Ralph and Dale Earnhardt from all of those roles:

We—Dale and I—just seemed to have a mutual respect for each other. He knew that I knew his dad real well and that we'd raced against each other. And I'd tried to help him some in his tougher days. And he publicly thanked me, along with others who had helped him in his career. How did I help him? I loaned him money, for one thing.

That wasn't all that uncommon. I was promoting the racetracks at Hickory and Metrolina Speedway in Charlotte, and he was racing more at Hickory. It was just tough to make it in the business. Sometimes when things wouldn't go too well and he didn't win much prize money, he didn't have sponsorship money to fall back on. So he had to go where he could to get some help. I loaned it to him never expecting to be paid back, because I never took a note.

He just agreed to come and run for a certain period of time at the tracks I was promoting. In some sense, it was payment in advance for him showing up at the racetrack. And he did.

Dick Thompson, longtime publicist at Martinsville Speedway, talked about Earnhardt's sometimes rough driving style:

I've been here for thirty-five years, and I was the racing writer at the *Roanoke Times* for nine years before that. So I precede Earnhardt; I go back to Fireball Roberts and Curtis Turner. I have to say that there are natural drivers and very exciting drivers who seem larger than life, and Earnhardt would have fit right in with Curtis Turner, Joe Weatherly, Junior Johnson, and the other early stars. He would have been right at home in the rough-and-tumble era, just as he fit in today.

It can be rough now, but racing is a lot more civilized today than it was back then. There were a lot of fights, and you took care of yourself with your fists and your fenders.

When Beckett Racing Monthly *started its collectibles magazine in 1994, I wrote BRM's first cover story for editor* **Mark Zeske.** *It was on Earnhardt's going after his seventh title. Zeske discusses the Intimidator's role in racing:*

I don't think there's anybody who admires Richard Petty more than I do. He's a great man with all of these pluses: He lifted the sport up; he was its spokesman and its ambassador. He was great for fans, and he signed tons of autographs. He worked hard on television, made lots of appearances, met presidents.

But, somehow, Earnhardt outdid him, and I'm amazed. I think Richard Petty is fabulous. He has been the key to the sport, and he's meant so much to his home state. To think Dale could do more, that's mind-boggling.

After Earnhardt died, NASCAR redoubled its efforts to improve safety, and many insiders will say that racing's much safer now. **Randy LaJoie,** *a two-time Busch Series champion, talks about it:*

With his passing, he's saved dozens of lives already. It's a shame that nobody paid attention before. We (lost) five or six guys before him; I guess their lives weren't good enough, worthy enough, to implement changes.

Derrike Cope *was running second when Earnhardt blew a tire on the last lap of the 1990 Daytona 500. Earnhardt was denied again, and Cope joined Tiny Lund, Mario Andretti, Sterling Marlin, and others in getting his first victory in stock-car racing's biggest event:*

Earnhardt always demanded respect. You didn't always like him—and I don't say that as a personal thing—as a competitor, you didn't always like the way things played out, but certainly you respected his talents.

Even when I won Daytona, you marveled at the man's ability. When he lost the left-rear tire at 200 miles an hour in the corner, he saved the race car and didn't hit the fence. You have to admire that, because you know the tendencies of a car during that period of time. He was unique.

2

Young Dale

"He was just so much like his daddy."

— Ned Jarrett

The young Dale Earnhardt wasn't much like the one we remember. He was shy, unsure of himself in social situations. He didn't have the supreme racing confidence of his later years, and he wasn't an entrepreneur. He was just a kid from the mill town of Kannapolis, North Carolina, who wanted to follow his daddy onto the racetracks.

Richard Sowers *attended J. W. Cannon Junior High in Kannapolis, North Carolina, with Earnhardt, who quit school after the eighth grade. Sowers, now an author of books about racing, worked as a journalist and once was chief publicist at Atlanta Motor Speedway, one of Earnhardt's best tracks:*

I knew him as one of a bunch of kids who'd get together and play baseball, pickup type games. Was he any good in baseball? Let's put it this way, I think he picked the right sport.

Back then, Dale was kind of quiet. It was not like we were best friends hanging around; he was one of forty to fifty kids that age I knew.

Dale was quiet, but that's not so surprising. Anybody that's thrown into the spotlight at a young age has a chance to be shy. College athletes fit that category. I haven't covered golf in years, but I imagine Tiger Woods is a lot more comfortable now than he was a few years ago.

For years Earnhardt said he loved cars and nothing else, not stick-and-ball sports and certainly not school. **Sowers** *saw that in Dale:*

Oh, yeah, he was into cars even then, because of his father. But when you grow up as Ralph Earnhardt's kid, any form of auto racing is terribly expensive to get into. When you have inner-city games of basketball, if one kid has a ball and you have a goal, you can play. In racing it takes one car per driver to make a race, and a car costs more. But being Ralph Earnhardt's son, Dale had an inclination and advantage in racing. The same would apply to Davey Allison and Kyle Petty and Sterling Marlin. People just naturally assume you're going to become a race-car driver.

If I wanted to become a racer, there's no way. I didn't have any way to race. If you're twelve years old and you tell your parents you want to become a race-car driver, hey, you still gotta have the money. If your father happens to be Richard Petty or Ralph Earnhardt, the probability becomes more probable.

Sowers isn't surprised Earnhardt took so long to hit his stride. Dale was twenty-nine when he reached NASCAR's top rung full time, and, if you think about it, that's younger than some guys. Dave Blaney was thirty-seven, Harry Gant thirty-nine, and Dick Trickle forty-eight:

There was a time when you had to be thirty-one or thirty-two to get a competitive ride, and that's changed a bit. The age of drivers who get competitive rides is going down, and I credit the success of Jeff Gordon for that. The drivers are definitely getting younger, but, for a long time, you really had to be twenty-eight to twenty-nine at the youngest to get a ride.

Humpy Wheeler, president/general manager at Lowe's Motor Speedway since 1975, knew Dale Earnhardt early:

His father (Ralph) was a good friend of mine, so I knew him when he was a little boy. Later when I was operating Concord Speedway, he ran races there. That's where I got to know him as an adult first. His father died right after that, and, a couple of years later, he was here at the speedway (which was then called Charlotte Motor Speedway). He was just starting his Winston Cup career at that time.

Wheeler, on the young Earnhardt:

I don't know if it was shyness . . . it takes most people a while to mature socially. I don't know that he was a whole lot shier than a lot of young people his age. People are a lot different today. They've been brought up on TV, and racing's more sophisticated than it was. Shyness was a pretty elemental trait in those days. There were very few young race drivers then who weren't quiet and sort of nervous about the whole thing, being thrust out there.

―――――※―――――

*Earnhardt was a twenty-nine-year-old rookie in 1979; by comparison, Jeff Gordon was a three-time champion, two-time Daytona 500 winner and fifty-two-time NASCAR race winner at age twenty-nine. In explanation, **Wheeler** went back to the 1970s, when Richard Petty was still "the King," and David Pearson, Cale Yarborough, Bobby Allison, Darrell Waltrip, and Buddy Baker were the big names, and they won most of the races:*

This was back in the days when the Winston Cup circuit didn't have a lot of money in it. The factories had pulled out for the 1970 season, and, from '70 to '77, there were few sponsors and little money. And there was a big gap between the first five or six cars and the rest of the world. So it was hard to look good (and move into Winston Cup full time) unless you got up in that top five or six, which a young driver would not be.

It was a difficult time for drivers to come forth. We did not have a Busch circuit, per se, in those days. There was the Sportsman circuit. In Winston Cup most guys raced their Saturday-night car or a second-hand Winston Cup car. It was hard for a driver to look good in Winston Cup, much harder than it is now. A thirty-fifth-place car today could possibly take the lead at someplace easy to drive like Talladega. But in those days, it was awfully difficult for someone to see your talent if the only thing he ran was Winston Cup or Sportsman. Back in those days, Saturday-night racing meant something. If a guy ran well at certain racetracks against big-time competition, there was much more interchange between the short tracks and the big tracks. There is hardly none of that today.

He (Earnhardt) was raw because his real forte on short tracks was dirt. The reason he did so well on dirt was that dirt was primarily what he ran for a long time—Concord (North Carolina) Speedway, Myrtle Beach (Speedway in South Carolina), Metrolina (Speedway in Charlotte)—places like that, and the local competition was pretty fierce. If you could go over to Concord and win races or go down to Myrtle Beach and do well, you were doing something. And he did that. The word kept getting around that he was pretty good.

Charlotte rolled around in the '77 and '78 period, and we were trying to get him a ride with somebody. He raced a lot, but he didn't look good. He was not in equipment where he could look good, because the guys couldn't afford it. In '78, Rod Osterlund saw him win a 100-lap race at Metrolina, and he was driving a dirt car owned by his former father-in-law, Robert Gee. He came from the back of the pack to win the race.

I was there that night; it was the night after the Southern 500 at Darlington. Osterlund decided to put him in a Sportsman race at Charlotte. Dave Marcis was driving for Osterlund back then. Earnhardt did real well in the race. So, the last race of the year, Osterlund entered two cars at Atlanta, and Marcis was in one and Earnhardt was in the other. He did well there—I don't know how he finished, but he looked good in the race. Right after that, (Osterlund) let Marcis go and Earnhardt got the ride.

※

Many people remember Ralph Earnhardt as a hell-bent-for-leather driver, just like his son, but **Wheeler** *recalls the senior Earnhardt saving his equipment to race another day:*

I remember him when he first started dirt-track racing. His dad never made much money in racing, though he made a living. Back then, few people would be a full-time race driver who was just running short tracks. Ralph was one of the first to do that.

Dale's driving style was quite different from Ralph's. Ralph was a pretty conservative race driver. I think that's because he was trying to make a living, and he was in his own car. He won a lot of races, though. If he ran a 100-lap race on Columbia Speedway's half-mile dirt track, he'd be running second or third until the last few laps, then he'd pass the guys and eke out the win. I think he could have won by a much greater margin, but he didn't want to take any chances with the family business.

When Dale started, he was pretty wild and woolly. He was quite different from Ralph. I'm sure Ralph tried to calm him down, and to some extent I'm sure he was able to do that. But you know Ralph died suddenly when Dale was twenty-two, and that sort of left him out there with not much money and some old dirt cars. He really had as tough time as anybody I know of who got into Winston Cup racing.

As a matter of fact he started running NASCAR at Hickory and Asheville, tracks that were paved. He knew he'd have to learn to drive on paved tracks. In '78, he ended up destroying a car at Asheville, and that's when he went to work for Robert Gee, his father-in-law. He started doing body work on cars.

Finally, Dale talked Robert into letting him use an old dirt car without a motor. He went back on dirt. And that's what led him to the Osterlund ride.

Once Earnhardt got to Cup, he won the 1979 Rookie of the Year award and the 1980 series title. Then he struggled for a few years, **Wheeler** *recalls:*

He won his first championship too fast. He simply wasn't

ready for it in 1980, his second year. He was completely unprepared, and he knew it. We (track promoters and racing people) got on him bad. I think we expected the Winston Cup champion to act a certain way, and he was just being Earnhardt at a very early stage of his career.

I'll never forget, I was giving him hell one time, and he stopped me and said, "Look, I don't need for you to tell me what to do. I need help. That's what I need." I stopped and thought, "I'm not approaching him in the right way." I changed my approach; everybody else did, too, and that helped him get through this period. It was just part of the maturing process.

⌇

Wheeler says that Earnhardt matured between his first championship, in 1980, and his second, in 1986. Two marriages had ended, and he married his third (and last) wife, Teresa, who became his mate and his business partner:

He obviously matured quite a bit. He had a couple of marriages go sour before 1980. I forget when he married Teresa. I think in '82. I've never known a really good or great race driver who didn't have substantial help from his wife. Race drivers lose constantly, no matter how good they are, and somebody has to pick them up on Monday. The crew chief, not; the car owner, not; particularly in those days. It's a lonesome business. He had a sponsor, but the sponsor was not too happy about not winning. Somebody had to help, and it's usually the wife who winds up having more influence on the driver than we'd suspect, even today.

⌇

Wheeler once commented that David Pearson changed less than any driver he'd ever seen. He said that Earnhardt changed the most:

Even from when he raced dirt, he (Pearson) was pretty solid and thinking about how to beat everybody versus how to knock walls down, or overdriving, as Earnhardt did. Earnhardt went from being wild and wreck-prone . . . he still takes risks, of course, but he doesn't do it as often.

Nowadays, there's a lot of thinking in Earnhardt's driving. He's totally into tire management, which is the way racing has gone.

***

Tom Higgins, retired motorsports writer for the Charlotte Observer, *says he, reporter Steve Waid, and publicist Joe Whitlock were asked to recruit Earnhardt for a Christmas parade in Concord, North Carolina, not far from Charlotte (now Lowe's) Motor Speedway. Concord is also near Kannapolis, Earnhardt's hometown:*

This was in the early 1980s, and he was still pretty shy. This was Christmas 1980, about a month after he'd won his first championship, and they asked him to be the grand marshal of the Concord Christmas parade. He'd only do it if we used Joe Whitlock's car, which had a sunroof. Whitlock drove, and Dale stood up in the backseat with his torso sticking out of the sunroof. Steve and I rode in the back seat and mixed the drinks. He drank nothing but Sundrop and Jack Daniel's, his favorite drink at the time. We had a hell of a time, and the people went nuts over him, although nothing like they did later on. He was still the hometown hero, even then.

***

Higgins saw Earnhardt grow from a rough kid from a textile mill town to an articulate one-man conglomerate:

I've said repeatedly since his death that he came further in life than anybody I've personally known. When he started, he was painfully shy, and he got to be really good as a speaker. The other night, I saw Richard Petty, Darrell Waltrip, and Jeff Gordon on the *Larry King Live* show (on CNN), and they showed some tape on Earnhardt and they talked about him quite a bit. He was very articulate just before his death.

---

*Few people saw Earnhardt the way **Gary Hargett** got to see him. Ralph Earnhardt convinced Hargett to give up race-car driving to be a mechanic, and the two men worked together. Hargett, who still lives in the country in Marshville, North Carolina, later was Earnhardt's car owner in Late Model Sportsman, which evolved into Busch Grand National in 1982. His other Sportsman driver was Harry Gant, and Hargett says that Gant was a better driver, at least back then:*

There are a lot of them (stories about Earnhardt), but you can't print them. He was just rough; he tore up a lot of stuff (cars), but he won races. There wasn't anything smooth about him.

I knew the family. When I first got into racing, Ralph helped me. I got to know Ralph good; of course, Dale was coming along then, too. Ralph was probably harder on Dale than I would have been. They never really got along good. Ralph was a real quiet fellow; he'd tell you one time how you was supposed to do something, and he wasn't going to tell you a lot after that. They'd argue; he'd try to tell Dale what to do. Of course, Dale was running dirt then; he never ran asphalt until after Ralph died. And he bought an asphalt car from Harry Gant. The reason I got to helping him—it was a kind of an odd deal.

I'd been around him a lot at the racetracks but had never really worked with him. And he came to my shop one day; he was going to Savannah (Georgia), wanted to know if I'd ride with him. I knew something was up then—he wouldn't stop to ask—but he was by himself going to Savannah to race. He said he had $7 on him. I thought that, if he was that determined to do it, I'd go ahead and help him a little bit. I just started then, started helping him some. I was in the tire business then, Goodyear dirt tires. I sponsored him that first year, then we built a car together, that orange and white car. We raced together until he got his ride with (Rod) Osterlund in Winston Cup (in 1979).

Hargett says he liked Earnhardt, both as a young man and a superstar, but it's interesting to hear his opinion of the man:

Back then, he was almost exactly like he was when he got rich. I told him a lot of times that he was always an asshole, then he got to be a rich asshole. A lot of people change, but he really didn't never change. He was hard-headed; it was his way or no way. There was no doubt in his mind that he was the best there ever was. He was like that from the get-go. He raced just like we had ten cars back at the shop, and we had one old car that we just kept beating back together. It never came to his mind that, if we'd tear up that car, we'd be out of racing. And that's the way he always was. He only had one thing on his mind; he'd either outrun everybody that was there or tear up the car trying.

We couldn't work together every day. If we did, we got in a fight. I think we just kinda tolerated each other. I knew what I was doing, and I think he knew what I was doing. I knew he could drive, and we sort of put up with each other. But we were still good friends; it was just a head-butting deal. If we'd stay together long enough, we'd get into a fight about something, but the next day we'd start all over again.

But I enjoyed racing with him; we just had different

opinions about stuff, the car and whatever. We could get along. And I knew that when we went to the racetrack, if we didn't win, it wasn't going to be from the lack of effort. We may have to put a new body on the car, but there was no doubt that he was going there to win the race.

Hargett remembers that 200-lap race in Savannah, Georgia, that featured an illustrious field—among them were David Pearson, Harry Gant, Butch Lindley, LeeRoy Yarbrough, Buddy Baker and others. Pearson won the pole, and Earnhardt qualified second. Dale followed Pearson the whole race. Then at the end of the race:

I went and got a set of tires for Earnhardt. I made a deal with him (the tire man); I said I would send him a check when I got home—I didn't bring any money with me. He said "no problem." Earnhardt said, "I got to win this race." I said, "No way." And he said, "I'm broke; I got to win this race." He qualified second; Pearson was on the pole.

And he run behind him (Pearson) for 199 laps, and they get the white flag and they got into turn one and Earnhardt turned him (Pearson) the wrong way and stuck him into the fence and come on around and won the race. Pearson was my hero at the time, and still is. I just chewed him up and said, "Why in the world would you do something like that?" He (Earnhardt) didn't even bat an eye. He said, "(Expletive) him, he's got money, and I'm broke." That's just the way he looked at things. We got into the truck and tried to beat the crowd out of there before we got killed. That's the way he was looking (at it); he *was* going to win the race.

He had the most confidence of anybody I *ever* was involved with. But when I raced with Gant, we won a lot more races than with Earnhardt. It was an automatic deal; we knew we'd win. Harry never had to bend nothing (cars);

he'd never tear up nothing; and we'd win races. We won over 200 races in four years; Dale won eighteen races (in three years). Wrecks and whatever was the only reason we never won more. Three of those (four) years, (with Gant) we ran 120 races a year. We ran three and four races a night all over the country. We give away, I know, two national championships (with Gant) because we ran for the money, instead of points.

Then, it was total points for ever how much you run. If they paid a $5,000, $6,000, or $7,000 race with regular points, that's where we'd go run. And we didn't go to a double-point race with something like $2,000 to win. We ran all over the country. And we (Gant and Hargett) won about everywhere we went.

Dale and I ran at least twice a week, and most of the time three times a week. We didn't travel all that much. The regular deal was that we ran at Columbia (South Carolina), Savannah (Georgia), and then Myrtle Beach (South Carolina) or Hickory (North Carolina) on Saturday night. Columbia, at that time, ran on Thursday night, so we could run Thursday, Friday, and Saturday. One year we ran Myrtle Beach the whole year (with Earnhardt), and we won the (track) championship there. But at that time, tow-truck gas cost from thirty-eight cents to forty-five cents a gallon; you didn't think anything about traveling then, the way we do now.

Hargett's Web site, http://www.garyhargettracing.com, has a ton of information and photos from the Hargett/Earnhardt Late Model Sportsman era. There's a business card with the No. 8 car and Hargett's and Earnhardt's phone numbers.

There's also the story of how Hargett became Dale Earnhardt's mentor of Dale Jr. in 1993. Hargett and Dale Jr. raced Late Model at Myrtle Beach Speedway, and the Web site has a photo of a skinny sixteen-year-old Dale Jr. standing in front of a green No. 3. In three seasons, Hargett and Earnhardt Jr. had twelve poles, three victories, fifty-nine top-five finishes, and ninety top-ten finishes in 113 races.

Dale Earnhardt Jr., from a 2004 Boston Globe *interview:*

"I used to work with a guy named Gary Hargett when I was racing Late Models, and he got to be like a grandfather to me. I couldn't imagine going to the racetrack without him, but the day came when I had to go to the racetrack without that man, and it was the hardest thing I ever did. From then on out, I realized that things were going to change, and they never were going to stay the same."

Hargett, on Earnhardt working on cars:

He did all the motor work. He was a *good* engine builder. We'd buy all our parts off Winston Cup people, which at that time we ran the same kinda motors, small-block Chevrolet. We'd either buy parts off (Rod) Osterlund or Blue Max (the team that helped Rusty Wallace win the 1989 Winston Cup title) or somebody around there, and Dale would do the machine work and put them together. He was a *good* engine man.

Longtime television broadcaster **Ken Squier** *recalls Earnhardt going to Canada for a race in the mid-seventies, before he became famous:*

I remember him going to a NASCAR Sportsman race in Canada at Cayuga Speedway. He missed practice completely, and they flew him in. At the track there were a lot of regulars who knew their way around it, a big half-mile (track) near Hamilton, Ontario. He'd never been on it, he'd never seen it. They brought a car up, and I think someone else even qualified it. I think he won by two laps, just ran everybody into the ground. And he didn't seem to abuse the car.

This was just at the beginning (of his big-time career). He'd just had that big crash in Johnny Ray's car at Atlanta (in 1976). It was that period. In those days, he was a lot like Morgan Shepherd. He had a helmet, he had a T-shirt, he had the desire to race, and he was looking for rides any way he could get them. He just knew he could make it, and that was about all he had.

Tony Eury Sr., the crew chief for Dale Earnhardt Jr., grew up knowing Earnhardt, because Tony's father, Ralph Eury, and Ralph Earnhardt had worked together:

My father raced, and Ralph Earnhardt built his motors. Ralph was kind of quiet and kind of different from most of the drivers. He wasn't a conversationalist. He didn't have a whole lot to say. If he didn't want you around, he just wouldn't talk to you so you would leave. He had to pay for all his own equipment, and he would take good care of his equipment. He didn't get out there and really charge. He would run second all night to keep from beating his car up and beat 'em on the last lap or whatever he had to do to win the race. The circumstances were a lot different when he raced. We always parked beside him. Ralph and my daddy were really close.

I drove six years. I ran a modified class on dirt. I won six races in six years. The first two years I didn't win. I just did it as a hobby. I started racing in 1975 and quit in '81.

Dale and I played in the yard when my daddy was picking up motors. That's how I met Dale, going over there picking up motors. I started helping Dale part time in 1976. I went back in 1982 and started working on his Busch cars. I was working a day job and worked over there at night. I didn't go to work full time for him until 1986. I had a retirement plan where I was working, and I wouldn't go to work for him until I got my retirement.

I just had to work there fifteen years, and I had already been there twelve. I was working at Great Dane Trailers in Charlotte, North Carolina. I was a mechanic. Dale worked there, too, for a while. He was a mechanic, too. He's a pretty good mechanic, but he's a better driver. I'm a better mechanic. I quit racing because I ran out of money.[1]

<hr/>

Adds **Eury:**

I helped Dale a couple of races in '82. He didn't have any full-time help. Everybody just kind of hung out and helped him at night. Three of us hung out there. Dale quit driving a Busch car in 1994, and Jeff Green came in 1995. Steve Park came then and won three races, and then Junior started driving the Busch car. He won seven races the first year and six races the second year, and he won the championship both years. He had driven Late Model Stocks in Myrtle Beach before he got into Busch, and we'd help him out during the week with those cars. Dale made him work on his own stuff.

He (Dale Jr.) didn't win a whole lot of races, but he was consistent every week. He wrecked his Street Stock car one time, and he wrecked it pretty bad. They got Sharpies out and wrote all over the car, all over the decals, all over it, just like a bunch of kids. They brought it back and Dale saw it and asked why they had written all over it. They told him it was wrecked and they were just having some fun. Dale told them the car wasn't hurt and they were going to fix it. They got the frame machine out and fixed it.[2]

———≫⫶≪———

Bob Moore, a former employee of R. J. Reynolds Tobacco Company's marketing arm, says that the late T. Wayne Robertson was a strong influence on Earnhardt. Robertson, who died in 1998, led RJR's sports marketing branch and was responsible for The Winston all-star race, plus the Winston Million and No Bull Five promotions:

They were real close. Dale went to Wayne quite a few times for advice, especially during the eighties when Earnhardt first was successful. Wayne was a big help telling Dale what he needed to do to take advantage of his popularity. Dale Earnhardt, when he was a kid, didn't have two nickels to his name. Later, when Dale had money, Wayne was a big help with Dale's major decision-making in the eighties and early nineties.

———≫⫶≪———

Morris Metcalfe, former chief scorer/timer for NASCAR, officiated races featuring Earnhardt for a quarter century, starting when Dale was just coming up:

The first time I noticed Dale was when he'd show up with a little cream-colored Chevelle, No. 8, in honor of his daddy. I remember going somewhere down east, like Wilson, North Carolina, and here he was, himself and two kids with him (as crew). They were just trying to get started. They didn't have a pot to piss in. They didn't have a scorer. He had two people with him as his pit crew, and we had to get somebody to score his car. That was a Late Model Sportsman race, in the mid- to late-1970s.

Buddy Baker was a star racer when Earnhardt was a rookie in 1979. In fact, Baker won the Daytona 500 the next year, and he said he felt obligated to help the up-and-coming Earnhardt:

Earnhardt would just come up and ask you questions. We thought the world of Earnhardt, and we knew he was going to be a superstar. You tell them as much as you can, but he was just such a quick study on everything that it was just a matter of time before he'd be kicking our fannies pretty good.

When he was first starting out, he was humble, and he'd ask you every question he wanted to know. I thought enough of him, and I knew Ralph, too, that it was almost an obligation to try to help as much as I could. I'm sure Richard Petty did the same, and I'm sure Pearson had a part of Dale Earnhardt's life. Bobby Allison had a part of it, and I had a small part of it.

While we're all as fond of Dale Earnhardt as we are, he made himself into the star he was. Once he made the pinnacle, I don't know anybody who has made the impact on the sport that he has. I raced with three generations. Fireball Roberts and my dad, Buck, were heroes of mine. I raced Pearson and Petty and all of that bunch. As far as fan admiration, there was nobody ever close to a guy from a small town like Kannapolis, North Carolina. It was the old thing, "I think I can, I think I can," and then, all of a sudden, "I know I can."

He just had that certain appeal to the common man that Richard Petty had at one time, and then Earnhardt moved in there. Even while Richard was running, I think Earnhardt drew even, or maybe a little ahead. I've actually watched people boo when they announced his name and then cheer like hell when he took the lead. He was that type of guy. I think they wanted to make him mad so he'd do on the racetrack what he did as well as he did. That same guy would put on that black hat and wear it for the race.

I've seen them do the same with Jeff Gordon, too, by the way: boo like hell and then put their hat on.

---

*Racing historian **Bob Latford** said that he offered advice during Dale's pre-Intimidator days:*

Basically, I was a friend, and I'd give him some advice on the politics of racing. Oh, yeah, he listened. He understood how things worked, and that's one of the hardest things for new people coming in to grasp, especially on the Cup level as the sport grew. He became more political late in his career, and part of that was the realization of his role as champion. That's something that Darrell (Waltrip) and I had talked about when he was going for that third championship, that, as the champion, there was a great deal of responsibility to represent the sport.

If there's a function at the White House and they want somebody from NASCAR there, they want the champion. So you've *got* to be able to represent your sport in those type situations. Or if there's a major function, they want the champion, and he has to be able to speak and not be a "dese, dem, and dose" orator.

I think he was a good champion, but he carried the role a little differently. He could be charming when the situation called for it. He was a lot like (A. J.) Foyt was—he was so intent on what he had to do and the amount of focus it required, he became tough to deal with when you wanted him to do something on your schedule, not his. Like Foyt, he could be one of the best interviews at the track, if you approached him "when you have time," understanding that he was working also.

Most of the people who had trouble with Foyt or Earn-hardt were the ones who wanted him to work on their schedule, not the other way around.

※

Latford, on Earnhardt's early years in Cup racing:

Like so many of the early guys, he could drive the hell out of a race car. But having to talk at a sales meeting or having to talk to an executive of a company, that was not his forte. And it became important to be as good a talker as a driver in the late seventies, shortly after he first came in.

When he was driving for Rod Osterlund in 1980 for his first championship, Osterlund wasn't worried about a sponsor. Basically, he sponsored himself with his large construction business out west. So Dale had to establish himself. His going to Victory Lane and having to talk at press conferences helped him develop his later speaking style.

Joe Whitlock, who then had the Wrangler account, talked to him a lot. Dale wasn't driving for Wrangler, but he and Whitlock were friends on Lake Norman. Earnhardt didn't live that far from Joe. Even then, Earnhardt had a place on the lake, and Joe had another one even farther out. They'd get together for a fish fry or a chicken bog, and Earnhardt could relax. He didn't have to worry about autographs; he was just another one of the young guys coming up. So that was really a good time for him.

Earnhardt was a shy guy, typical of what you'd expect to come off the short tracks, especially the dirt tracks. He was much like Bobby Isaac, who was from Catawba, North Carolina, near Hickory. Like so many of the guys, he raced at Hickory; Columbia, South Carolina; Asheville, North Carolina; Greenville-Pickens in South Carolina—places where it was easy to tow a trailer 200 or 300 miles, something like that. Most of the guys did. That was how they would learn their skills, before we got this influx of guys from the Midwest, Wisconsin, Michigan, up that way.

Most of the racing people knew Ralph because of his prowess on dirt, even though Ralph actually left and raced on the outlaw, non-NASCAR tracks. They were closer by, and he could make more money to support Martha and the kids.

Ken Squier, like Latford, saw a parallel between Earnhardt and Bobby Isaac, another Tarheel. Here, he talks about their lack of education and their ability to communicate:

I don't think that stuff (rough communication skills) is bad. I think he was shy. I always thought he was like Pearson and Isaac. The best answers I ever got come from Bobby Isaac. Bobby Isaac couldn't read, but he thought so much about what was going on and made it very, very special to me. He was not going to embarrass himself with some fellow who could write and do stories.

Isaac was that way, and, for a long time, I thought Earnhardt had a lot of that. He worked hard not to embarrass himself; I think that's why he drove so well. He didn't have to say anything because he did it with what he drove. But Isaac was the same, and Pearson was the same. They didn't have to say a lot because they did what they did, and they did it well.

A writer once told me—a man I deeply respected—that the best answers he ever got in his sports interviews came from Joe Louis. Louis was supposed to be a guy who didn't say much, who mumbled. And he said the most meaningful answers he got, he got from Joe Louis. That always impressed me, and that's what I thought I heard from Isaac, and I think there was a great deal of the same thing in Earnhardt. Those people are very, very proud. They are not going to say a whole lot and have somebody make fun of them, their accent, or their lack of education. So, instead, they go out and do what they do and do it at a level that raises the bar.

And then, as the years went by, his confidence level came along. He got some support from his family, and he actually became a pretty funny guy. He had a lot to say and

When Dale Earnhardt drove for Wrangler, he was billed as "One Tough Customer" and then "the Intimidator."

began to feel comfortable that he could say it. And, at the same time, he understood that being a little reserved and not giving himself totally up was a way that really gained attention. He knew that what he was going to give you was valuable, and he made you make a judgment. If you ran away, then he had you. Then he knew it was just as well he didn't give it to you, anyway. (Later on) he always surrounded himself with people who could help him. He was smart enough to know what he didn't know.

---

*Hall of Fame driver **Ned Jarrett** saw Earnhardt when Dale's dad, Ralph, and Dale raced in the Carolinas:*

I knew his dad (Ralph), and I'd see young Dale around the tracks some. The kids didn't go with their dads a lot back then. I remember him as a kid. He was sort of between my two sons age-wise, a little younger than Glenn and older than Dale.

But I remember him getting started driving race cars, and I soon learned he'd be someone to be reckoned with in the sport because he had obvious talent. I've said a number of times since then, in recent years and for the last ten years, any opportunity I'd get, if there was ever a chip off the old block, there was the classic example. He was just so much like his daddy in mannerisms, especially on the racetrack. They drove exactly alike; they gave no quarter and didn't expect any. There was never any doubt in my mind that he'd make it big in the sport.

---

*Hall of Fame driver/car owner **Junior Johnson** had an influence on Earnhardt's career, although Dale never drove for him. In fact, Johnson apparently told Richard Childress that he needed to get out of his race car and put Earnhardt in it:*

I wouldn't be surprised if several people helped Earnhardt a tremendous lot. Rod Osterlund helped him get moving. I've helped Earnhardt get rides, sponsors. I helped hook him up with Bud Moore and Richard Childress—with Richard twice. It was a friend thing. I knew Richard a long time, and I knew Earnhardt's father. I'd do anything to help. I was in a position to help. You're friends with people, and you want to see them survive.

3

TALES OF DALE

"It was almost like visiting with the king or the president."
— CHRIS POWELL

One of my favorite Earnhardt stories is Dale's supposed intimidation of Jeff Gordon and Gordon's reaction. Gordon won the first Brickyard 400, in 1994, and Earnhardt won the next year. Earnhardt got on TV and told a talk-show host that he was first man to win the Brickyard 400. At one point, a rumor was circulating that Gordon was gay, and that apparently came out of the Earnhardt camp. Gordon, who was painfully young and youthful-looking then, took it well enough that the whole intimidation thing died out.

At a NASCAR banquet one year, Gordon drank a milk toast to Earnhardt, who responded with champagne. Gordon was certainly no milquetoast, and Earnhardt recognized that. The two actually became business partners, and in photos you can see Earnhardt's affection for Gordon.

Earnhardt had seventy-six Cup victories. Who would later pass him for sixth place on the all-time victory list? Gordon, of course.

In the nineties, we always figured that Earnhardt, like the rest of us, would see his talent fade at some point. Like many other greats before him, he'd stay too long, and I'd write a magazine article entitled "The Lion in Winter." Just the opposite happened. Earnhardt, who would have turned fifty on April 29, 2001, was still a force at the time of his too-early demise.

Here are a few assorted stories to remember him by.

Geoff Bodine, Earnhardt's arch rival in the 1980s, remembers the incident with Dale and the handcuffs . . . yes, we did say handcuffs. It's an arresting story:

We were in Louisville, Kentucky, at the old Louisville track, going to a race on an off weekend. There were six of us there, and we were doing some interviews up in their little media center. We walked out on a balcony they had, and he grabbed some handcuffs from a security guard and walked to me when I wasn't looking and put one end to my hand and one end to the railing. He started laughing; of course *everybody* started laughing except me. That made me pretty upset.

It was kinda embarrassing, number one, and number two, I have a little claustrophobia. I didn't feel comfortable being chained, handcuffed to that railing. Immediately, I said, "Hey, get these things off me." He didn't do it right away. I said, "Listen, get these things off me right now." He was chuckling, and they could see I was pretty upset, so everyone kinda stood back to see what happened. He eventually uncuffed me, obviously. But that started a war that night for the race. In the heat race, he tried to spin me out, and in the feature race he tried to spin me out. That was a fun night. The race fans got a good show out of that one.

Bodine, on his relationship with Earnhardt:

That was pretty interesting. We started out as friends. When I first moved down (from Chemung, New York, to North Carolina), we went to dinner with him. My kids and their mother stayed there at the lake for a weekend and had a good time. But as soon as we started winning and being competitive and a challenge, things changed. He started the bump and run, and of course that changed things. So we went through a rough time for a while.

We actually rode some horses with him. (My brother) Todd had a horse farm. We were over there one time, and I had a couple horses. He and Dale Jr.—it was quite a while ago; Dale Jr. was just a little guy—we rode some horses together. Away from the track, we weren't buddies, but we respected each other. At the track, it was a different situation. It was competition, and Dale didn't like to get beat.

He'd come behind you and grab you. That was his signature, I guess, to come up from behind, put his arm around you, and put the choke hold on you. Or else grab you by the shoulder and squeeze; he was a pretty tough guy. It was fun. What I read from that was that he cared, he respected you, he wasn't trying to hurt you. But we never hung out; we were never buddy-buddy after the first year or two. He knew his limits. You learn your limits with people.

Larry McReynolds, now a TV announcer for Fox, was Earnhardt's crew chief for a few years in the nineties, and he and Earnhardt won the 1998 Daytona 500 together:

My first race with him was '97 in the Daytona 500. Of course, we know the years he tried and tried and tried to win, going there. I was fortunate enough that I had won the 500 in '92 with Davey Allison. I was pretty pumped up going there, knowing how great of a race car and engines Richard Childress normally had for Daytona and Talladega, the restrictor-plate races, knowing how Dale Earnhardt was probably better than anyone (at the restrictor-plate races); I was pretty pumped up.

We had had an up and down day in the 500. We had some problems on some pit stops. With about twenty-five (laps) to go, we had no more stops we needed to make, and we were leading the race. I can remember, with about seventeen or eighteen to go, looking up at Richard Childress and said, "What do you think?" He looked at me and said, "Been here too many times before. Been there, done that." Sure enough, with about eleven to go, I totally understood what he was talking about. We were upside down on our roof.

So they got to Dale, and Dale got out of the car. The car actually landed on its wheels; it flipped and barrel-rolled a couple of times. But he got up in the ambulance. The spotter said, "Larry, he's out of the car. Richard, he's out of the car. He walked to the ambulance. The car's pretty destroyed."

We were all walking down behind the pits. And you know how you're walking and something out of the corner of your eye catches your eye that you go, "There's no way"? We were almost to the end of the walkway behind the pits in the garage area; I was actually going over to the infield care center to check on him. I saw a black car go down pit road, and I'm thinking, "No, there's no way." I walked out on pit road and looked back down, and there was our car sitting in our pit box. He was in the car, screaming, "Where are you guys at? Just get me back out there."

When he got up in the ambulance, he looked out of the ambulance before they pulled off, looked at the car, and it was like, "Dadgum, that thing's sitting on four wheels and tires. It ain't even got a flat tire." So the maintenance work or cleanup-crew guy who was sitting in his car while they were hauling it in, he told him, "Get the hell out of my car." I guess the guy didn't know what to do, so he got out of the car. Dale got in it, cranked it up, and brought it around to the pits to have some repair work done where we could go out there and finish the race.

By finishing that race, even though we didn't win a race in 1997, we finished fifth in the points. And one of the reasons we finished fifth in the points is that we had no DNFs (did not finish) at the end of a race. And it all started at Daytona.

~☞~

McReynolds talks about one of the exhibition races that NASCAR ran in Japan in the 1990s:

Another funny story: After the season was over in '97, we went over to Suzuka, Japan. Dale was not really a big fan of being over there, but obviously he was part of the chosen group that went. It meant a lot to Bill (France) Jr. for him to be over there, and though he wasn't into it, he went. It was not something that was high on his list.

We were told, because of the logistics of going over there, that we would qualify and race, no matter, rain or shine. To be prepared, because they took rain tires over there. Sure enough, we raced in early November, and you had to ship the car in early to mid-October. And we had made all of the accommodations for the rainy weather. You had to put a windshield wiper on the left side; you had to make accommodations for blowers to defog the inside of the rear window, and you had to put a stoplight on it that you had to hook up.

We got over, and Saturday, which was the main practice day, it was monsooning. It was raining nonstop, but NASCAR said, "Look, guys, we're going to qualify and practice." And Dale screwed around and screwed around and screwed around; didn't want to go out. Finally, I said, "Dale, we've gotta qualify in this mess."

Back in the shop, I didn't think a whole lot about the windshield wiper. I said, "Mount it up at the top; it'd be much easier to mount up at the top." When he came down that front straightaway, the windshield wiper, because of the speed coming down that straightaway, it was up there oscillating back and forth. He had it on, but it was going back and forth like an antenna. He came on the radio and said, "Well, my pack of geniuses, this isn't going to work." "Ten-four, Dale, bring it on in here. I know what we need to do now."

*Longtime Cup driver **Ken Schrader** is a racer, not a fisherman, but he remembers a fishing outing from about a dozen years ago:*

My wife's daddy (Tom Pokrafke) was in town, and we was going to take him and his friend—they were both in their late 70s or early 80s—and my little girl (Dorothy) over to Earnhardt's place to go fishing. This was like Tuesday before the (Coca-Cola) 600. We were supposed to be there at one, and at twelve thirty he started calling—I only live about six miles away—and said, "Where in the hell are you? Where in the hell are you?" I said, "Dammit, I'm coming; I haven't left yet, I'm on time." He said, "Get over here."

So we get over there, and he couldn't be a more gracious host as far as making sure you had a good time. We went down to the pond. We got his little girl (Taylor Nicole) and mine (Dorothy), which were a year apart—at that time, they were maybe five and six. We go down to go fishing, and my father-in-law, Earnhardt, baits up his hook and everything. Tom throws out his hook, and, heck, it wasn't twenty seconds and he was reeling in a big old catfish, and the girls are reeling in fish. And Earnhardt's just going back and forth, taking fish off and rebaiting hooks.

After my father-in-law caught something like three fish, after the last one he pulled in, he set the rod down after Earnhardt took the fish off the hook. We said, "What's wrong, Tom?" He said, "I don't want to fish no more." He'd caught three in ten minutes. We said, "Why not? We're catching a bunch of them." He said, "I don't like fishing like this." Earnhardt said, "What's wrong?", and Tom said, "I like it when I throw a hook out and sit a while." I thought Earnhardt would die laughing; I thought he'd fall in the pond laughing.

He was trying to make sure everybody had a good time. But them guys, it was too much work for them.

Randy LaJoie, a two-time Busch Series champion, recalls his own fears and Earnhardt's humanity:

I was at Dover, racing my own car in the Busch Series, and he was driving in the Busch Series. And I got a lap down early in the event. He was running second, and I was running behind him. I said, "Okay, I'm going to pass him." (My car) was better than him then. I got up to his door a few times, and he'd pass me going into the corner. I thought, *What the hell is he doing? He's running this place wide open.* Then I said to myself, *If he can do it, I can do it.*

The next time I got to his door, I never lifted. We got into the third turn. I went in there wide open. I went up the racetrack a little bit. I got into his door, and he got into my door. And I (pulled away) and ended up finishing seventh; I think he finished second.

At the time, they had only one parts truck there, and it was in the Cup garage. So I had to go down and pay my bill. And as I was walking back to the garage, Earnhardt came out of his hauler. *"LaJoie, come here!"* And I thought he was going to kick my ass for running over him. He came over and put his arm around me and said, *"That's* the way to pass somebody." It made my day.

Ron Hornaday, who became a three-time Craftsman Truck Series champion, has a story behind the story. Hornaday did Richard Childress a good turn, and Childress returned the favor:

We were up at a (three-eighths-mile) racetrack up there in Colorado, and they had an exhibition deal with Richard Childress and a couple of other big-name owners. Richard got in a car, and—I don't know how to use the word—it wasn't a top-quality car. (There was) a car I'd sold to a guy who had won the championship the year before, I talked him into letting Richard drive it, and Richard ended up winning the race. Richard said, "Hornaday, anything I can do for you for giving me that car . . ." I said, "Talk to Dale for me." He said, "I'll do that." The next day, I got a phone call from Dale.

Hornaday likes to tell the tale of him getting a Truck Series ride for Dale Earnhardt in 1994. This was when Hornaday had the shop Victory Circle Race Cars in California, and Earnhardt had trouble leaving a telephone message:

He saw me on *Winter Heat* (on television). A kid who was working for me at the shop hung up on him. We had this guy we worked closely with who would call and mess with him: *"Hey, this is Richard Petty."* He hung up, because he thought it was him. Dale called back and said, "No, this is really Dale Earnhardt. Is he home?" "No, he hasn't come back from the races yet." He got pretty excited.

When I showed up at one o'clock, I had to go to the bathroom real bad, and he said, "You can't go to the bathroom. Dale's going to call at one o'clock. He's going to call you at one o'clock." Dale did call when I was in the bathroom; we'd just got off the airplane. I came out to talk to him. Everybody was quiet in the whole shop. I was just saying, "Yes sir, yes sir . . . all of that stuff." Just everybody being excited at the shop.

We had one more race to run in *Winter Heat*. And Dale said, "I'm going to fly you out here and talk to you, get you to drive my truck next year." I said, "I got one more race this weekend. I gotta get my truck done." He said, "Aw, you can get the other guys to do it." I had a couple of buddies, working on the championship. He said, "I'll get you back in time." I had first-class tickets, and at the airport, he picked me up in a Silverado pickup truck, and he was signing autographs for some people, and he was in a tuxedo. He was doing a commercial with his seven championship trophies; he had four in the back and three in the backseat—it was an extended cab.

We were driving up the road, and we were passing a couple of people, and he took the back roads to his shop. It was my first time in North Carolina, and I didn't know where he was going. He passed a couple of cars, and he got up to this truck in front of him, and he ran into the back of it. He tried to pass him again, and he pulled over, and he ran into the back of him again. The guy pulls into a little dirt road, and (Dale) pulls into his shop there. I go, "What was that all about?" and he said, "Oh, that guy's dating my daughter, and I don't like him."

He took me down (to the shop), and showed me all his 400 acres with all the deer on it. We probably talked for an hour. He said, "You want to do the deal?" We went in to talk to Doug Richert. He dropped me off at the door. I'd never met Doug or anything. We just started talking and working on race cars. I stayed about a year in Doug Richert's house, and I was working for Dale and Teresa Earnhardt.

Jeff Gordon likes to tell a story about an International Race of Champions event several years ago at Daytona. Gordon was running three-abreast between Ken Schrader and Earnhardt, and three cars couldn't make it through the turns side by side:

Someone was going to have to back out of the throttle and let the other two go. I looked to my right and saw Schrader looking straight ahead. No help there. I looked to my left, and Earnhardt was grinning at me. Dale was sending a message: "It's up to you, big boy." I also knew he wasn't going to lift (his foot off the gas pedal) and that I was going to have to be the one to lift. And, sure enough, I was. I'll never forget that day.

Dr. Joe Mattioli, chairman of the board and CEO of Pocono Raceway, recalls Earnhardt's first win at Pocono:

When he won his first race here, his son Dale Jr. must have been twelve years old or so, and the kid couldn't get in Victory Lane. So we saw him, my wife (Rose) did, and she grabbed ahold of him and took him to the top of the podium where his father was getting the trophy, and we got them together. In all our pictures, we have a picture of young Dale and his father, and we still treasure it. That was sort of an unusual day and a nice day.

———— ❦ ————

Earnhardt had plenty of friends outside the auto-racing community, notably Atlanta Braves third-base coach Ned Yost; former Braves Jeff Blauser and Jody Davis; country music stars Kix Brooks and Ronnie Dunn, Travis Tritt, and Delbert McClinton; and television journalist Brian Williams.

Yost met Earnhardt in the mid-1980s when he was hunting with Davis, a catcher. Davis asked if he could bring a friend, Earnhardt. **Ned Yost** *remembers a hunting trip with Earnhardt. Dale had a sponsor commitment, but he wanted to extend his trip to Iowa, and the original excuse was the weather:*

Finally, we looked at him and said, "Dale, we really didn't want to admit this, but we'll say it now anyway. We don't want you to go because we love you. We love you, man. We can't help it; we just love you." He got this huge smile on his face, and I think he understood what it was. We just didn't want him to go. I'm sure glad I got a chance to say that."[1]

———— ❦ ————

Yost *also recalled Earnhardt talking about Ernie Irvan's near-fatal crash in 1994:*

I remember sitting on the back porch where we were at. It was three in the morning, and Dale said, "You know, if that can happen to Ernie Irvan, it can happen to me." And in the back of my mind, I'm thinking, *There's no way it can happen to you. You are, literally, in my mind, invincible.*[2]

———— ❦ ————

Yost reacted strongly after he learned that Earnhardt was dead:

I wanted to start bawling and screaming, but it felt surreal. It didn't feel like it was really happening.[3]

A day later, Yost sounded almost at peace:

I don't really feel bad for him. I know his faith, so I know he's in good hands right now. I feel bad for myself. I won't get to call him up anymore. One phone call to him would energize me for weeks.[4]

Around 2000, a NASCAR fan gave Travis Tritt a black Sam Bass guitar with Earnhardt's face on the front. He added it to his collection, but he didn't play it until Dale died. Then he decided to begin each performance of his tour by strapping on the guitar and singing a song in memory of Earnhardt. He changed the lyrics to his opening number, "Put Some Drive in Your Country," and the final line became "I miss Dale Earnhardt; I wish he was still alive":

Dale's death was extremely disturbing to me and my family. I met Dale years ago when he called me to tell me that my song "I'm Gonna Be Somebody" was a huge inspiration to both him and his son.[5]

Tritt says he and Earnhardt were mutual fans. In May, he talked about him again:

Dale Earnhardt was what made NASCAR exciting for me. He was my favorite driver. I had the privilege of meeting him on several occasions and was honored to find out that Dale and his family were fans of my music. He told me that "I'm Gonna Be Somebody" was one of his favorite songs. I told him that I only wished I could "be somebody" as big to the music world as he was to racing.[6]

Humpy Wheeler, president and general manager of Lowe's Motor Speedway, on Earnhardt's rivalries and non-rivalries:

Lots of people tried to intimidate him. By the time Earnhardt came along, Darrell Waltrip's career was rolling, and Dale was one of the young guys trying to take a job away from him. Darrell hadn't totally established himself as a superstar, but he was a star when Earnhardt got going. Darrell was not a combative guy on the track, as you know, and if he fought anyone on the track, it'd be during the last ten laps. They crossed swords many times. They didn't have the rivalry that Cale and Darrell had, but he was a nemesis.

I guess Rusty Wallace was his biggest rival, as well as Tim Richmond, as far as his contemporaries. As for the older drivers, I'd say Bobby Allison, whose last race was in '88. There was some rivalry there, because Bobby Allison was one driver nobody could intimidate. There was no way to do that. He had a lot of intimidation himself.

One rivalry that never happened, that we all thought was going to happen, was Earnhardt and Jeff Gordon. Because you could see Jeff Gordon coming from a mile away. Earnhardt had his piece of the pie. He was the man, and here comes this young upstart, but it never happened.

It would have been great to see those guys driving the old cars with bias-ply tires, but it wasn't meant to be. It's pretty interesting how many races they won, but the rivalry never developed, although we all thought it would. Earnhardt picked on Gordon for a while, and he knew he was getting to Jeff. So Gordon thought, *He knows he's getting to me, so I'm going to back off and let him say what he wants to.*

At that point Dale stopped needling him, and they developed a mutual respect. They had an interesting relationship, because they did a lot of business deals and stuff that nobody knows about.

Jim Hunter, now NASCAR's chief publicist, was president of Darlington Raceway when Earnhardt was dominating there in the nineties:

I remember one year at Darlington in practice and qualifying—he may not have been the slowest car, but he was one of them—and naturally he was in a bad mood. Late that afternoon after qualifying was over, (track publicist) Russell Branham and I went over to his motor coach just to ask him if he knew what was wrong.

We knocked on the door of the motor coach, and he said, "If you've come to give me any sympathy, I don't need any." I said, "I didn't come to give you any sympathy; I come to shoot the bull." And he opened the door, and he was in the motor coach by himself. He was cooking a steak, and he was pretty ticked at himself. He couldn't figure why the car was so slow. He wound up finishing second or third in the race, and he drove the car sideways the whole day, which was an Earnhardt thing. He drove Darlington like it was a dirt track, a big dirt track.

Longtime radio personality Mark Garrow remembers that Earnhardt wasn't an easy guy to interview, but he was strangely easy to talk to after the 1990 Daytona 500, perhaps Earnhardt's most bitter defeat:

(One memory was) in 1990, when he lost the race (to Derrike Cope) at Daytona. Dale could be kind of prickly with the press, so when something wasn't going right or something bad happened, you had to be careful. One remarkable thing about Dale's career is how he handled that loss. He wanted to win in the worst way, and he'd dominated that race. I figured that, after the race, he'd basically slam the car-hauler door and walk off, and we might get a comment from him at Rockingham the following week.

But I'll never forget the fact that he stood in that garage at Daytona, and people were kind of hesitant to approach him, but myself and a handful of others did that. And he talked about the race and his disappointment for a good fifteen to twenty minutes.

Part of that was he was a stand-up guy, but part was he was a guy who was totally shell shocked. So instead of an angry reaction, slamming doors and whatnot, he was actually reserved and almost resigned to the fate that maybe that was the race he was never going to win. Instead of being all fired up and mad, he very calmly, bit by bit, point by point, went through what had to be as agonizing a defeat as any professional race driver has had to endure, because of the importance of the race and how badly he wanted to win it.

As a matter of fact, after we walked away, he was *still standing there.* That goes back to shell shock. I'm sure he was angry, frustrated and resigned to his fate. He probably had a lot of things running around there. But I remember talking to him fifteen or twenty minutes and walking away and him still standing there in that garage. It was one of those surreal moments in the twenty-five years of my career at this level. That's something you won't forget—and I haven't.

Garrow remembers the famous, or infamous, water-bottle incident between Rusty Wallace and Earnhardt:

I was in the middle of a rugby scrum during the famous water-bottle-throwing incident with Rusty Wallace. I'm the only guy who had actual audio of what was said during the water-bottle-throwing escapade. But it was kind of funny; the only way I could describe it to people is that it was like a rugby scrum.

You have Rusty starting to get out of his car, and Earnhardt was talking to people. I was there, maybe another media guy, and his crew chief was Andy Petree. Andy was there, and Earnhardt is talking to Andy. And all of a sudden, Rusty whipped a water bottle at Earnhardt; it bounced off the (car) roof a little bit, and it caught Dale a little flying by there. And Rusty jumped in there—he was really upset about Dale spinning him early in the race.

Dale was just listening, and Andy Petree was just pushing him, like, "Come on man, you know he didn't do it on purpose; you know that." Again, they were in this tight little pack like a rugby scrum. It was Rusty and his crew chief, with Andy and Earnhardt in the middle; they were the core, if you will, the pit of a giant peach that wrapped all around everybody.

As they came together, more and more people gathered around. So what became three people in the circle became ten people in the circle, became twenty people in the circle, and right in the middle of it was Rusty hacking at Earnhardt: "You spun me out on purpose because you knew I was going to beat you." And Earnhardt going, "Come on, man, I wouldn't do that."

Rusty was hot and flinging four-letter words; he was definitely upset. And Earnhardt was just smiling: "Come on, man, just call me Monday. We'll talk it out; we'll get it fixed." And Rusty's, "You're not calling *me* on Monday. I'm not calling you on Monday. Get outta here." And Dale was smiling at him, "Come on, man, you can call me on Monday and we'll talk about it." And Rusty's hot. He didn't want to have anything to do with that. And Earnhardt walked away with a "that's the way that goes," that little Earnhardt smirk he had.

Rusty was living in one of Earnhardt's houses at the time, until Rusty's house on Lake Norman was finished, so they were great friends.

⌁

Chris Powell, now vice president/general manager at Las Vegas Motor Speedway, was the chief motorsports publicist for then-series sponsor Winston in the early nineties. His job this particular day was to round up Earnhardt for a get-together at a racetrack:

One time I was taking him out to the Winston track house at a racetrack to do an interview. I won't say which track, but we were going out to the track house, and there might have been a couple of thousand fans crammed in there. The people who run the pavilion, the tent thing, would announce that they were going to have such-and-such driver in here at 10 a.m. I had Dale in the front seat, and we were going through the tunnel to the speedway. But we can't move because there are so many pedestrians walking along the roadway.

And I thought he was going to get mad. He was a fairly impatient guy; that's what made him a great race-car driver. I thought, *Earnhardt's going to get upset and tell me to start blowing the horn, and I hate doing that.* We hadn't budged for about thirty seconds, and he said, "You know, these track operators ought to build sidewalks for these people to walk on. They're out here paying their hard-earned money to come out here today, and they're having to walk on the street. If these track operators would build more sidewalks, people could walk and we could drive along."

And it settled me down, because I was nervous that he was going to be upset and tell me to blow the horn or "Let's turn around," or "I ain't doing this again." Instead, he was just as patient as he could be. And then we went in and did the interview, and he was as great as he always is.

—————

Randy LaJoie, the two-time Busch Series champion, recalls an incident in which the drivers were on pit road at Daytona International Speedway and they hadn't gotten into their cars yet:

It was right before the Daytona 300 race, and Dale and I were starting side by side. During the prerace, he came over and put his arm around me. We were looking up; there was a pretty big wind. He says "LaJoie, that plane's not moving." It was a plane that was carrying a banner. I said, "It has to be moving. Otherwise, it'd fall out of the sky." But he said, "But look at it."

So we were both looking at this airplane up there. Somebody took a picture of us; it was one of the people who was taking pictures for my mom. My mom had maybe fifty of them made up for the fan club members. And I brought them over to Dale (after the race) to see if he'd sign them for me. I wound up spending two hours on the farm with him, had a half a dozen beers. We went inside and he signed the pictures, and he said, "I gotta keep one; you gotta sign one for me." I said, "I can do that." He was just a regular guy.

—————

Stevie Waltrip, the wife of Darrell Waltrip, placed a Bible verse in Dale Earnhardt's No. 3 Chevrolet before the 2001

*Daytona 500. It was Proverbs 18:10: "The name of the Lord
is a strong tower, the righteous man runs into it and is safe."
Mrs. Waltrip had done this before; it pleased and comforted
the Intimidator. Each time, she signed it: "To my friend Dale.
I love you, big guy":*

Years ago I started giving Dale a Bible Scripture before each
race, and he had come to expect it. Last Sunday before the
race, I was trapped back behind a big crowd of people in the
infield, and Dale and Teresa looked back and saw me. They
motioned me to come over, and just before Dale got in his
car I gave him his Scripture.

Sometimes I would try to come up with something
motivational or inspirational. Last Sunday I was riding to
the track on a bus and, since it was February 18, I decided
to look in Proverbs 18. My eye fell on that passage and I
decided that was the one I'd give Dale. I wrote it down on a
little card with the stickum on the back because he liked to
stick them on his dashboard.

If it was getting close to race time and I hadn't given it
(his Bible verse) to him, he'd look around for me and say,
"Hey, where's my Bible verse?" One year at North Wilkesboro I was running late and didn't get down to the track
until they were about to start the race. Dale actually got out
of his car and came looking for me. He grabbed his verse
and ran back and climbed back in his car just in time to
start the race.[7]

Mike Bolton, the outdoors writer for the Birmingham
(Alabama) News, *got to know Earnhardt through their
mutual friend, Neil Bonnett. Bolton says that when Bonnett
died in 1994, Earnhardt was devastated. In fact, he wrote
about it in 2000, just before Earnhardt won his last race,
at Talladega:*

I could tell it really affected him. As a matter of fact, I've got something here I'll read to you. I went skeet shooting with Earnhardt last October, a couple days before he won the Talladega race.

"You know, I miss my old buddy," he said. "I was just thinking about him. It's hard to come to this place in May and October now." He said, "I'll always love the outdoors, but I'll tell you, it lost something for me when Neil left. I still like to go hunting and fishing to get away from everything, but I don't think I'll ever enjoy it like I did." He said, "I took my son fishing, and I enjoyed that. I took my eleven-year-old daughter, Taylor, hunting the other day, and she got her first buck. I wouldn't give anything for that, but it's still not the same, though."

He said, "I have two brothers that I love dearly, but what Neil and I had was special. It was not a relationship where either one of us had to ask or tell. It wasn't a matter of 'I want' or 'I need.' It was a matter of 'we did.' Instead of 'let's go there,' we just went."

I'd seen a Realtree decal on the No. 3 Richard Childress Racing Chevrolet—I didn't even know what Realtree Outdoors was at the time. Then Realtree announced a full sponsorship with **Dave Marcis** *when the Winston Cup Media Tour went to Earnhardt's little shop in the mid-1990s:*

Him (Earnhardt) and Richard Childress told Bill Jordan of Realtree to sponsor me. Realtree wasn't big enough to fully sponsor Childress's team, but it was big enough to sponsor a little team like mine. So Richard and Dale suggested he get ahold of me, and that's how our relationship began with Realtree.

Marcis talked about his friendship with Earnhardt:

Probably him and I were the two best buddies in the garage, because we hunted together and fished together. We spent a lot of time together and talked, and I did a lot of testing for him at Daytona and Talladega in Childress' car. So we were pretty close.

One time, he called up (my wife) Helen on a Thursday afternoon and told her to tell me to be at the airport tomorrow morning at six thirty; we were going hunting. I had no clue how, where, or what, or a doggone thing, but he said don't be late. I got my hunting stuff together; I assumed we were going for whitetails (deer), because we'd talked about it, although we'd never made no definite dates or anything.

I was there at six thirty, and he finally showed up at seven thirty (Marcis laughs). We got on the plane, and he says, "We were going to Texas hunting whitetails." He said that Bill's (Realtree Outdoors owner Bill Jordan) going to meet up, so off we went to Texas.

I think we hunted three days. It must have been an off weekend (from racing). Bill and Dale had each purchased a trophy hunt and a deer that the landowner maybe wants out of the herd maybe because it doesn't have a perfect rack; he wants the genes out of the gene pool. Both Bill and Dale let me shoot that particular deer, and they each shot the trophy deer. It was great for me, because I couldn't afford to go myself.

———⟡———

Marcis, on Earnhardt getting ahead of his friends:

He was as aggressive at hunting as he was at driving a race car. He always had to be ahead of you. If you were in the woods, he had to be ahead of you. If you were standing on the corner waiting to buy your license, he had to be ahead of you. If you said you were getting up at five o'clock, he'd say, "That's fine," and that rascal would have to be up at four thirty so he'd be up before you, then he'd spend the day picking on you because you weren't up. Same with breakfast. If they said breakfast was at such and such a time, he'd be there early just to be ahead of you.

We were hunting turkeys one time in Alabama—and he had flown a helicopter in then, him and his pilot—and he said he was going to stay only one day. I got a turkey that day, and he didn't. All of a sudden, from not being able to stay another day, he could all of a sudden stay another day. He wasn't going to the racetrack with me having a turkey and him not. We were racing at Talladega. So he stayed the next morning, and he got one.

Bill (Jordan, Realtree Outdoors owner) tried to get films of us hunting, but they always had trouble with Dale. They'd be calling the turkeys, and the turkeys would be gobbling, but Dale didn't have the patience for that bird to come in. He'd start crawling on his hands and knees, and Bill would say, "Dale, Dale, don't do that. You're screwing us up. We can't film you from over there." Earnhardt would keep on crawling (Marcis laughs). There'd be a big *boom*, and Bill would say, "There he goes again; we ain't got nothing on film again."

Chris Powell says he sometimes felt like he was visiting royalty when he went to see Earnhardt:

One thing he'd do when I was doing PR for Winston, he'd put his arm around me and say, "How come you don't come by and see me? Why don't you check in?" I did that a couple of times, but I didn't feel he thought I was necessarily the person he wanted knocking at the door of the hauler.

One day in Bristol it was raining, so I went by and knocked on the door of the lounge in the hauler. I didn't hear anybody, so I stuck my head in there, and he said, "Come on in." He was looking over the results from the truck race the night before. He was going down the list, giving an assessment of the young drivers. That was a lot of fun.

And, at the time, Kenny Irwin was running well in the truck series, and Dale was saying, "He's going to be a good race-car driver." I said, "This guy (Steve) Park, who's driving for you, what about him?" He said, "He's a racer; I can tell just watching him. He's not a driver; he's a racer."

When you got Earnhardt at the right time, and you know this, he could be so engaging. It was almost like visiting with the king or the president. For a guy with so little education, he was really smart and wily, both on the racetrack and off.

Paul "Little Bud" Moore, who was a driver when Earnhardt came along, became close friends with Dale. They did a little business together, and they did the "7-and-7" promotion between Earnhardt and Richard Petty. But then they drifted apart. Until the 2001 Daytona 500 weekend, they hadn't talked in a while:

He and I were into cars, and he liked cars. His last words to me were on Friday morning before the Daytona 500. He and I had a person come between us, and we had not talked in quite some time, probably two years. It's really ironic how this happened. We used to be awful close. Something told me that morning, "Go to the racetrack and find him, this is the time to do this," and I did. It worked out perfect, and we pulled out chairs and were talking. Dale Jr. came out and listened to the conversation, and I was glad he heard it.

Toward the end of the conversation, he knew I had a lot of old cars and signage, and he does, too. And he said, "When we get home, I'm going to build me and you another building, and we're going to put all of that stuff in that building." He said, "We need to start enjoying this stuff. It's time to do that some." It's ironic that he'd say that. I knew how much he always wanted to, and how much he liked all of that stuff.

With seven championships, Earnhardt should have gotten used to going to New York for the Cup banquet. **Chris Powell** *recalls Dale getting excited on Times Square when they were doing publicity for his 1994 title:*

He got that little-boy look in his eyes occasionally. It was Friday at lunch, the afternoon before the banquet that night. You've seen it a thousand times, we had the champion's photo shoot at Times Square. We turned onto Broadway, and we were still eight to ten blocks from Times Square, riding in the limo.

There was a Jumbotron at Times Square showing a thirty-minute loop of season highlights from Earnhardt's team. When he saw it, he got this great gleam in his eye, like a little kid at Christmas. "Look there, Teresa!" he said. "Look at us up there!" He got as excited as we mortals do when we are excited. I was happy we did that video up that day because he was as excited about it as anybody.

Former Charlotte Observer *motorsports writer* **Tom Higgins** *remembers a story that revealed Earnhardt's mindset and his toughness:*

When he busted his knee at Pocono, Earnhardt went home

and went to see a doctor, and he said, "My knee is swollen as big as a basketball. Take a look at it and see what's wrong." They took x-rays, and the doctor said, "My God, man, you've got a barrel fracture." He said it had to be as painful as hell if he put an ounce of weight on it. The doctor talked about an operation, but Dale said, "I can't have it operated on, I've got to race at Talladega." The doctor said, "There's no way in hell you can race on that."

Dale went to see a surgeon, and he told Dale the same thing. Dale was persuasive, and they put a splint on the knee, and Dale ran in the race. He was so afraid that NASCAR would find out how bad hurt he was, so he hid in a Lincoln Town Car. He stretched out in the back when he wasn't practicing or qualifying so they wouldn't see him.

He came home and was operated on the Monday after the race, and they put nuts and bolts in the knee.

And Earnhardt continued to race.

Roger Bear, who is now president of Keystone Marketing, was in charge of R. J. Reynolds's Winston Racing Series when he took a wild ride with Earnhardt:

I don't remember the year, but it was long before Dale became famous. Dale was racing a Late Model car in Coeburn, Virginia, in a Saturday night race, and I was up there. I had an airplane ticket, and I was going to Auburndale, Florida, the next day. It's in south-central Florida, and they had a flat, quarter-mile track, also a NASCAR-sanctioned track. There was going to be a big Late Model race the next day, I'm not sure where, but I think it was in South Boston, Virginia, and that's where Harry Gant and all the rest of them were going.

Before this race in Coeburn, Virginia, I was talking to Dale, and he asked if I was going to this other race the next night. I said, "No, I gotta go to Auburndale," and he said, "Well, if I do well here, maybe I'll go to Auburndale, too." I said, "If you do well and want to go down there, I'll help you drive," never figuring he'd want to do that, because it was a long way from Coeburn to Auburndale.

At the end of the race, Dale had done decently, finished third or fourth, and he was standing in line to get his money at the pay window. He called me over and asked, "Hey, do you think the Auburndale promoter will give me a deal?" He thought he could get appearance money. I said, "Well, it's ten thirty at night and his crowd's probably gone, so I'd say there's no way to promote it, but I'll call and find out." I called, and the promoter said to tell him he couldn't give him a deal, but he'd guarantee his expenses.

Dale, at that time, hauled his car on an open trailer behind a truck. It had rail sides and a place for his gas can, tires, tools, and whatever else he carried with him. Then there was a bench seat in the front of the truck. And there was an opening between the cab and this tarpaulin area where he could crawl in there with his sleeping bag or cot. It was Dale, me, his brother, and Bob Tomlinson, who went on to be team manager for Cale Yarborough, but then he worked for Cannon Mills. It was the four of us in the truck. Dale said, "I'm going to climb in the back and go to sleep," so he gave his brother directions on how to get down into Georgia down to I-85.

His brother took a wrong turn, and we were on some roads where the brakes were just smoking going down the mountain, and Dale stuck his head up after we were about an hour and a half into the trip. He realized the brakes were stinking, and he said to his brother, "Where in the world are you?" His brother said, "I don't know, but I think we made a wrong turn." He said, "Pull over," and he got behind the wheel, and down the mountain we went. We flew down that mountain, and we wound up someplace in North Carolina, where we hooked up with I-85. Finally, we got to Anderson, South Carolina, and he pulled over and said, "Roger, you drive. You ever drive one of these?" And I said, "No." He said, "Well, just get going."

Dale later would tell the story this way: "When I went to sleep, Roger had both hands tightly on the wheel, hanging on for dear life as he was driving down the road at sixty or sixty-five miles an hour." He said, "At that speed, I knew we'd never make it. When I woke up south of Atlanta, he's going one arm out the window, one hand on the wheel, yakking on the CB and driving eighty-five miles an hour." And he said, "I figured we'd make it then."

I drove a while, and then he woke up and drove the rest of the way in. I was just exhausted, and I'm sure he was, too.

So he dropped me off, went out there and set the fastest time in qualifying, got spun out by the local hero, lost a lap, made up the lap and came back to finish second. It was an incredible feat, and, to my mind, it was one of the great races I ever saw Dale Earnhardt run.

It's my story, and it was kinda his story, too, because he'd always tell it every time we got together.

Ed Clark, president/general manager of Atlanta Motor Speedway, remembers a conversation at the 2000 Cup banquet in New York:

It was unusual for Dale to stick around at the banquet. Usually, he'd get his stuff together and go home. I was at the party afterwards; Dale and Teresa were there, and he said, "Let's go get something to eat and talk." We did, and Dale talked about everything from the kids to the farm to the team he was building. He asked how things are going here (at Atlanta Motor Speedway). We'd had a couple of tough events here with the weather, and we started talking about the challenge of promoting races here.

Very unlike the Dale Earnhardt I knew in the early years, Dale said, "You gotta quit worrying about that. Your job is to find something good every day. Life's too short; enjoy it. Make it fun for those around you. If you do that, everything will fall in line." It was like a different Dale Earnhardt talking. Since that conversation, I have realized so many times that the last couple years of Dale's life, that's really what he was doing in so many cases.

It was the first time that he was satisfied that he had gotten to where he wanted to get. His team was doing well. His kids were racing and doing well. A lot of things were good, and he was enjoying life. Not that he was any less intense when he pulled the helmet on. You know how intense he was. But I'd never seen that side of him until the last couple of years. It may have been there; I just hadn't had the opportunity to see it, and it stuck with me.

Max Helton, *formerly of Motor Racing Outreach, remembers Earnhardt after a famous wreck:*

You always expected him to be above that (dying in an accident). You always expected him to have a heart attack, anything but a car wreck. I guess that's because we'd seen him walk away from so much stuff he'd been through.

I think one of the worst crashes of his life was at Talladega a few years ago. It was a several-car incident, but he was tapped by Sterling Marlin, who had been tapped by Ernie Irvan. He got turned into the wall and turned upside down, and he got hit several times while he was upside down. It was a bad accident.

I went to the infield care center, and they'd brought the

others in before they brought in Earnhardt. Earnhardt was the last one to come in, and here he comes walking in, holding his shoulder, because he'd hurt his shoulder and ribs. He was sore, and yet he went around to check if the other drivers were okay before he'd let them check him to see how he was. I thought, *Man, this guy is incredible! Before he'll let the doctors check him, he checks on the other drivers and gives them high-fives.*

Then he proceeded back to his bed so they could check him out. That just shows you his thoughts of other people.

Clark chuckles when he remembers a post-race incident at North Carolina Speedway:

It was at Rockingham, and you know how all the guys fly their planes and land at the drag strip across the road. I'm standing at the top of the concourse, and people are just filing out like crazy. Right in the middle of them come Dale and Teresa; Dale's got a cap pulled down over his eyes, and he's got their daughter Taylor on his shoulders. They're going along with the flow of the crowd, and he saw me and we made eye contact, and he gave me a look that said, "Don't you dare!" Because he'd have been stuck there three hours signing autographs! And nobody recognized him. He was just someone in the crowd. But I could have gotten him good.

Ron Hornaday, who raced the Craftsman Truck Series for Earnhardt, talks about his favorite memories of Dale:

Everything. There's not a bad memory at all. A lot of times we'd sit around on Monday night, and we'd talk about what we did all week long. Me winning a championship and twenty-five races for him. And I won an ARCA race and two Busch races for him.

He really treated me like part of the family. And we had a lot of business deals where he took care of me. He really gave me the right direction to go in racing; gave me a lot of wisdom.

---

*Longtime motorsports announcer **Eli Gold** became friends with Earnhardt after making an apology:*

It was in the early eighties, when Dale didn't need my help in getting on the wrong side of the fans—he seemed to be doing that pretty well himself. He was being booed by the fans—there wasn't a love relationship with the fans then.

We were at Rockingham, and I was the turn announcer for Motor Racing Network in turns one and two. Dale was coming off turn two outside Benny Parsons, and Benny was on the inside groove and was leading the race. It was late in the afternoon, and Earnhardt, from my angle, bumped Benny two or three times coming off turn two, heading down the backstretch late in the race. Benny went on to win or finish second, I don't remember which, but he had a good finish.

I saw Benny in the infield after the race. I said, "Congratulations on your finish. Earnhardt roughed you up a little bit there, didn't he?" This wasn't on the air; this was just me and Benny talking. He said, "The boy never touched me." I said, "Come on, you couldn't have slipped a piece of paper between you." He said, "He might have been that close, but he never touched me." Here I had been on the air, and I didn't editorialize, but I made it clear that Earnhardt was bumping against Benny. I'm sure I saw what I saw, but I must not have had the right angle.

I felt bad because he didn't need help getting the fans ticked off at this point. When I got back home to Alabama, I called Earnhardt on Monday at his house, and I told him what I had said. I offered an apology. I said, "I could have sworn you touched him, but Benny says you never did," and Dale swore he never did. He said, "You've got to be very careful, because you don't understand how many people formulate an opinion on what guys on the radio or in the media say. I don't mind a comment as long as it's correct."

I learned a good lesson from that, to be careful about what you say. Interestingly, that became the starting point for a good working friendship with Dale. I don't want to say that he and I went to dinner all the time; we rarely did, so I'm not passing myself off as his all-time best buddy. But we had a good relationship right up until the day he died.

---

*After **Dale Earnhardt Jr.** won in 2000 in Texas, Dale Sr. visited him in Victory Lane. Earnhardt showed his excitement and his love for his son:*

He just told me he loved me, and he wanted to make sure I took the time to enjoy this and relax a little bit with what we accomplished today. You can get so swept up with what's going on around you that you really don't enjoy it yourself personally, so he just wanted me to take a minute and do this and celebrate how I wanted to celebrate. That was pretty smart on his part to be thinking about that at that particular time.[8]

***Buddy Baker** smiles when he recalls Dale Jr.'s first Cup victory and Dale Sr.'s reaction, at Texas in 2000:*

He loved his son, and his son loved him. You could see that in Texas last year when Dale Jr. won his first Winston Cup race there. It was so apparent. No one had seen that part of Earnhardt at all. One tough customer became one proud papa. And I said it on TV. I said, "You're finally getting to see the part of Earnhardt that nobody gets to see."

Earnhardt had his share of rivals. **Humpy Wheeler** *explains:*

The Bodine-Earnhardt feud didn't start at Charlotte or start on any track. But they kept crossing each other's paths. Geoff was in his prime at the time—he was a good driver—and, in those days, they'd run awfully close together.

I regard that whole deal as the North versus the South, Geoff from Chemung, New York, and Dale from Kannapolis, North Carolina. Bodine was one of the first guys from out of the area who came down here and told us that we didn't have a monopoly on good race-car drivers in the South or the Carolinas. I always thought Earnhardt looked like a Confederate soldier anyway. It was a North-South Yankee deal.

I don't know who wrecked who, but it happened so many times. They got together time after time, and it was the nearest thing we had to the rivalries between Richard Petty and Bobby Allison or David Pearson. It didn't seem like they could stand each other on the racetrack. Eventually, over a period of time, they developed a mutual respect for each other.

Perhaps the most interesting relationship Earnhardt had was with Tim Richmond. Tim drove a race car a lot like Dale, took the car to the end of its limits. He knew how to drive a loose race car, which is what made Earnhardt great.

---

*Russell Branham, the former publicist at Darlington
Raceway, says Earnhardt loved that track:*

It was my job to sell race tickets, and he was a great tool in
selling tickets. He loved that place; they were so much like,
like two peas in a pod. He was the Man in Black, and it was
the Lady in Black. The track was Too Tough to Tame, and
no one was tougher than Dale. He listened to old drivers
and followed their lead—race the racetrack, and if you
have a problem, you say, "Yeah, the old lady slapped me
around." That's why we utilized him in so many commercials, newspaper advertisements, and in our DarlingToons
on the radio.

He loved to make me squirm. If I needed him for a
photo or to do something on radio, he'd say, "Why should I
do it for you?" I'd say, "You're going to get me fired." He'd
say, "That's your problem." I'd say, "You gotta help me,"
and he'd never fail. He'd end the conversation, and he'd
make me wait and squirm, but he always did it, whether it
was a photo, a press release, a writer to talk to, or a social
function.

We had a good rapport with him, and the number-one
reason was Jim (Hunter, the track president from 1992
until early 2001). Jim's known him a long time, from the
days when (publicist) Joe Whitlock worked with him. Dale
had a hard time with the media. Jim knew him when he
was a nobody, and Jim helped my relationship with him.
He helped me get to know another side of him.

And there are several reasons he had a closeness with
Darlington. Number one, even before Jim got there, I think
he was close to the racetrack itself. Since he was from the
old school—and remember what that place meant in the
history of the sport—he wanted to achieve success there,
but he also wanted to help the place out as much as he
could to keep it afloat. He remembered the years in the

fifties, sixties, and seventies. He remembered the greats racing there. He remembered going there as a kid. He told me, "I remember all that stuff. There's no place that has more history than this place." And the fact that it was only down the road from where he grew up . . .

I think he had a special place for Darlington in his heart, and he'd always have fun. He'd do what we asked him to do, but he'd have fun doing it.

———※———

A couple of years before Earnhardt's death, **Tom Higgins** *and fellow motorsports writer Steve Waid authored a book on Hall of Fame driver/car owner Junior Johnson. Junior could count Cup champions Darrell Waltrip, Cale Yarborough, Bill Elliott, and Terry Labonte among his drivers, and Cale and DW won three titles each for Johnson. But because of bad timing and a sponsor's reticence, he never hired Earnhardt:*

Junior (Johnson) once tried to hire Dale, but Budweiser would have no part of him. Junior wanted to hire Earnhardt when he hired Terry Labonte. But Dale was so controversial at that time that Bud didn't want him. It's ironic that Budweiser wound up paying $10 million to $11 million a year to sponsor his son (Dale Jr.). I guess Bud got to liking Dale better over the years.

———※———

Earnhardt often would relax and just enjoy some camaraderie with **Russell Branham** *and others:*

Sometimes he talked about the race car three or four minutes, and that's all he said about racing. Then the conversation turned to other business, maybe his chicken farm business, which he enjoyed. He talked about the wildlife reserve on his property. He talked about hunting and fishing, and sometimes he'd talk about other things. He didn't know my father, but he'd ask me about him; he'd ask about my family, and he'd want to know about other things. He'd get to know you better all the time.

⎯⎯⎯⎯⎯

Clay Campbell, president of Martinsville Speedway, had known Earnhardt since he was young and Dale was running Sportsman races at the track near the Virginia-North Carolina border:

It wasn't all that long ago, he was up here for two or three days of a testing session. The first day, he said, "How about if I bring my fishing pole and let's go fishing tomorrow?" Sure enough, he did. He brought his rod and tackle, and, when we broke for lunch, we fished for about an hour. He caught something; I didn't. I kinda expected that.

I remember when he first got into Winston Cup, and, again, he was here testing. I keep bringing those up because that's a good time to sit around and talk. The mood is more relaxed. After he started winning races in Winston Cup, we'd just sit around in his van, talking. He was having a grand time, finally making it to the top.

⎯⎯⎯⎯⎯

Doug Stackert, a television cameraman from Charlotte, North Carolina, was friends with Earnhardt for years. Naturally, Earnhardt liked to play tricks on him:

I was late getting credentials for Talladega, and Talladega ran before Charlotte. I wanted to get some preliminary footage from Talladega. It was the middle of the week, and I called the Talladega office. I'd never been to Talladega before, and I explained, "Look, I'm very sorry. I need credentials." This guy's talking to me, and he says, "We don't like Channel 36. You're not coming to Talladega." I said, "Wow! I know we're late and everything, but we need these credentials." And all of a sudden, he started laughing. Earnhardt had picked up the phone in the ticket office, and he was kidding with me.

During the 2001 media tour, **Dale Jr.** *talked about a dream in which he had won the Daytona 500:*

I'm pretty confident that I'm going to win the Daytona 500, because I've dreamed about it so much. You can call me crazy, but I'll be talking to you at the post-race interview, talking about how I did it.

Earnhardt *was asked what he thought of Junior's dream:*

He ought to dream; he sleeps enough!

Clay Campbell, *on Earnhardt's willingness to help the speedway:*

He helped me in a number of ways with different innovations we've come up with here. The one pit road we came up with a few years ago, Dale was very instrumental in that. In fact, we met in Rockingham one October and sat in front of his transporter, and he made a drawing of what he envisioned it should be. And what we have today is pretty much what he came up with.

Dick Thompson, *longtime publicist at Martinsville Speedway:*

Martinsville is a tough track to drive, and the most impressed I've been with him is when we noticed one time during the race that Earnhardt was driving with just his left hand. He had his other hand resting on the roll bar, just like he was going for a Sunday drive. And he was going in and out of traffic. Everybody else was fighting their cars, and he was going *la, da-da, da-da.* He was something else.

<hr />

Idus Brendle, Earnhardt's fishing buddy, learned that Dale was as competitive off the track as he was on:

This is a vintage Earnhardt story: We would go to a pond up around Gadsden, Alabama, called 5W, and fish and talk about anything but car racing. He just loved to go bream fishing, and he'd always say that he'd be the one to catch the biggest fish. He was so competitive that he wasn't going to let anybody catch the biggest fish but him. And if you did catch one and he didn't, he'd be so mad that on the car ride back to the track he wouldn't talk to anybody.

So, on this particular day, we were going after shell-crackers, which are a little bigger than bream, and he catches this big shellcracker and gets it into the boat. So now he's holding it up and laughing, and it's the biggest fish anyone's got so far. We continued to do some fishing, and I got myself a big shellcracker, and he knows that mine is bigger than the one he got. So he goes over with his fishing pole, and he's hitting at my fishing pole, trying to knock the fish off.

Finally, he gets his pole entangled in my line and breaks my pole. Naturally, the fish is gone, and at the end of the day he's the one who ends up with the biggest shellcracker. The next day, we're at his garage at Talladega, and he goes over to (Richard) Childress and some of his crew guys and says, "Go over and ask Idus who caught the biggest fish yesterday."[9]

Dick Thompson says Earnhardt and Junior Johnson differed on who was the hardest-charging driver ever:

I always loved to watch Junior Johnson race; he and Earnhardt drove a lot alike. One day, Junior came in the office to see (track president) Clay Campbell, and I said in a loud voice, "There's Junior Johnson, the hardest charger in NASCAR history." Junior shook his head no and said, "No, Dale is." A few minutes later, Junior left, and Dale Earnhardt came in, also looking for Clay. Again, in a loud voice, I said, "There's Dale Earnhardt, the hardest charger in NASCAR history." He said, "No, Junior Johnson was." I always thought that was ironic.

*Racing artist **Sam Bass** says he's done seventy-five or eighty paintings of Earnhardt, and here he talks about his handshake deals with Earnhardt:*

No, we never had any hard, fast contractual agreements. That was the one thing that was so great about Dale, was you always knew where you stood with him. And I always felt especially honored and proud to have a relationship with him, because he'd call on me to do a lot of neat things, special things to him. It was really cool to get a call or a project from Dale Earnhardt himself personally.

***Bass** continues on business with Earnhardt:*

He had an incredible desire to know everything about

everything, to know it inside out. And he *did*. There were amazing things that he'd talk about, that he'd know up and down. When we moved into the gallery where we are now, he visited and walked around, and he was telling me about how to redo the ductwork and redo the air conditioning, how to save on everything, on the construction and layout of the building, how to improve efficiency. That'll be seven years this October. I'll forever be repaying the debt to Dale Earnhardt for what he's done for me and my career over the years.

We had been told we'd have to move out of that old building across from the racetrack (Lowe's Motor Speedway), and I was struggling about where to move to. Earnhardt heard me talking about it on a radio show, about me outgrowing my space, and he called in to the radio show. "If you've gotta move, I've got a property to talk about." Honestly, I thought he was kidding, but it turned out to be the property he allowed me to buy was the site I'm on now. I'll always be in his debt. There's no way in the world I could have purchased it.

He was a truly incredible, incredible person. I feel so fortunate to have known and worked with him.

Racing artist **Garry Hill** *has done many paintings about NASCAR history, and he's rubbed fenders with Earnhardt off track often enough:*

"My most favorite Earnhardt story came from Richmond in 1989. I'd go to the all-star race for the series sponsor every year, first Winston, (R. J.) Reynolds (Tobacco Co.), and now Nextel. In '89, the program was still in its infancy. Earnhardt won the '87 all-star race. I was working on the '89 race; it was Rusty Wallace and Darrell Waltrip, with the infamous spin when Rusty got into Darrell in turn four at

Charlotte. I did a preliminary before the final painting, and I ran the preliminary by everybody to see what they wanted. And I had taken that preliminary drawing to Richmond. This was after the final practice on Saturday, and I was showing it to Rusty and Barry Dodson, Rusty's crew chief then, and a couple of Goodyear (Tire Co.) people standing around, too.

Here comes Earnhardt, and he says "What ya got?" I told him I had a preliminary drawing for the all-star race, and I showed it to Earnhardt. "What do you think?" He looked at it. It was about the 27 (Wallace) and the 17 (Waltrip), with Earnhardt and (Bill) Elliott back in turns three and four. With their position on the track, Earnhardt and Elliott, the further away the car is, the smaller it'll get. He looked at it and said, "I think the 3 car needs to be bigger." I was the same kind of guy. I told him, "If you had been closer, the car would have been bigger."

You know how competitive he was. It was like a cartoon character, starting from his toes to his ears turning red. He didn't expect that kinda reply. He turned and walked off; then, he came back, and he had that Earnhardt swagger, like a gunslinger. He turned around and came back. He said, "I'll tell you one damned thing, if I *had* been closer, I would have hit them all in the ass." That was the epitome of Dale Earnhardt's driving style. Comparatively, it's sterile today. But Dale didn't know anything else but winning. He'd put the bumper to you, then later come back and apologize and sugar coat it.

<hr />

*More **Hill**, on dealing with Earnhardt, with Dale constantly testing everyone:*

If you stood your ground and would play his game, you'd be his buddy. Otherwise, he didn't give you the time of day.

Bass, on another painting:

My other favorite Earnhardt piece would be the one *Fade to Black*. It's kind of a long, vertical piece. It shows him leaning against the car, and you sort of pan up, and there's a

INTERNATIONAL MOTORSPORTS HALL OF FAME

A few years before his death, Earnhardt shaved off his moustache so he could go snorkeling. Here, it hadn't quite grown back.

pit-crew scene behind him. And when you get to the top of the piece, you're looking right into his eyes. He's in his helmet and got his goggles on. It's so dark and black that, when you first glance at the painting, you don't necessarily see it.

Remember the off-season that Earnhardt went snorkeling and had to shave the mustache to wear the underwater mask? He didn't seem like Earnhardt, did he? When I see a curling mustache and a sideways look from actor Sam Elliott, who often plays cowboys, I think of Earnhardt. If Elliott didn't have such a gravelly voice, he could have played Earnhardt in a movie—with a darkened mustache, of course.

Jim Hunter, now chief publicist for NASCAR, and racing artist **Sam Bass** both compare Earnhardt to John Wayne's screen persona and to the Western genre in general, and artist **Garry Hill** talked about gunslingers when he mentioned Earnhardt and other drivers from the past:

Hunter: He was a tough guy. (He was) like John Wayne, in all his movie roles, a tough guy on the exterior, a hero, but then a real caring person underneath. That's how I'd typify Dale Earnhardt.

Bass: I had one painting entitled *The Magnificent Seven*, after his seventh championship. It had a Western look, a scene of him walking across the desert. There was a mountain range in the background, and in the foreground there are the seven cars that he won the seven championships with. It was like the movie *Tombstone*, as far as style, with the tattered edges. It had a real Western look to it. Many people referred to him as the sport's John Wayne, as tough as nails. And I thought it would be cool to have him walking across the desert and have it like horses running across the desert in front of him.

Hill: (My paintings) are an effort to keep the history of the sport—Earnhardt, Richard Petty, Cale Yarborough. You don't buy a picture of a race car; you buy a piece of history. And that effort continues today. I go back and look at the photographs. Those guys were gunslingers; we don't have any gunslingers anymore.

4

DEVILISH DALE

"Slow this damned thing down!"

—DALE EARNHARDT

S ometimes it wasn't safe to be around Dale Earnhardt. He loved to play jokes, particularly on people he liked. And Earnhardt, the man with the unparalleled racing skills, also was a master prankster.

One year I was at North Carolina Speedway in Rockingham, and I was standing in the Cup garage between Earnhardt's garage stall and someone else's. Suddenly I felt a *whoosh* of air and something brushed my pants leg—didn't even touch me. I looked up, and there was Earnhardt's car, charging from practice into his garage stall! I never asked him if it was on purpose, but he smiled every time he passed me from then on.

Jay Wells was a publicist for North Carolina Motor Speedway in Rockingham when he took a temporary assignment with Charlotte Motor Speedway in the early 1980s. They needed a publicist for the Coca-Cola 600, and Wells volunteered. The problem was that Wells couldn't afford to keep up his home in the Rockingham area *and* a hotel room in the Charlotte area. So Joe Whitlock, then chief publicist at CMS, introduced Wells to Earnhardt, who said that Wells could stay in his basement. When visitors showed up, Wells might poke his head out, and Earnhardt would say that Wells was the troll who guarded his bridge. So the five-foot-six Wells was stuck with a nickname for life.

It got worse later, though, when he was working the Skoal Bandit account for U.S. Tobacco. He showed up somewhere one day, and someone (not Earnhardt) said, "It's the Troll from Skoal . . . the *Skoal Troll*."

Jay Wells talks further about the nickname:

I wore it like a badge of honor. Everybody kinda had a nickname of their own, (and I had) "the Troll," "the Skoal Troll." And it still lives with me to this day. I haven't worked with U.S. Tobacco since 1995. It's been twelve years, and people still say, "Come here, Skoal Troll."

*Most people have a crazy Earnhardt story. **Wells** can go them one better with a story about Earnhardt driving a car backwards. Relax, though; apparently he didn't put a front bumper to another guy's rear bumper:*

I can honestly say that he had a true sixth sense about what was in front of him, in back of him, from side to side. I have never seen anybody drive down the highway like that.

One thing I remember is going to a little barbecue in Mooresville. Then we went to his race shop in Kannapolis. We'd been drinking Jack Daniel's, and Earnhardt had a Pontiac Trans Am, like *Smokey and the Bandit*. He started smoking the tires, but then the transmission locked up. What do we do? What do we do? How we going to get home? He said, "Hold on," and he started driving from Mooresville backwards!

It was about eleven o'clock, and Cannon Mills was having a shift change. Earnhardt said, "This guy's going too slow," and he'd pass him! Going backwards, he'd pass a car. He'd come up behind another one, and he'd say, "Hold on!" and he'd pass another one. I turned the bottle straight up; I was about twenty-four years old at that point.

But then he got a little nervous, and he said, "Let me know if you see a highway patrolman." He was afraid we'd get caught, so he parked a while, maybe thirty minutes. Then we started again and went backwards through downtown at twelve or twelve thirty. It was about fourteen miles. (Wells pauses as he thinks about the memory.) He had the ability to do amazing things.

<hr />

Wells talks about living in Earnhardt's basement and going on a quick fishing trip:

I'd say the whole two and a half months I stayed there (with Earnhardt), probably we stayed in it twice. Every other night, it was like going here, going there, seeing this person, seeing that person. Or else we were at the racetrack.

Here's another funny time: I was at the house, and it was my last Sunday off before I had to work three straight weekends in early May. And Earnhardt had gotten in around four thirty or five o'clock, had driven all night long. And it was early May, so it was still cool in the mornings.

He comes rousing me out of bed, saying, "Let's go; we're going fishing." "What?!"

So we got in that bass boat and we got out there, and it's about fifty-two degrees in the morning (Wells laughs). And on a bass boat, there's not enough clothes you can put on, especially after leaving a nice, warm bed. He didn't want to go out there by himself. When the sun was coming up and it was getting warm, I'd get a little toasty warm. I'd doze off asleep, and all of a sudden that fishing pole would be almost between my eyes. *Tchoo!* (He'd) just whisk it by my face, and it'd wake you right up. He was still aggravating in his own way; he could keep you awake, no matter what.

Wells *talks about Earnhardt's less-devilish side:*

He had amazing generosity. He didn't know me well, but, on the word of a friend (Joe Whitlock), I had that opportunity, and we became life-long friends. I miss him. I miss a helicopter buzzing my house on a regular basis. I do miss him very much. He gave me a lot of strength and knowledge in my small, little world. And (he) gave me a lot of perseverance to just be the best you can be. I'll always owe him that much. He was always right there for you.

Russell Branham *was the publicist for Darlington Raceway for ten years, starting in the fall of 1989. He got to know Earnhardt pretty well, and, mostly, he learned that Dale loved a joke.*

Late in Branham's stint at Darlington, he decided that he needed something to protect his head and neck from the fierce South Carolina sun. Jim Hunter, the track president from

*1992 until the 2001 spring race, suggested they get straw hats
and put wide bands on them with "Darlington" on them. So
they had their own trademark.*

*Branham made the mistake of going into the garage
wearing that hat:*

The drivers come in early Friday morning, and I was walking through the garage area. Dale sees me from a distance. He looks at me and gives me that little come-here sign with his first finger. I'm thinking, What does he want? Already this morning, he's going to get on me for something. He looks at me and says, "Where in the world did you get that ugly, pitiful hat?" I tell him that it's our new trademark, but he says we need get rid of it, that it's the ugliest thing.

---

*On race day, **Branham's** guiding the drivers up onto the stage
for drivers' introductions. Earnhardt sees him and gives him
the curling finger—"Come here." Russell bends down, and
Earnhardt steals the hat off his head:*

I'm wanting it back, because I have wet-hat head, but he says, "No, I'm going to wear it." He puts it on his head and walks across the stage, waving to the crowd with it. And I'm thinking he'll bring it back to me. He comes back to me, takes it off his head, and he fakes putting it on mine. "You're not getting this back," he says, and he walks away. The first thing he does is a TV interview for ESPN. He's asked about the hat, and he says, "I stole it off my buddy Russell's head, and he's paying me for the advertisement." Just making a good joke out of it. I never saw that hat again that weekend. It was gone.

Two weeks after the race, Earnhardt calls and says he's going to keep the hat on his boat. Hunter buys them some replacement hats, and Branham goes to the fall race that year wearing a straw Darlington hat.

Earnhardt qualifies at the back of the field, so Hunter and Branham decide to visit his bus that night to see how he's doing. Earnhardt, it turns out, has grilled himself a steak and is washing dishes. They knock on the door, Earnhardt sees them, and he lets them in. First thing, he rushes off and comes back with the hat he had taken from Branham.

He says, "Russell, I want you to know that I didn't get rid of that hat. I've been wearing it at racetracks."

DARLINGTON RACEWAY

Earnhardt gave Darlington publicist Russell Branham plenty of grief about this hat. But he must have liked it; he wore it enough.

*The raceway bought Dale a bunch of the hats. He wore some, telling people that he was doing advertising for the track, and he gave others to friends. Said **Branham**:*

Apparently, it wasn't such an ugly hat.

*This story might have gone in "The Angel in Black" chapter, instead. **Leonard Wood** of the Wood Brothers says he always had to be careful with Earnhardt:*

He was very aggressive on the track, but he had a big heart off the track. A lot of people didn't know that, unless you talked to him personally. But he liked to pick on me. If I broke a rib, he'd find out about it, somebody would tell him. He'd come up and grab me from behind and was gonna squeeze my ribs real hard. And I didn't know that he knew they was broke, but he didn't squeeze me too hard; he was just making like he was. Of course, I enjoyed picking with him, too. You wouldn't call him a prankster; he liked to pick in a nice way.

Earnhardt was a good and devoted outdoorsman. It was his hobby, and it probably was what kept him calm and sane. But, as it often happens, Earnhardt took his hobbies to extremes.
*   **Tom Higgins** remembers being included on a trip to Las Vegas after Earnhardt won the 1980 Cup title. Dale, who had just won the Rookie of the Year championship the previous year, didn't have the patience to stay in Vegas and enjoy the slot machines. The outdoors called:*

I was able to go to Vegas with him and his brothers, and (radio announcer) Barney Hall was along. Sam Moses from *Sports Illustrated*, too. We got over there and the plan was he was going to stay two days. I had spent the whole night at the poker machine, and I was still down there at the machine early in the morning, and here goes Earnhardt out with his bag. "Where you going?" He said, "I've had enough of this. This isn't for me. I'm going home and go deer huntin'."

So he went on, but his brothers stayed out there. He left after only a few hours. He left all the ballyhoo and the glitz. Even though he'd just won the championship, he came home. He told me, "By this time tomorrow, I'll be sitting in the top of a tree in Chester County, South Carolina, deer huntin'." That's what he did.

In Higgins's favorite Earnhardt story, **Higgins**, *Joe Whitlock (Earnhardt's first publicist and agent), and Earnhardt were going to a conservation meeting at Santee Cooper in South Carolina. They were going to take Higgins's two-week-old station wagon, since, otherwise, they'd have to squeeze themselves into the cab of a pickup truck. Arthur Smith, a musician who was then famous in the South, had asked Whitlock and Higgins to bring Earnhardt to a meeting that was to feature Clemson football coach Danny Ford and country music star Porter Wagoner and his band:*

Earnhardt said we could only take the station wagon if he could drive. Fool-like, I threw him the keys. It was an adventure from the time we left my driveway. I didn't think I was going to live another minute. We took a back way from (Higgins's home in Mint Hill, North Carolina) to Heath Springs, South Carolina. Then we went on down to Camden, and he was doing some outrageous stuff. It wasn't really all that dangerous; it was just outrageous.

Publicist Joe Whitlock and Higgins played a trick on Dale.
We won't reveal the joke but will say only that Earnhardt was
*yelling at **Higgins** to tell him the end of the story:*

He kept on pressing me to do it, and finally he grabbed me
by the collar of my shirt, pulled me over to him, and said,
"Dammit, I said tell me how he got killed!"

Higgins fed Earnhardt the punch line of the joke—again,
we won't tell it here—and Earnhardt became livid when he
realized they'd duped him:

He was infuriated, and we were doing about ninety miles
an hour. We'd set him up; Whitlock and I were just rolling
in laughter, he'd bit so well. He slammed on the brakes,
turned it hard-left, and we did two or three 360s, and we
ended up off the shoulder of the road, with sand and dust
flying. I said, "Good God, are you crazy?" He said, "Did you
think that was funny?" I said, "No! Hell no, I didn't think
that was funny," and he said, "I didn't think your joke was
too damn funny, either. I don't like jokes like that; don't you
ever pull another one on me." I said, "Don't worry, I won't."

But that's not the end of the story. After traveling down
the road three or four miles, they hear a thumping sound.
Casually, Earnhardt tells them that he's flat-spotted all four
tires, and the right-front tire is ready to blow out. It does, as
***Higgins** continues:*

He said, "We're going to have to change it." By now, I was a
little bit ticked off. I said, "Before you get that 'we' stuff, Mr.
Winston Cup Champion, you can get out there and change
it yourself." So he went out there, laughing like hell, and

put that little ol' donut on it, and we went on into the marina where the meeting was to be held. The sheriff and his deputy are there, so Earnhardt gave the deputy $80 to go into Moncks Corner and buy a tire.

On the way back, Dale went to sleep, and the car drove like a buckboard. It was bouncing around, hard to steer. When we got home, my wife was waiting when we got there, and she said, "Oh, Dale, how are you doing?" He said, "I'm fine, but Tom's mad as hell. I've tore the car all to pieces." And she laughed. She drove it to work that night, and the minute she got to work, she called and said, "What in the hell is wrong with that car?"

*It turns out that **Higgins** had to replace the other tires, plus the front end was out of line, a shock was broken, and the dashboard was loose:*

He laughed about that for years. I saw him a couple of years later—I still had the station wagon—and he waved me down when I was leaving Charlotte Motor Speedway. He was getting ready to leave after qualifying, and he was walking to his car. I stopped, and he patted the station wagon on the hood a couple of times, and he said, "It's about time to take this thing to Santee Cooper again."

He was mischievous. He had a lot of the little devilment in him.

*Yes, Earnhardt was a prankster, and other people liked to play tricks on him, too. Take driver **Sterling Marlin**:*

I was telling the guys (crew) a while ago, we could beat and bang on Sunday and see each other the next week at the racetrack and be joking and carrying on. About two years ago, we were in Sonoma, California, and at the time, there was no garage area and he had parked his—we thought it was his rental car at the time—real close to our race car.

We snuck over to Goodyear to get a bunch of wheel weights and put on his wheels, halfway around them. Him and Teresa jump in the car to go to the airport, and I think (crew chief) Larry McReynolds was with him at the time. And he said Dale was so mad he could bite a ten-penny nail in two because he couldn't run but about twenty-five miles per hour because it would shake the car all to pieces.

He found out I kinda had something to do with it. He got me the next week, and he said, "I'm going to catch you when you're away from your lake house, and I'm going to put a goat in it." It was always a fun side to Dale Earnhardt. He was a prankster, and he was always fun-loving and cutting up.[1]

Higgins wasn't the only man to get into a car with Dale driving. **Russell Branham** *did it twice at Darlington Raceway, and one of those rides might be one of the best performances ever for the Intimidator:*

If you remember, in 1995, we had just repaved the race-track. It was the first full paving since the inception of the track. Ricky Rudd had been there a couple of weeks before because of a tire test, and he said the new track felt good. Prior to 1995, throughout the late eighties and nineties, there was no one better at Darlington than Dale. He was dirt-tracking his way around the track and winning a lot of races. He was ruining the nickname "Too Tough to Tame." In a way, he knew the track needed repaving, but in another way, he didn't want it repaved because he'd been so dominant.

Branham knew that Earnhardt was inside the track testing, so he drove a Pontiac Transport van into the infield. That was a mistake:

He makes that little finger motion to me, and he says, "Man, y'all have messed the track up. I don't like it, the way the grooves are. Somebody didn't do their homework." I knew that wasn't so, because the guy overseeing the project used to be the superintendent for Indianapolis. He'd done a hundred fifty jobs; he was an expert. I said, "Dale, I don't understand what you're talking about. We just need time to let it cure. Ricky Rudd ran on it, and he said it was great." Dale asked me where the keys to my vehicle were; he wanted to drive out there and show me what was wrong.

So we got in the van and eased out on the track. He went to the corner and parked. He'd get out and show me the seams. It was Japanese to me, what he was saying. Then he said, "Do you want to feel it?" Here, I'm thinking we're going to go around sixty to seventy miles an hour, and I don't know what we're looking for. He gasses it up, and, within three to four laps, the speedometer was locked. Here we are, in a van with thin tires, and he's decided to take me for a joyride.

We go into the corner wide open, with smoke billowing everywhere. You can smell rubber, there's smoke in the vents, and the tires are screaming. I'm holding on to the little handle above the window and trying to keep my composure. He knows I'm scared to death, and he gives me that devilish grin. That's when I knew I was in good hands. To him, this wasn't anything. He had his sun shades on, and he gave me this look like "I gotcha." I held my composure, but I said a few bad words.

Needless to say, we didn't go back out there that day. That afternoon, he crashed his race car in turn three . . . destroyed the car.

I never thought I'd go around out there again, until another incident came along. This was in 1998, for the spring race. That was the year that, number one, Little Earnhardt was a rookie in Busch, and he'd never driven Darlington; number two, Steve Park was hurt in Atlanta, and Ron Hornaday was going to drive the Pennzoil car. Hornaday normally drove Dale's truck. Dale decided to come down; he was testing Richard Childress's car. This was about a week and a half before the race. Also, Little Earnhardt was going to test, as well as Hornaday, who had not seen the track as well.

Dale calls the day before he's coming and says he's bringing Little E and Hornaday. He said, "Can you pick me up in the morning?" He was going to fly in in his helicopter and land in the infield. At the time it never dawned on me he wanted me to pick him up for a reason. The thing was, the garage is right there, so why does he need me to pick him up and take him into the garage? I guess it was about eight fifteen, and Sammie Yarborough, the track superintendent, called me and said, "Russell, Earnhardt's flying in."

I jumped into a car, a Pontiac Bonneville. I drove inside the track. The chopper's still running, and they get in the car. Big E gets in the front seat on the passenger side, and the others are in the back. We go toward pit road, and I'm going to take them to the garage, and all of a sudden, Dale says, "Why don't you go out on the racetrack?" He says, "I want to show these guys the line. They've never been on the track before; Hornaday's never seen the place. I just want to give them a little lesson on what they need to do and what they need to look for."

I said, "Sure." I felt pretty good about that. I got one of the best ever in the sport asking to drive 'em. No problem at all. So I get up to seventy, and we go into the corner. Over my ten years there, I gave many track rides in the pace car, so I'm thinking I know the line.

So, as I go into the corner, I get close to the white line. I let the car drift up. I'm trying to be just like Dale. I'm trying to show him, "I know how to do this!" Finally, he looks over at me, and he said, "Where did you learn how to drive this place?" I said, "From watching you guys, and I'm looking at the rubber from the last race." He says, "The rubber you're looking at is from the guys who haven't won here before." He said, "You're looking at the wrong rubber. Those guys don't know how to get around this place as fast as I do."

He said, "Speed up, and in what is now turn one, you've got to go below the white line. Then let the car kick up." So I speeded up to eighty or eighty-five. We go into the corner, and he says, "Russell, you're still not doing it right." And, in the meantime, he's trying to tell them what to look for. They're leaning forward, like children in the back seat looking out. Finally, when Dale tells me I'm *still* not doing it right.

Well, there's a big console in a Pontiac Bonneville. Still sitting in the passenger seat, Dale lifts his left foot and leg over the console and puts his foot on the gas, and he tells me to move mine. He then tells me to take my hands off the steering wheel. He grabs it with his left hand, and so he proceeds to mash the gas. I think, Here we go again. We're wide open again, and he's locked the blamed speedometer.

I'm behind the wheel, but I have absolutely no control over anything. The man who has control is driving with his left foot draped across the console, and also driving with one hand, and it being his left hand. Needless to say, I was a little bit nervous. But I was comfortable with him, I guess because of what I'd done with him a couple of years before. He looks over at me and says, "Russell, are you scared?" I said, "No, I'm not scared. Keep driving, keep driving."

I'm trying to act Mr. Cool. But to see him do this physically—and at the same time, he's being a teacher, telling Little Earnhardt and Hornaday what they need to do to get around that racetrack. It was like school was in session. It was like the students were on the playground listening to him, and he was playing. It was absolutely amazing to see him at work doing that. There again, those old tires were screaming, and there's the smell of rubber.

This is a racetrack car; and if it gets crashed, I'm in hot water. But what do you say to a seven-time Winston Cup champion and Darlington's all-time winner? It was impressive, unbelievable. If he was going to do it to anyone, I knew he was going to do it to me, because he loved to pull my chain. He loved to joke with me. Two or three years ago, I asked him, "Why do you pick on me; why do you make me to beg you to do things?" He said, "If I didn't pick on you, it would mean I didn't like you." I took it as a huge compliment. He always, *always* made me squirm.

When asked about that story at the 2007 media tour in Charlotte, Ron Hornaday nodded and said, "Oh, he did that to everybody."

But even Earnhardt would get a little panicky while riding with someone else. **Buddy Baker** *has such a story:*

I had this bass boat out of Florida, and it had the biggest motor you could put on it. I went and got Earnhardt one day, and I said, "Let's try this boat out." I was riding along on the lake, and that thing was like a bullet. We got near marker eleven up here on Lake Norman, and all of a sudden, the boat took a hard left and went around the corner. And he said, "I don't believe I'd turn this thing that hard running that fast." I said, "Earnhardt, I never turned it," and he said, "Slow this damned thing down!"

I didn't turn it. The boat was actually airborne, and the boat turned itself.

I rode back with him from Myrtle Beach (South Carolina) one time, and it was in the wee hours of the morning.

I tell you, I've been on a lot of trips from the beach, but nothing like that. He was driving. Not that it was anything dangerous, because it was not. But some of the corners he went through, I think he was cutting up a little bit with me. I think the Goodyear stickers were off the sides of the tires. But I wasn't going to say anything, even if the sparks flew off the wheels! Because, really and truly, I knew he wasn't going to do anything to hurt himself.

Radio personality **Mark Garrow** *remembers the infamous Earnhardt-Terry Labonte finish at Bristol in 1999, when Earnhardt said he was only trying to rattle Terry's cage:*

It was the night Earnhardt knocked Terry Labonte out of the way at Bristol, when Terry was passing him on the last lap. Even some of his own fans thought it was unsportsmanlike when Earnhardt wrecked him. . . . People took sides, and it wasn't fifty-fifty. Some diehard Earnhardt fans were cheering, but most were booing. There was a lot of controversy. Dale had a lot of questions to answer in Victory Lane.

After that, he was transported to the press box in turn three. I was told this by public relations director Wayne Estes, I believe. I was told the story that Earnhardt was escorted to the elevator, and (car owner) Richard Childress and Wayne were with him in the elevator. People were yelling, and it was animated. When they closed the doors, they were in the quiet of the elevator—the noise was shut out. Earnhardt looked at Richard Childress and said, "God, I loved it." That's Dale Earnhardt.

Wayne Estes, *now Bristol Motor Speedway's vice president for events, offers a slightly edited version of the elevator incident following the '99 Battle of Bristol:*

That's close. Childress wasn't there. There were Earnhardt and me and probably six deputies. Every one of the deputies wanted to be part of the entourage to protect Earnhardt. Every deputy who could get loose and be part of the detail got to Victory Lane. It took two cars to get everyone to the press box. The deputies were holding hands, outstretched, to keep people from Earnhardt. There must have been six or seven deputies.

When the doors to the elevator closed, Earnhardt leaned back against the wall, closed his eyes, and said, "Man, that's my music." Fans were screaming and hollering. They were throwing t-shirts over fences. They were taking Earnhardt t-shirts off their backs, not just there, but all over the track. But I guess they got over it eventually.

When we had our fortieth anniversary celebration, we sent out an open-ended invitation for fans to pick the most memorable moment ever at the Bristol track. We were deluged with entries, and the two top vote getters were Earnhardt and Labonte in '99 and Earnhardt and Labonte in '95. Ninety-five was the one where John Boy & Billy wrote the song about it to the tune of (the Charlie Daniels Band song) "Uneasy Rider." I think it was called the "Bristol Song," all about that night.

It was raining that night, and at the meeting NASCAR told the drivers that, if everybody behaved, we'd make halfway and we'd get the race in. Well, we got all 500 laps in, and Earnhardt hit everybody on the track but the pace car—I'm not sure, but maybe he hit it, too. I have a picture on the wall of Rusty (Wallace) spinning; that's the night Rusty threw the water bottle (at Earnhardt). The song's funny, and it's about that night.

Somebody was holding Labonte up; Labonte was going to win by a straightaway (over the second-place car). Earnhardt has been sent back a couple of times for hitting people. NASCAR didn't park him for five laps; they just sent him to the back of the longest line. Well, he came charging through the field for one last run, and Labonte was being held up and that cost him momentum. Earnhardt hit him and turned him, and he hit the wall hard as he crossed the finish line. Terry came around and drove the car to Victory Lane with a crumpled hood.

Estes says that Labonte later watched the video of the last three laps of that 1995 race:

He was angry, and he made a reference to the SOB who held him up (Estes laughs).

Estes was reminded about Labonte's reputation as the calm "Ice Man," but Earnhardt managed to turn the ice into fire:

He (Labonte) had a temper, too, man.

Eddie Gossage, now president/general manager of Texas Motor Speedway, was a twenty-two-year-old working at the Bristol track when he got into a situation he couldn't handle:

It was 1982, and I was managing Bristol at the time. It was race week, probably Tuesday or so, early in the week. I'm driving home; it's dusk. I'm driving down the road at about sixty miles an hour, just kind of oblivious to everything.

Bam! Somebody hits me in the rear. I look in the mirror, and it's Earnhardt! He was in town, visiting friends, and he had happened upon me in traffic. He just gave me the old chrome horn, just like he'd do on the racetrack to other folks. He just stayed right on my bumper for the rest of the way, just grinning at me, that kind of thing.

What do you do? Do you speed up? No, I can't outrun Dale Earnhardt. Do you slow down and give him a brake check? No, he's got all this talent, and I'm just this silly kid driving down the road. I just sat there and let him ride on my bumper. There was nothing else I could do. That was typical Dale.

~~~

Jerry Gappens, the longtime publicist for Lowe's Motor Speedway, recalls track president Humpy Wheeler wanting to get Earnhardt for a couple of functions, but Earnhardt's schedule didn't permit it. Wheeler, who had a good relationship with Earnhardt, was a little upset, and that got back to Dale. That's when Gappens got an intimidating visit:

This is the most I've ever been intimidated by Earnhardt: I was trying to hook up with him for a press conference and an autograph session for one of our big Auto Fairs. Typical bad luck: every time I wanted him to do something, he had a conflict and couldn't do it. I was working through his publicist and Don Hawk, his business manager at the time. Humpy wanted to know about Earnhardt, and I said, "He was busy and couldn't do it, blah, blah, blah." That kinda made Humpy mad.

Well, Earnhardt always comes here to get his tickets. He had a condo here, and Humpy would give him his tickets. Earnhardt'd make a tour through the speedway offices, say hi to people, pick up his tickets, sign stuff for employees. After I told Humpy about not being able to get Earnhardt over this three-month stretch, it made him mad. Dale had a lot of respect for Humpy; he and Humpy were very close. Humpy said, "I'll talk to him the next time I see him. He's not too big to help out."

I'm on the phone one afternoon, and the door was open. All of a sudden, Earnhardt walks through my door, followed closely by Don Hawk. Earnhardt stops, shuts the door, and locks it. I think, *Oh, my goodness, this is big here.* He's towering over my desk, so I say, "How are you doing?" He says, "I'm doing fine. I just want to find out what our problem is." I said, "What problem is that?" He said, "I don't know. I just went to Humpy's office, and I'm sideways with Humpy." That's exactly how he said it, "sideways with Humpy." He said, "I don't need to be sideways with Humpy. He mentioned some press stuff that didn't get done. I want to try to straighten it out."

I gave him the three situations we were talking about. He says, "Here we go: If you need a press conference, call J. R. Rhodes, my publicist. If you need an autograph, call Don Hawk. Hawk, give him your numbers." Hawk gave me his business number, his home phone number, his cell-phone number. I had about six numbers for Don Hawk.

He said, "Jerry, all I ask is that you give me enough advance notice so I can get it on my schedule, because my schedule is cramped." I said, "I understand," and he said, "I don't need to be sideways with Humpy. This is my home track, and I don't want to be sideways with anybody here. I want to help out, just like I always have. We have an understanding. And I understand my role in that." So he says, "Are we square?" And I say, "Yes, sir." And he reached over and pinched my nose, twisted my nose a little bit. If he liked people, he always pestered them a bit.

I'd just been put in charge of public relations. Eddie Gossage had just gone to Texas to be the general manager there, and I thought, *Here I have one of Winston Cup's best drivers in my office, and he's going to whip my butt right here.* It was a real businesslike conversation, and he gave me that real crappy Earnhardt-like grin. After it was over, he even asked me about my pictures of my kids, what they did, what they liked. He looked around the office because of the racing mementos.

After that, he always helped us out, but I understood where he got the name "the Intimidator."

Chris Powell, who now runs Las Vegas Motor Speedway, often acted as a gofer for the media when he was a publicist for R. J. Reynolds Tobacco Company:

In 1995 at Indianapolis, we were up there for the second Brickyard 400. When we got there—(Jeff) Gordon had won the inaugural race in '94, so here it is in '95 (and) Gordon's leading the points and everything—on Friday it was raining, and the writers didn't have anything to write about. And somebody said, "Do you think you can get Earnhardt to come in?" I said, "I don't know, but I'll try."

So I go to his motor home and knock on the door. Teresa answers, and she says, "Come in." I step up in the motor home. It's Teresa, Dale, and Taylor—she was seven or eight at the time—and there were four or five other acquaintances of his there. And he says in that way that only Earnhardt could, "What do you want?" And I said, "Well, Dale, it's raining outside, and our friends in the media don't have anything to write about. I was wondering if I could get you to come to the interview room and talk as the defending NASCAR Winston Cup champion."

He says, "I ain't going in there. All they'll want to talk about is Gordon this and Gordon that. I ain't going." So he kinda went off on a tangent. While he was doing it—and he could be fairly gruff—everybody was looking at me to see my reaction, because he lit into me a little bit.

While everybody's looking at me and he's talking, he winked at me. And that was his way of saying, "Hey, I understand why you're coming in to ask. And I ain't mad at you for asking." It was his way of softening the thing. He got a kick using that gruff exterior to see how his pals and buddies would react when he took off on a lowly PR guy. He didn't go in, but he did, however, win the race the next day.

David Green, who has covered motorsports for print and online media, has two stories about Earnhardt's legendary ability to make life hard on reporters:

I know he was a very playful type of guy, and at Talladega Chuck Williams of the Columbus, Georgia, newspaper and I were trying to pin Earnhardt down to try to talk to him, and we couldn't get him to stand still from running around and throwing water balloons. He was tossing them over the hauler and trying to hit people over the head with them, and we were having to chase him around and try to work our questions in around his game.

Yeah, we got him, as much as you could pin Earnhardt down in those situations, as you well know. If you weren't one of the select few people he'd sit down with, you just had to catch him on the run.

I also remember a Watkins Glen race, where he was in a hurry to get out, as we all know he could be. And he came barreling into the exit of the garage. Instead of going down pit road and going into the entrance like everybody else was doing, he knew nobody was going out of the garage area, and he just went barreling in there and ran into a security guard and knocked him over. Just in that effort to get away before somebody could stick a microphone or tape recorder under his nose. Everybody had the same kind of stories about him.

*To be fair, let's look at **Earnhardt**'s explanation of that incident with the Watkins Glen security guard:*

The guy started one way, and I went the other, then I turned back and went the other way. I couldn't tell which way he was going to go. He was trying to dodge me. He fell and bumped his head, but I didn't hit him.[2]

*Even longtime television announcer **Ken Squier** found Earnhardt tough to interview:*

He didn't want to do it, but it was always a sly thing with him. He was always in a hurry. "You gotta hurry up," because, usually, television can take forever to set up. "I'm awful busy. I got things to do." He limited that (interviews), and I think that worked in his favor. He realized there was strength in not being that available, and it fit the mode of being the Intimidator. It made the time he was available more precious. He understood that very, very well.

As much as he tried to intimidate other racers, he did his best to intimidate the press or anybody that was there. And he rather enjoyed that. It was as much fun as the racing part. He had a good time with that.

And he got more secure as time went along. I think his wife had a lot to do with that. I think Teresa helped him. Originally, he was timid about that kind of stuff. When Joe Whitlock worked for him, I think he understood that, that he was a timid person, more like Bobby Isaac and David Pearson. But, as he began to win, that changed. He began to get a better sense of himself, and he was able to use that to his advantage.

Sometimes it wasn't safe to stand in Victory Lane with Earnhardt. **Larry Balewski,** *then the publicist at Daytona International Speedway, was handing Earnhardt the appropriate hats after the Intimidator won the 1990 July Fourth race, the Pepsi 400:*

Plasti-Kote used to bring spray cans into Victory Lane. Earnhardt got his picture taken in the Plasti-Kote hat and handed it to me. Then I put it on, and he spray-painted it! (Balewski paused in telling the story to let the picture—and the paint—sink in.)

I still have that hat.

Mike Bolton, *the outdoors writer for the* Birmingham News, *recalls an encounter between Earnhardt and his buddy Neil Bonnett:*

They did a lot of hunting together, and Neil bought a new ATV, a four-wheeler. And Dale got to Neil's house about two o'clock in the morning, saw it, and decided he wanted one. Dale said he had to have one, and Neil said, "We can get one later on." He said, "No, I need one right now."

So they went down to the shop where Neil bought his, and they got the emergency number off the door. They called him (the store owner) at two o'clock in the morning and woke him up, told him he had to come down there, because Dale Earnhardt wanted an ATV. So he came down there and sold him one.

Well, they went to a hunting club, and they were riding along a dirt road. Neil was being careful to dodge the puddles and the tree limbs, because it was brand new and he didn't want to scratch it up. All of a sudden, Earnhardt took a hard right and slammed into Neil, knocked him off the road. That thing flipped upside down and rolled down an embankment into a creek.

Neil, jumped up, mad as hell, wanting to know what he was doing. He said, "I could tell you were worried about putting a scratch on that, so I decided we'd go ahead and get that over with." He ran him off the road, tore the fenders off it, brand new.

5

RACING WITH THE MAN

"Dale Earnhardt would give an aspirin a headache."
—BUDDY BAKER

I saw two incidents in person that shaped my memory of Dale Earnhardt. Once, I was sitting in the Darlington Raceway press box. Earnhardt was leading, and he was coming up on lapped traffic in turn one. I figured Earnhardt would catch them in turn two and pass them down the straight stretch.

He didn't wait. He dove between the two cars in turn one and was ahead in turn two. In the back straight, he was pulling away. I described the incident to Deb Williams, then the editor for *Winston Cup Scene* (and the person who always sat to my right at Darlington), and she said that was just Earnhardt being Earnhardt. I thought I'd never see that again, but a few years later Jeff Gordon was in the exact same situation on the exact same spot on the track. And he pulled the same move. I guess it was just Gordon being Earnhardt.

The other incident came at what was then Charlotte Motor Speedway—it's now Lowe's Motor Speedway. There was a big wreck on the front stretch, and Earnhardt was one of many cars spinning through the trioval grass. Earnhardt was heading backwards toward two non-moving cars in the grass, and, *amazingly, his car weaved between the two cars to avoid them!* Earnhardt kept going, did a sort of reverse highway patrolman's spin to straighten his car, and he calmly drove to his pit on pit road. Wow.

You probably remember the infamous incident at Bristol in 1999 when Earnhardt bumped Terry Labonte, spun Terry out, and won the race. Regarding the incident with Labonte, Dale just sheepishly said he was trying to rattle Terry's cage. Earnhardt haters roared their displeasure, but the victory stood.

I was then working at a North Carolina newspaper near where Labonte lives, and I received a call from someone with a gentle voice asking if the sports editor was there. I said, "This sounds like Terry." He said, "It *is* Terry." I said that, yes, the sports editor was there, but he was talking to Bob Labonte, Terry's dad, on the phone. In a hushed tone, Terry said, "Is Daddy mad?" I told him that the sports editor hadn't said anything in ten minutes, just listened, so I assumed that Daddy was mad.

But Earnhardt had earned a tough reputation on the racetrack *long* before Bristol 1999.

Once, Earnhardt's car was belching smoke during a twenty-lap Busch Clash all-star race, but Earnhardt ignored the black flag. He kept running and wound up in a final-lap crash with Buddy Baker and Terry Labonte. Baker was incensed.

"Dale Earnhardt would give an aspirin a headache," he said.[1]

Here are a few more stories about Earnhardt on the racetrack:

Geoff Bodine and Earnhardt had some glorious battles in the eighties, although NASCAR didn't seem to approve. At least one incident from the Bodine-Earnhardt feud— one involving two rental cars—was used in the 1990 movie Days of Thunder. *That's not exactly what happened— they only had one rental car, and no one got wrecked when they met with NASCAR boss Bill France Jr.—but that's Hollywood for you. Here, Geoff talks about The Feud:*

Dale started the bump and run, and I started the penalty box, because he bumped me and I bumped him, and I got in trouble. It took me a while to figure out that that wasn't working. He'd get away with it, and I'd get in trouble. We kept doing it. (Car owner) Rick Hendrick got upset with Dale running into his cars all the time, causing us trouble, and he said, "Look, if you don't figure out a way to stop this, I'm going to find another driver who will." He put the pressure on me to do something, to figure out how to get Dale into trouble, and that's what happened at Charlotte that weekend before the meeting (with France).

In the Busch race, he spun me out. I didn't wreck, but I spun out. Everyone thought I'd wreck him, but I didn't. I finally learned that the guy that retaliated, threw the second punch, he got in trouble. I didn't throw a punch; I didn't hit him in the Saturday (Busch) race. It took me a while; I'm not real smart, but I try not to be stupid.

In Sunday's race, I hit him first. I didn't wreck him; I just got him a little sideways. That made him mad, and we went into turn three, and he just put me straight into the wall. And that's when Bill Jr. called us all up that night—he actually called (car owners) Rick Hendrick and Richard

Childress up—and said to "get your drivers down here, we're going to have a meeting."

He got us together, and he showed us video of the two races that weekend. On Saturday, Dale ran into me and spun me out, and Sunday he drove me into the wall. (France) was very clear. He told us both, "Look, this is NASCAR; this is how I make my living. And you're messing with the way I make my living, and I don't appreciate it. I'm going to tell you guys how you're going to act from here on out."

He told us he didn't want bumping anymore, he didn't want to see us near each other. He said, "I don't want to see you guys on the same track. If you get close, I'll have to bring you in (the pits) and make sure your steering's right. And if you touch, if you bump, the consequences are going to be pretty steep."

So the rest of that year, Dale and I stayed away from each other. He put the bump and run on hold that year. If you think back to the rest of that season, he behaved and I behaved. It had to be after I won Daytona (in 1986), so it was '87, I believe. It was before the movie *Days of Thunder* came out, of course.

But that's what happened. He brought up bump and run, and I wasn't smart enough to figure out . . . it took me a while to figure out that I'd get in trouble, and that's when they came up with that darned penalty box. I got put there with some other guys.

Bodine recalls the rental-car caper in Days of Thunder:

I told them (the movie people) the story about, after the meeting, Bill threw me set of car keys and said, "Hey, you two guys need to ride together. We're all going to dinner." Dale and I weren't saying a whole lot. We were following the parade to dinner. Dale reached over and whapped me on the shoulder and said, "Hey, go up there and give him a shot." I said, "What?" He wanted me to go up there and give him the bump and run. I said, "Are you crazy? We just got our butts chewed out, and you want me to go up there and give him a shot?" I said, "I'll pull over, and you can do it." He said, "No, that's okay, let's keep going."

It was funny and all that, but when I told the writers, they put us in two cars (in the movie), and we wrecked each other on the way to dinner. That really didn't happen, but he wanted me to give (France) a shot in the butt on the way to dinner.

***

Bodine was asked if Earnhardt was more careful with him after the meeting with France:

You know, for a long while he was. I was driving for Bud Moore at Bristol. The late Alan Kulwicki was leading; I was running second. Dale had a flat and was a lap down. So he was coming up through the pack, and he got to me, and I raced him for a couple laps. I thought, *What am I racing him for? Let Alan race him for a while; let Alan hold him back.* So I moved up the track and motioned him by and he spun me out for no reason.

Back then, people had scanners, and everyone was listening. Richard Childress said, "What happened?" Earnhardt said, "Ah, Bodine was in my way; I just put him out." He admitted right on the radio what he'd done. And that was the first time since the meeting in Daytona that he did anything. Up until then, he didn't bump-and-run me. That day, for some reason, he just felt like turning me around, for no reason, because I'd moved out of his way. That was (car owner) Bud Moore, so that was '92, I believe. Bud went over and asked him, "Why'd you do that to the driver in my car?"

That was totally wrong, but that was Dale. But he did that to everybody; it wasn't just me. If you didn't get way out of his way, he'd bump you and turn you around. He thought it was supposed to be that way.

Unfortunately, a lot of these young guys have picked that up—to try to emulate Dale. There'll never be another Dale Earnhardt. Some of these guys think they can be, and they'll get up there and bump and run. NASCAR's got themselves in a box; they can't stop it. They might have a little bit, but the bump and run's just a part of racing. Bumping and running's okay, but bumpin' and wreckin', that's where you cross the line.

But, as you know, we've seen that kind of driving the last several years. If you bump a guy on the last lap, spin a guy out, wreck him, it don't matter. It all started with Dale. He's the guy who got away with it, so all of these young guys think that's the way to drive. I never believed in that philosophy of driving; I tried to pass guys clean and fair, outsmart them, outdrive them. My philosophy on the bump and run is, that's called demolition derby; that's called bumper cars. That's not called NASCAR.

* * *

*David Pearson reminded me that he won in Earnhardt's
No. 2 Rod Osterlund car before Earnhardt did. Dale broke
two collarbones and had a bruised heart in a crash at Pocono
his rookie year, 1979, and missed four races. Pearson filled in
and picked up the 105th and last victory of his legendary
career at Darlington. Still, Pearson raced against Earnhardt
late in David's career. Here, Pearson talks about racing with
Earnhardt:*

I was good friends with him, and I talked to him quite a bit. In fact, I drove his car when he got hurt that time. I won a race for in that car before he did, in Osterlund's car. We were just good friends, and every time we went around the racetrack together, we talked about things.

I run with his dad on dirt tracks. Yeah, he (Dale) was a lot like him (Ralph). He was tough to outrun, and his dad was tough. His dad laid the bumper on you if he got the chance. He wouldn't try to put you out of the race, but he'd pull you over. Richard (Petty) and I were always close friends. We raced hard together. We wouldn't knock you out for meanness or anything like that. If we got a nose under somebody, we'd move them over. Yeah, I feel he (Dale) did a lot of it (for meanness); I really do. (Did he bump Pearson?) No, not as I know of. I don't recall.

It depends on who he was running with. He nearly (clobbered) Rusty two or three times, and Rusty never would pay him back. He thought the world of Rusty, and Rusty did of him. I always pulled for Rusty a little bit until he came up and said Earnhardt was the best driver out there. And if you think somebody's better out there on that racetrack, they're going to beat you. I always felt that, when I got in a car, I was as good as the next one. But Rusty always said that Earnhardt was the best, you know. Yeah, he shouldn't have done that. When they hit you, you gotta get them back. If you don't, they'll know they can keep on doing it.

***

Bobby Allison raced in the sixties, seventies, and eighties, won three Daytona 500s and was the 1983 Winston Cup champion. Some people say he was the one driver Earnhardt couldn't intimidate:

On the racetrack Earnhardt was a great competitor, you know. And he tried to intimidate everybody, and I think I did quite well with him on that part of it. We ran good. I was able to be ahead of him on some of those things. And he won from early on. And he not only won the races, but he looked after the point thing (standings) very well. He won the Rookie of the Year with (Rod) Osterlund, then won the Winston Cup title with Osterlund the next year. I probably was (a little surprised).

He tried to intimidate me, and he didn't achieve that. He slid up under me at Talladega one time through (turns) three and four, coming for the checkered flag. A lot of people would have lifted (off the gas), and I didn't and beat him back to the flag.

I could control my car with small bumps from people anyway. I had been through some things earlier. Petty would bump you a little bit there when it would do him some good, and he'd bump you if you got around him on the racetrack. Sometimes it'd be way back early in the race, in the middle of the race, or whenever. On the short tracks, there were several we rubbed wheels with . . . several guys that ran the Alabama circuit early on. They didn't run into anybody to do any harm; they just raced close. And, every once in a while, there was a little bump or a little rub. And it just helped me understand that and deal with it.

Allison said he knew the bumping wasn't personal:

He was just running hard and was a little over the line occasionally. And a lot of times when that happened, they'd lift off the gas and he'd go on. I felt I understood what the deal was, and I felt I could control my car and continue to go at full throttle.

We all remember Earnhardt bumping everybody else, but
Jay Wells, Earnhardt's good friend, remembers an incident

between Earnhardt and Bobby Allison in which Dale was the bumpee, not the bumper:

I was doing pit notes at Pocono; this was 1980. And Bobby Allison, in his own way, could be very aggravating, not really hurting, not really spinning you out, but just bumping you, just bumping you. I'd never seen Earnhardt go up to a driver after a race and say, "Why'd you keep bumping me all the time?" And Bobby's going like, "Did I touch you?" He said, "Yeah, you kept hitting me down the straightaway, in turn one, in turn two, in turn three, here come that bumpin'." Bobby said, "I hit you? I swear I don't remember that." He said, "You sure you didn't back into me?"

It was like the big fight with Cale Yarborough at Daytona in '79. He was so aggravating, it was like, *He ain't going to win this argument.* And Bobby's looking at him, "What are you talking about? I didn't hit you." And I remember Bobby just thumping him, thumping him, thumping him. I guess that's where Earnhardt learned it, from other people, that thump-bump—"I'm here!"

Buddy Baker, a Hall of Fame driver, taught Earnhardt some lessons on and off the track. These lessons had nothing to do with the aforementioned Busch Clash, however:

One time I raced Earnhardt for the win at Talladega. I was leading, and he was trying to make a run on me, and I just went up the bank on the straightaway on the last lap. He thought I was giving him racing room, but what I was doing was taking the draft away from him. He thought about it, and he figured it out on his own. About a year later, he said, "You son of a gun, you took the draft and went up the hill with it. And your car was quicker, and I didn't realize what was going on, but you'll never beat me like that again."

But I thought that, if I could run up the hill and make him run head-on into the wind, he'd slow down and I'd win. It happened that way, but, like he said, it never happened again.

He was a quick study. We talked a lot when he was real young about drafting, and we rode on the lake together and talked about the major speedways. When he won a couple of times at Talladega, he acknowledged my help at major speedways. It was flattering as all heck, but he had so much natural talent that all he needed to do was get some direction.

<hr>

*Most racing folk knew that short-track legend **Dick Trickle** liked to smoke under caution:*

You know, I've been known to smoke, and usually I have a cigarette during yellow. Usually, when the race goes green, I'll flick the cigarette up in the air out the window. And after a race, I forget which race it was, Earnhardt come up to me kinda jokingly and said, "Trickle, on that restart, when you flipped that cigarette, it came in my car," which I know it didn't. You couldn't hardly get it to do that if you tried. I was going to, sometime when we were side by side under yellow or something, but I never got to do it because we lost him.

<hr>

*Earnhardt got his ride with Rod Osterlund because the crew chief was fired and an angered **Dave Marcis** quit the team. Later, Earnhardt and Marcis actually became friends because of a spinout at Martinsville. In fact, it was the famous race in which Earnhardt spun out but still wound up winning; and* *this is another case of Earnhardt admiring someone who stood up to him:*

At Martinsville, we had a difference there. He kept leaning on me and leaning on me, leaning on me, so finally I got upset with him and spun him out. He got all bowed up about it, upset, and he wouldn't talk to me for a while. We was at Rockingham, I believe it was, and he come up to me and put his arm around me, and said, "That deal at Martinsville, I had it coming. I'm sorry about that." And he said, "You handled it the way you're supposed to handle it. My daddy always said don't carry a grudge down the road; take care of it right away, and get it over with so you can get back to your business." He said, "I respect you for that," and we became the very best of friends after that.

Yeah, I was real surprised, because I felt he had it coming, and I felt he *knew* he had it coming. You know, I was just a little guy trying to make ends meet, and goldarnit, when somebody tears up your race car and keeps banging on you for no reason, I mean . . . I raced him hard and everybody hard. I always had a reputation for racing hard; my opinion was that's what the race fan came to see. I just raced everybody hard. I gave them plenty of track. I was courteous. I didn't lean on them, but I raced them hard, even if I was down a lap. I was there to race; that's the only way I know, and that's how I was brought up, to do your best.

So anyhow, Dale and I became very, very good friends after that. I think he realized that we had to get along with everybody; I mean we competed with each other every week for almost a year at a time. We didn't have much time off. We were all together, and we needed to get along with each other. We always had differences, but as far as I was concerned, we always sat down and talked about it.

It's kinda funny how it worked out, how good of friends we became after that. I wanted to talk after it happened, and he wouldn't talk to me at the time.

Marcis, on another incident:

One time after that, I guess at Rockingham, he gave me a shot in the rear when he came by me; I gave him a shot in the rear on the straightaway. And after the race, he said, "I knew I was going to get that shot in the rear."

Benny Parsons, the 1973 Cup champion and 1975 Daytona 500 winner, was an established star when Earnhardt joined Cup racing full time in 1979:

He never put me into the wall, but he sure ran into me a few times. I remember racing at Talladega in 1981. I was driving a Ford Thunderbird, and Dale was in a Chevrolet. To get that Thunderbird to run, you had to jack the back end way up in the air to try to get the front end as low as possible. I was leading Dale going down the backstretch, and about the time we drove into turn three, the engine began to rev up. He literally had driven right up under the rear end of the Thunderbird and lifted the rear tires off the ground. Yes, that was a bad thing. It scared me to death. I got back under control, and we went on.

Parsons, on Dale's philosophy:

Earnhardt's thing early in his career was, "I'm out here to win, and that's it. If I have to move them out of the way, that's okay." I don't remember anybody else like that.

Parsons, on Earnhardt's driving style:

It was amazing how sideways he was the first couple of years he ran, especially the first year. I remember Charlotte in 1980 in the 500-mile race, he came up and passed me for position, somewhere in the top five, pretty early in the race, and he went into turn one like he was on a dirt track. The car was sideways getting down into the corner. I said, "I'm not going to have to worry about racing him because you can't drive a car like that all day here at Charlotte. He'll be gone before this thing's too far gone." And he won the race.

Jack Ingram, the Hall of Fame driver who had the nickname "Ironman" before Terry Labonte came along, saw a rough-and-ready Earnhardt when both raced Late Model Sportsman and, later, Busch Grand National:

Frankly, based on his performance in Late Model Sportsman, I didn't think he had much of a chance. Then I wound up racing against him in Charlotte in his own car, and he didn't look much good. But then he got a chance to drive Charlotte's Late Model Sportsman race in one of Rod Osterlund's cars. He had two ex-Winston Cup cars; back then, they'd go out of style in two or three years. Dave Marcis was the regular driver for Osterlund, and Dale drove the other car. And I was in the race, too.

Dale probably should have won the race, but he didn't. He outran a lot of really good drivers that day, including Marcis, who was driving as good or better a car as the one Dale had. That's when I knew he could be a factor on superspeedways, but that was several years after he began racing in Late Model Sportsman.

The first time I raced against him, Dale had been running on dirt. Ralph told me that he looks like he's going to be a pretty good driver if he stays out of trouble. Anyway, he bought a car from Harry Gant, and he told Harry and I that he thought that, if he had one of our cars, he could outrun us. He bought that car and went to Columbia, South Carolina, and he didn't keep up, and he wound up wrecking it. He seemed to do a lot of that. He came off a little ol' dirt track without much competition, and Late Model Sportsman probably had the most competition.

Most of the then-Grand National drivers would run in weekly races: Harry Gant, myself, Bobby Allison, David Pearson, and just on and on. Just about everyone except Richard Petty. You'd go to those races, and it was tough. Dale showed up at Charlotte in that Osterlund car; he had a car that was sure enough good enough, and he made the most out of it. And that resulted in him getting a Winston Cup ride with Osterlund. The rest of it's basically history.

Ingram discusses Earnhardt's tenacity:

Earnhardt was tenacious in taking advantage of a situation that come in front of him, regardless of the consequences. It got to the point in that kind of racing where you either take it or somebody will take it from you, and he took his share of it. He'd do whatever it takes. If he had to bump somebody or whatever, that's what he'd do. When the time came for somebody to bump him, he'd move out of the way. He wouldn't let them take him out. All of them good drivers does that.

When I was driving, if I was going for the win, no, I wouldn't let someone go around me. If that happened four to five laps earlier and they came up fast on me, yes, I'd let

Dale Earnhardt posted twenty-six top-five and thirty top-ten finishes at Atlanta Motor Speedway, setting a track record with nine Cup wins between 1980, his first, and 2000 (left), his last.

Dale Earnhardt was one of the biggest winners at Darlington Raceway, with nine Cup victories and two Busch wins. The only bigger winner is David Pearson, who tallied ten Cup wins. Earnhardt always liked to make sure he was the first to send in his entry to Darlington each year, and he was quick to do publicity for the track.

The Intimidator could be reticent with media representatives, but sometimes print, radio, and TV reporters would catch him in a smiling mood, as they did here.

Earnhardt had nineteen fruitless years in the Daytona 500, but he made up for it when he celebrated his victory in the 1998 race.

Dale Earnhardt only had three chances to run at Texas Motor Speedway, but he posted one win and two top-ten finishes. In 2000, he was in Victory Lane at TMS (above right) to help Dale Jr. celebrate his first Cup victory.
• Before the March 2000 race at Las Vegas Motor Speedway, the Intimidator pointed out something on the track to driver Bobby Labonte (right), who would capture the Cup championship that year.

Dale Earnhardt Jr. drives past a memorial to his father at Las Vegas Motor Speedway in 2001.

Dale Earnhardt has a strong presence on the mural in the lobby of the Winston Cup Museum in Winston-Salem, North Carolina. Earnhardt recorded seventy-six victories during the Winston Cup era, second only to Darrell Waltrip's eighty-four wins.

The Dale Trail helps fans find nearly twenty special places in and around Kannapolis, North Carolina, Dale Earnhardt's hometown. Among the hot spots on the trail are Dale Earnhardt Boulevard, Ralph Earnhardt's grave, Car Town (where Dale grew up), Dale Earnhardt Plaza, NC 3, and Richard Childress Racing, among many other places.

The centerpiece of Dale Earnhardt Plaza in Kannapolis is a nine-foot, 900-pound bronze statue (above left) depicting Dale as hometown folks knew him—in Wrangler jeans, boots, and a short-sleeve shirt with button-down collar. Fans have paid their respects in a field of bricks (below) in the plaza, which also includes a memorial (above right) donated by fans from New York and Vermont.

Quick Silver, one of several paintings of Dale Earnhardt by renowned racing artist Sam Bass.

him go. That's better than getting spun out or getting in a problem, or racing with him and losing second place. At the end of the race, you can't let them go.

Earnhardt—I'm not saying he was the most talented driver, but he was the most talented at taking advantage of a situation. I raced with people who probably could do a little more with a race car than he could, but he wound up getting more at the racetrack than most people because he went there to win; regardless of what happened, he went there to win. All of us did, but a lot of people didn't go to the extremes he did to win.

But he won. He won them championships. He was the biggest man in his time, that's for sure.

INTERNATIONAL MOTORSPORTS HALL OF FAME

This is the classic Intimidator pose as Earnhardt waited to go racing.

Hut Stricklin, an Alabama native who raced against Earnhardt from the late 1980s to the early 21st century, remembers two Earnhardts. The first was a good guy to race against. The other was someone to watch out for:

You know, I always felt that he was the type of guy that, if you'd show him respect, he showed you respect. He was just a driver that drove as hard as he could go every lap; he just got every ounce he could get out of it every time in was on the racetrack. Doing that, he'd run into people. Yeah, he sure did (run into Stricklin), a few times.

One of the most memorable ones, I remember very well, was in, I guess, '91. I was driving for Bobby Allison. I was running second in the Daytona 500 behind (eventual race winner) Davey Allison. We'd had an extremely fast car the whole week leading to the 500. We were coming off turn four. Davey and I were tucked in there, and Earnhardt was behind me. The three of us were running nose to tail. And Dale just run into the back end of me, off turn four; it spun me out. I didn't hit anything, but I had four flat tires when it was all over.

He always had a knack where he could make it look like people backed into him rather than him hitting you. NASCAR officials asked him about it, and Bobby was hot. He (Earnhardt) said, "They backed out of the gas right in front of me, and I couldn't stop." It didn't happen. He was that aggressive; he didn't cut anyone any slack. He'd run a half-inch off your bumper continuously; that's where he'd run. A few (other) people tried to race like that, but they didn't have the natural ability.

A lot of people tried to pattern their style after him. I know Ernie Irvan came on board in an aggressive way, and he tried to pattern his driving style after Dale a lot, I think. But he couldn't do it the way Dale could, where when something happened, it looked like it was the other guy's fault."

*The first time I got to talk to Earnhardt was after a 1990
race at Atlanta Motor Speedway.* **Morgan Shepherd** *was
leading the race under caution, with Earnhardt second.
Alan Kulwicki, in a lapped car, ran Shepherd up the track
on the restart; Earnhardt dropped to the apron and bottomed
out, but he passed both men and won the race. In the press
box, I asked Earnhardt if he was surprised when the hole
opened up, and he gave me an unprintable response. Teresa
punched Dale on the shoulder, and he looked contrite.
Shepherd remembers that incident:*

I was mad at Kulwicki. He was a lap down, and he ran me
up the track and allowed Earnhardt to get under me and get
past. It knocked me out of a shot at winning the race.

Shepherd, *a winner of four career Cup races, got Earnhardt's
respect, but it was hard won. His favorite memory of Earnhardt
came later that same season:*

It's probably when he got into me when I was driving the
90 (Junie Donlavey) car at Darlington. He got into me and
spun me out. At the next race, when we were at Richmond,
I went up to him and said, "Dale, if you touch my car again,
I'll hang you on the wall every time I get to you." He said,
"What are you talking about?" I said, "You know what I'm
talking about. Touch my car one more time." He said, "F—
you," and walked away, and I said, "You heard me."

That night there was a Busch race. You know that he
reached for everything he could, but when I got to him, he
got over and moved out of my way. I thought, *Wow, I can't
believe Dale'd move over and get out of my way.* The next
night (in the Cup race), he had qualified in front of me.
When I got to him, he moved over and got out of my way. I

outrun him both times. Anyway, he showed respect after that. I think there were few drivers he'd do that with. But you just had to show him where you stood and that you meant business.

I don't think we had trouble until 1995, I think, at Talladega. I was running third in the 21 Wood Brothers car, and he was running fourth. Coming down to a lap or two laps go, he tried squeezing me on the outside, and, of course, I didn't move, and Dale spun out. He finished twenty-first, which was *my* car number (with the Wood Brothers), and I finished third, which was *his* car number.

He lost the points lead, and R. J. Reynolds was offering a $100,000 bonus to the points leader. He was pretty mad with me; he felt like I took him out. But I showed him respect, and I expected him to show me respect. That was one of the times we got together, but he didn't try to retaliate because he knew my promise was good.

I reckon my other good memory of Earnhardt was when he ran second to me in Atlanta in '86, because that's when he was doing good (Earnhardt won eleven races and his second Cup title in 1986). I think Bill Elliott was third, and it was good to know I beat one of the best in racing and nobody had fallen out of the race.

Dale Earnhardt Jr., on racing with his dad and Jeff Gordon in March 2000 at Las Vegas:

When I turned and gathered the car up, Gordon was beside me and I slammed into the side of him. Dad was two cars back, so I was like, "I'll just get the heck out of the way here because I'm getting ready to wreck everybody." About a straightaway and a half later, Dad went by and he was shaking his finger out the window at me. You don't see that on television. The fans don't get to see that part of it. I guess that was where the father was going, "You'd better watch it. You'd better straighten up."[2]

—————◆—————

*Before the 1990 spring race at Charlotte, '90 Daytona 500
winner **Derrike Cope** said, "One of these days, we're going to
whip their butts, and we won't hear all of this crap anymore."
I wasn't able to run that column that week, so I saved it for
the next week, Dover. Yes, Cope won at Dover; unfortunately,
it was his last victory, so far, and he's probably heard that
"crap" about being lucky for more than seventeen years.
Still, Cope was in position to win the 1990 Daytona 500,
and he did. When he has had good equipment, say, with
Bob Whitcomb and Bobby Allison, he has run well:*

For me, it was just the fact of winning a race early in my career. I didn't have many races under my belt, and that, really, was my first full season. People don't realize what (crew chief) Buddy Parrott and I did all day. We had a car capable of winning; we knew we were the only car capable of passing Earnhardt in Happy Hour.

The key was: did I have the experience to get it to the end? I applaud Buddy, because I lifted (off the gas) all day, and Earnhardt ran wide open all day. That's why he was able to pull away in a runaway. And I was lifting all day because I was trying to take care of the car. Nobody else could seem to battle us, so we were simply biding our time. Buddy said there'd be a caution late and we'd have our opportunity, and that's exactly how it played out.

I was on used tires, and Earnhardt was on new tires, and I still stayed on his bumper. For me, it was self-gratification, the fact that we performed at a high level that day. We were in position to win that race, and fortune went our way.

—————◆—————

Cope also had a good car the year Earnhardt finally won the Daytona 500:

I felt I had a better car than he did the year he won it, in 1998. I ran up front with him. That race, I got wrecked by Jeff Burton on pit road; it was the same time when Dale Jarrett and Mark Martin got together on pit road. Earnhardt and I came in and pitted together. He was leading the race, and I was running second. Jeff Burton hit us on pit road and knocked us out of the race.

The next week at Rockingham, Earnhardt came up to me and hit me on the arm and said, "I'm damned glad you got hit on pit road. Otherwise, it might have been '90 all over again." That was like payback to me. I'd carried a lot of burden at Daytona the first time when I won because people said it was a fluke, that I didn't deserve to win and that I took something from Earnhardt that he desperately wanted. It was like he was saying, "You had a better car when I won it, and I had a better car when you won it, so I guess we're even." That's the way I took it.

<hr />

*Former Cup driver **Jerry Nadeau** was driving Richard Jackson's No. 1 car when he had his first encounter with Dale Earnhardt:*

It was my first race, at Michigan in 1997. Everything was the talk about me, this rookie driver just showing up and being the second-fastest guy in practice, and then everybody talked about me. And then I ended up crashing the car, totaled it in qualifying. In the race, I was competitive, considering the car I was in. And I was hurting Dale Earnhardt's chance of winning the race, but I was racing.

I remember I was passing him, and he was shaking his fist at me out the window, like, *Get the hell off the racetrack.*

You don't need to be here. I could just sense it. I didn't even realize it that it was Earnhardt, because, when you're racing, you don't care about that. But I remember him sticking his hand out the window and just shaking it. I think it's because I got too close, and I hurt his chances to win the race. Here I am, I'm a lap down, and he thought I didn't really need to be in the way. He never said anything to me after the race. After I got to know him, he said that you didn't want to get into the Winston Cup Series without having a name. That was like, "Welcome to the series"; he was just shaking his fist.

———※———

Max Helton, the founder of Motor Racing Outreach, never raced Earnhardt—he just calmed him down once or twice:

Back in 1988, when I came into the sport, there was very little done in a religious way in the racing community, and I got to know the drivers as I got more involved.

I think one of my initial contacts with Dale was when we were up in North Wilkesboro at a race. He and Ricky Rudd were running for the lead, I think on the last lap. They spun each other in turn two, and after the race they were fighting mad. I think Geoff Bodine went on to win the race.

I was kinda staying down between them to see what was going on and try to defuse any kind of fight if I could, and Dale leans over and says, "Max, maybe you'd want to leave. You might hear things you don't want to hear." And I say, "Dale, did it ever occur to you that God hears you anyway? I'm really insignificant."

There was no fight, and Rudd walked away.

From that moment on, he became a good friend of mine. He always called me in to talk about things, and it was a good relationship. That's how I got to know Dale Earnhardt.

*Derrike Cope, who won the 1990 Daytona 500 when
Earnhardt blew a tire on the last lap, says he's glad Dale
finally won the prestigious event:*

In some respects, I felt tied to Earnhardt. Until his win (in
1998), I was one of the main obstacles between the Daytona 500 and him. It's almost to the point to where you feel
bad that you won it, to some degree, just because he had
done everything else in racing that he could possibly do.

Thank God he did win it, because to do what he had
done and to get killed in the fashion that he did, it would
really have been unfair. I'm just very appreciative that he
won it.

*Mark Martin, himself a tenacious driver, talks about
Earnhardt's never-say-die attitude:*

Some of the fiercest and most successful drivers are also
the most aggravating on the track. Dale was incredibly
tenacious, and he drove me to rise to his level. He made me
want to be the best, because he made me want to beat him.
I have never in all of my experience raced against anyone
with as much desire to win as he had, and that's saying a
lot, because I've raced against them all.

He was so tenacious, but he was so different from that
away from the track. I was really fortunate to know that side
of him, because not everyone did. There was a softer side to
Dale that most people I know didn't know he had, but it
was there.[3]

*Cope said that when he drove for Allison and Whitcomb he
felt competitive with Earnhardt:*

When I've been in competitive cars, Dale and I ran together a lot. We've had our pushing and shoving matches. We've had our discussions, but I think that, over the years, he's respected me for some of the things I did. Knowing Dale, he likes that kind of stuff. He didn't want you to be a pushover. He wanted a battle.

Still, he wanted you to move over. Back then, as a young kid, you didn't care. You didn't want to give up. But as you get older, you realize there are times to race and times when you don't. I didn't realize that or didn't want to condone the fact that I needed to do that. So we definitely had our run-ins when I was in some better equipment.

***

*Former Cup driver **Jerry Nadeau** talks about Earnhardt's style:*

I'm sure that there's not a day that in every driver's mind they don't think of Earnhardt, because he was the master. It was too bad what happened. He was definitely not one of the drivers who'd wreck people. Yes, he was aggressive, and he had his own style that people didn't like. He was a great race-car driver, and he was very aggressive. I think everybody knew that, coming into the series.

But you knew you didn't want to race against Dale Earnhardt, because he was the master. And it was like, he'll make you mess up, or he'll make you crash. He was a guy who gave it 110 percent every week, and that's one thing I respect a lot about Dale. Jimmy Spencer was a little bit aggressive, but he didn't have the finesse that Earnhardt had.

If you'd look in your rearview mirror, you could see him in his half-helmet, sitting low in the car. And you'd see his eyes, and you kinda knew—*oh, shit, he's going to race you hard, so you need to get the hell out of the way.* He was good.

*Ned Jarrett's last-lap work during the 1993 Daytona 500
made the Dale & Dale Show a part of the Earnhardt legend:*

One of the best feelings I ever had came from him, and that
was after my son Dale beat him in the 1993 Daytona 500.
Everybody knows that story. I was working for CBS. They
turned me loose on the last lap and encouraged me to be a
dad. I went away from being a supposedly professional
announcer and cheered my son home, but that's what they
told me to do. The producer said, "Call your son home. Be a
daddy."

He was up beside Earnhardt when they got the white
flag (for the last lap), and they were side by side in turn one,
and that's when they turned it over to me. I said, "Get to the
inside. Don't let him get there. It's the Dale & Dale Show,
and you know who I'm pulling for: Dale Jarrett." Of course,
Dale Jarrett did go on to win the race. I felt bad about it
later, that I had not done Earnhardt and his fans justice, by
calling my son home. That's not the way it should have
been done, in my opinion. That's the way I felt.

The next week at Rockingham, I didn't get there until
Saturday, and I didn't see him on Saturday. On Sunday
morning, I stopped him when he was walking to the drivers' meeting. I said, "Dale, I need to talk to you a second."
He said, "Congratulations on Dale winning the race down
there." I said, "That's what I want to talk to you about. I sort
of threw you in the river." He said, "What do you mean?" I
said, "I'm an announcer, and I cheered Dale Jarrett home
to victory, and that's not the way it should be."

He pointed a finger at me, and he said, "Don't you forget that I'm a daddy, too." He just removed all of those bad
thoughts that I'd had about the race. It choked me up, and I
still choke up when I tell the story. It has always meant so
much to me that that's the way he felt about it.

Jarrett compares the driving styles of Curtis Turner, Junior Johnson, himself, and Earnhardt:

Dale had a tremendous amount of confidence in what he could do with an automobile, and, as a result, he could do more things with a car than anybody I've seen. We've talked about Curtis Turner, Junior Johnson, guys who were dramatic to watch in the early days. But Earnhardt could do more than anyone I've seen, get a car in position and get it back out without wrecking.

The last example I saw of that was the IROC race in February, two days before he was killed. And Dale Jarrett went on to win that race. One of the first things he mentioned in Victory Lane, he said, "He's the best race-car driver in the world. Nobody else could have brought that car out of the situation he was in and brought it back into the race." He said he knew Earnhardt was going to wreck. Dale (Jarrett) backed off. He said, "I just wanted to see what he was going to do, how he was going to get that car under control." The man just could do things with the car . . . he had a tremendous seat-of-the-pants feel on the racetrack.

Most of Turner's reputation came on dirt. It would have been interesting to see Dale Earnhardt on dirt. His dad was good on dirt. I'm sure it would have been dramatic. I managed to win a lot of races on dirt, but not in the same style of a Curtis Turner or a Junior Johnson. I wasn't too exciting to watch because I always thought a car was faster going straight than it was going sideways. Those guys would throw that car sideways, and it'd throw up those rooster tails. It was fun to watch those guys drive those cars. But I didn't do it that way.

*Cup car owner **Bill Davis** smiles when he thinks of a 2000 race at Pocono, when Earnhardt was leading and Jeremy Mayfield bumped his way past Dale on the last lap:*

Remember last year when Jeremy bumped him out of the way at Pocono, and he went up the track? By then, we'd fallen out of the race, and I was already back on the truck. We were parked next to the 3 (trailer in the garage), and I was standing there as we were loading up. And he comes wheeling up like he always does, at about a hundred miles an hour. He slid to a stop and looked at me. He gave me that big ol' smile and winked. I thought, *There you go, that's perfect.* It was two or three minutes after he'd gotten spun out on the last lap and, basically, he enjoyed it. He enjoyed it.

Davis has another favorite Pocono story about Earnhardt:

Probably my favorite Earnhardt story was at Pocono three years ago (1998). We (Ward Burton) had led 100-some laps, just had the best car there in the race. I think he led 160 of 200 laps. The last pit stop came with about twenty laps to go, and a bunch of cars put on two tires (for track position). We put on four tires, so we came out eighth, ninth, or tenth. Ward was passing his way through there, and he'd caught Johnny Benson and the 3 (Earnhardt), and they were racing hard.

We were just a whole lot better than they were. They were racing for about sixth or seventh place. We were going right back to the front, but Ward got impatient and went inside the 3 on the tunnel turn, and we ended up almost three wide. We got wrecked, and we were pretty crushed. We hadn't won many races, and here we thought we had that one won for sure.

After the race, some reporter came up and mouthed off about who you're racing with and you've gotta be careful around a black car with a 3 on it, something like that. The next Friday morning, we got to the racetrack, and you know how they pass around the paper, maybe *Winston Cup Scene* or maybe even a newspaper. I went to the trailer, and at nine o'clock, the back door swung open, and he came stomping in there. "Where the hell is B. D.?" They say, "Well, he's not here." He says, "Well, tell his ass I'm looking for him."

He caught me pretty shortly—he was on a mission to find me—and he just wore me out. He said, "I didn't wreck any people, blah, blah, blah." From then on, until fifteen minutes before the Daytona 500 this year, more than half the time when we'd meet, he'd get that smile and go, "I didn't do it." That was his standard phrase for two years now: "I didn't do it." He didn't say hello or nothing, just, "I didn't do it." We had many a laugh over that.

The last time I saw him, we were walking to the cars for the Daytona 500 this year (2001). Of course, he said, "I didn't do it," and he put his arm around my shoulders. I don't know what I said; "Good luck," or something like that. I was on my way to the spotters' stand, and he was on his way out to the drivers' intro.

Humpy Wheeler, on Earnhardt's evolving driving style:

Earnhardt got to the point where he quit fighting the car. He fought the car a while, even after he won his first championship. Richard Childress was a real master with Earnhardt, because he knew how to talk to him and calm him down, and also make him understand that you've got to be there at the 400-mile mark. That's when the race really starts.

No one really understands how much emotion there is in a race driver during a 500-mile race, and how you contain that emotion and how you put that emotion in its proper perspective. That's the absolute reason why you win most races.

You talk about Earnhardt trying to be an intimidator; there were lots of people who were trying to intimidate him. And he had to get through that, just like everybody else did.

---

*In the fall of 1999, **Jeff Gordon** held off Earnhardt to win at Martinsville Speedway. Here are Gordon's thoughts on seeing the black No. 3 Chevrolet in his mirror:*

It wasn't a pretty sight. I never had to be so smooth in a race car in all my life. It's so easy to tell yourself to drive it in deeper, but I was just trying to keep it on the bottom. The good thing is, we were good on long runs today. My car was driving up pretty good there up off the corner at the end. I knew it was going to be close.[4]

---

*During the same interview, **Gordon** recalled Earnhardt bumping his way past Gordon's teammate, Terry Labonte, on the last lap of the fall 1999 race at Bristol. It made Jeff nervous at Martinsville:*

In the closing laps, I felt him coming, and he was coming hard. I knew it was going to come right down to the wire. Going into the last corner, I've got to be honest with you, all I could think about was Terry Labonte. I was like, *Man, I hope he doesn't get to my bumper.* I knew I would be feeling a little bit of a nudge. You just expect that in short-track racing, especially with a hard racer like Dale. Instead, he waited until after I crossed the checkered flag to give me that nudge. I knew once I got to turn three that we were there. I just couldn't believe it. I really could not believe I was able to hold him off.[5]

Eli Gold was working for Motor Racing Network years ago when he got too close to Dale Earnhardt's car:

We're at Pocono, and Earnhardt is in a blue-and-gold car—I don't remember if he was driving for Rod Osterlund or for the Wrangler team. He's running side by side with Tim Richmond, coming down the long front straightaway, and they touched. The cars started flipping wildly, doing barrel rolls into turn one.

I'm on a wood scaffold, outside turn one, and Earnhardt's car is flipping wildly towards me. The car actually hit the wooden platform on which I was standing. Fortunately, it didn't devastate the platform or myself. I kept talking through this; sheet metal's flying everywhere. To this day, in my office, I have the whole right-front fender assembly of Earnhardt's car. There was shrapnel flying, and it nearly took my head off. Dale was injured, not severely, in the hellacious accident.

People had heard the broadcast, and they didn't know if I was going to survive. A television magazine took the video and took out the audio and put the MRN audio in there. It was a subject of conversation for a week or so. At each subsequent visit to Pocono, while I was a turn announcer, as the cars came by me on that wooden platform on the pace lap, Dale would scrunch down in the car so he could see me, and he'd wave at me on the pace lap. I waved back; I never did that for anybody else. The wave was Dale's way of saying, "I'll stay out of the broadcast booth; you stay out of my car." One of those things.

Kenny Wallace pushed Earnhardt to his seventy-sixth and last Cup victory, in the fall of 2000 at Talladega:

I'm very happy to have literally pushed Dale Earnhardt to his last Winston Cup win. I'm Kenny Wallace and that was the deal. It means a lot. I definitely would have liked to have won the race. But for Dale Earnhardt to have given me as much praise as he did in Victory Lane and all over the newspapers, it meant a great deal to me. I told this story a lot over the weekend, but Earnhardt put his arm around me and said, "What can I get you for Christmas?" I said, "Hey, just you thanking me. That's enough. You're Superman." It was a great endorsement from Dale Earnhardt.[6]

Wallace also credited Earnhardt with getting him his start:

Dale Earnhardt offered me the chance to drive his Busch Grand National Goodwrench car in 1988 at Martinsville. He said, "Kenny, if you drive my car at Martinsville, that will get you approved by NASCAR. Then you can go to Daytona and race." He let me drive that car, and I finished seventh. If it weren't for Dale Earnhardt, I would have never been in NASCAR racing, period.[7]

In the middle of the March 2000 race at Atlanta Motor Speedway, Mike Skinner got knocked out of the race, and he talked about Earnhardt. Later that day, Earnhardt edged Bobby Labonte in a dramatic finish for Dale's seventy-fifth victory:

I'd crash my mom to win my first race. Dale did what he had to do, and I did what I had to do. It's nothing he wouldn't have done to me. He's my teammate, and I wouldn't wreck him. It was too early in the race to be wrecking anybody, but I blocked him and he was probably a little farther alongside of me than I thought, but looking at the bumper, he wasn't too far up there. He raced me clean when the shoe was on the other foot. He gave me plenty of room.

My hat's off to Dale Earnhardt. I sure hope he wins this race. He's been an inspiration. A few years ago I figured they were going to name this place Earnhardt Speedway because he won all the races here.[8]

---

*Former racer **Paul "Little Bud" Moore** raced Ralph Earnhardt, and he's watched (and been friends with) Dale:*

I guess at the height of his career, Ralph Earnhardt was one of the toughest people I have ever seen drive a race car. That is where Dale gets it.

If I had to race against Dale, I'd have to race him just like we used to have to race Ralph. There wouldn't be but one way to race him, and that would be to stay away from him. It is just that simple.

The intimidation thing, yeah, he does it. There is no question about that. And his dad, he was an intimidator. I mean, he convinced me to stay the hell away from him. And he had a lot of other people convinced of that, too.[9]

---

*Former Cup driver **Rick Mast** once talked about the first time he raced against Earnhardt, in the Busch Grand National Series in the late 1980s:*

I remember running with him in the Busch cars. I'd heard what everyone had said, and I thought, *He must not be driving the same way with me that he does with the Cup guys, because he'll race with you.* He's the best driver to run with. He's a smart driver, always aware of what's going on around him.

⸻ ❦ ⸻

Tony Eury Sr., Earnhardt's longtime friend and the crew chief for Dale Earnhardt Jr., once compared the driving styles of Ralph Earnhardt, Dale Earnhardt, and Dale Jr.:

There's too much difference in the years to compare those three as drivers. I believe Junior takes care of his equipment a little bit better than Dale did at the same age. That's because we beat it into him. We stay on him pretty hard about saving equipment, and his daddy does, too. His daddy didn't have anybody doing that to him. Everybody knows Dale was pretty rough on his stuff when he first started. I always thought he was his own enemy. I think (crew chief) Jake Elder probably helped Dale out more than anybody.[10]

⸻ ❦ ⸻

Johnny Ray fielded one ride for Earnhardt in 1976, at Atlanta, but it was spectacular. In fact, it was one of the worst crashes of Earnhardt's career, and Dale probably got the worst purse of his career: $1,360. Ray and Earnhardt remained friends, went hunting occasionally, and Dale often visited Ray at his home near Talladega Superspeedway:

I used to drive myself years ago, and he was working in the shop where I kept my car. He worked for Robert Gee, his ex-father-in-law. I used to keep my car up at his shop and work on it out of there. After I got hurt at Daytona in '76, I kept the car, and Johnny Rutherford and people like that drove it a few times for me.

It came around to Atlanta. Dale and I had been talking, and I put him in my car at Atlanta. He done a good job there, just got in a racing accident, flipped it several times. I still had a neck brace on and couldn't get around too good. I went running over there where the accident was at. About the time I got there, the ambulance left with him. I ran back over to the hospital, a little care-center deal, and the guard there says, "You can't go in there," and I says, "I'm going."

I got the door open, and there sat Dale on a little cot. He had a cut finger; that was about all he got out of it. He said, "I messed your race car up, didn't I?" And I said, "You all right?" We built another car like that one, but then he got a chance to go with (car owner Rod) Osterlund. I said, "I don't have a sponsor, I don't have that kind of money, so you need to go." We remained good friends, though.

Dick Trickle, on racing Earnhardt and what Dale got away with:

He was the Intimidator, although it's pretty hard to intimidate your dad, isn't it? Me being a generation older than him, he never really did intimidate me. There was one occasion at Dover on a restart where he got into me and spun me. Of course, I was pretty unhappy because it was unnecessary. Nobody was going anywhere. It was like the first corner of a restart. I was pretty perturbed with him, and he knew it. He had more to lose than I did. Him and Rusty (Wallace) were pretty tight, and he got Rusty to come over and talk to me that next week. He knew that payback was probably going to be hell, and he tried to smooth things through Rusty. I could have returned the favor, but I let up on him a little bit.

He was a great driver and a great person. The biggest thing (was that) he got by with more than anyone else—

perhaps he earned it. But a lot of things he got by with on the track, I didn't blame him for; I blame NASCAR. Had Hut Stricklin done the same things, he'd have been sitting in the pits for five laps. I don't mean that in a derogative way, but I'm sure a lot of people saw it that way.

He gave a lot to racing. Richard Petty is probably the number-one ambassador for racing, but Dale Earnhardt is probably a favorite alongside of him. We had some good times, some good races. Got along quite well. We had one incident in racing. In twelve years I raced Cup, that's minor. Most guys had trouble with him every month; I only had trouble with him once. Like I said, it was pretty hard for him to him to intimidate me, being ten years older. And I'd been around, too.

6

DALE'S TURN

"I think the Martians came and took me away for a little while."

— DALE EARNHARDT

One of my favorite Dale Earnhardt stories happened nearly four years before his death, and it shocked everyone at the time.

In 1997 at Darlington Raceway, the Southern 500 started without Earnhardt. Oh, he was in his No. 3 Chevrolet, but he wasn't all there. He passed out, and his car bumped along the wall. He was taken to a hospital for tests. They never found the reason for the blackout.

In typical Earnhardt fashion, Dale put a strange twist on the whole thing. He attributed the problem to an alien abduction.

"I think the Martians came and took me away for a little while," Earnhardt said just before the 1998 Southern 500, "but they won't get me again. I'm going back for revenge this time around."

As far as we know, the Martians left him alone after that.

———⟨⟩———

*Here's a poignant set of quotes from **Earnhardt** that makes one think of the last lap of the 2001 Daytona 500. Dale knew how to protect himself, and it still didn't help him:*

Anything you can do for safety is great. We've had a switch in the car that you can turn off ever since I've been racing. Anything you can do will help. If the speedway wants to step up to the plate and put some barriers in the corner that are Styrofoam or whatever, like Flemington short track did, that's great. Whether NASCAR would make it mandatory, it would be hard for them to do that. The switch we have now is on the steering wheel instead of on the dash. I can reach my switches on the dash.

That's the problem when you're confronted with a situation like when the throttle hangs. I went through the fence at Richmond several years ago with the throttle hung. The reaction time is very small. It's within hundredths of a second. For a driver to be able to react and do the right thing to save him or the car is really tough. Will the driver remember or will he just lock up?

And that's the response of a driver. It's like you guys going down the highway and somebody steps out in front of you, pulls out in front of you or whatever, it's your reaction. What do you do? Do you panic and lock the car up or do you steer clear? It's all in reaction time. It's all in drivers in that split second of making that decision.

It's the same thing on the racetrack in racing. If you remember the things to do, you can probably save yourself from hitting that wall or hitting that wall hard. Dale Jr. did the same thing at Pocono in practice. The car pushed out and got on the edge and he locked the car up and hit the wall harder. If he had just drove it on through, he would have hit the wall with the right side and probably bruised the car more than you could race it, but it probably wouldn't have bruised him.

I'm comfortable with the helmet and safety equipment I have in the car. I've hit the wall pretty hard in several instances and gotten through it. I think the full-face helmets are different. They put a different stress on the neck and the head. That's everybody's argument. It's to everybody's liking. I think if you run a full-face helmet, that thing is probably going to work good for you.[1]

After Earnhardt won the 1998 Daytona 500, he said he hadn't reached all of his goals:

Hell, no, we want to win that eighth championship. That's what my life and career has been all about, winning championships. Nobody has ever won eight before, and that's what we're shooting for. We think we've got a great shot at it this year, and then we'll keep going from there.

More on Daytona:

We cried a little on that lap coming in to get that checkered flag. It was pretty awesome. All the race teams were giving me high-fives.

This is it. There ain't nothing gonna top this. Well, maybe that eighth championship.

I cried a little bit in the race car on the way to the checkered flag. Well, maybe not cried, but at least my eyes watered up.

It was my time (to win the 500). I have been passed on the last lap (in 1993, for one instance), I have run out of gas (1986), and I have had a cut tire (1990). I don't care how we won it, but that we won it.

It's a feeling you can't replace. It's eluded us for so many years. The drama and excitement of it all has built so much over the years. There have been a lot of emotions played out down here at Daytona with the letdowns we've had.

I never believed, when guys told me how it felt to win the 500. I never believed, but I do now. It sure feels good.

You won't have to wake me (tomorrow). I ain't going to bed.[2]

On religion:

I am aging well. I believe my faith in God has carried me through better than anything. I am not the kind who goes out and shouts it, but it is like driving a race car. I believe I can do it, and I am confident I can do it. I am confident I will be okay. That is the way my religion is, too.[3]

On his fifty-nine-race losing streak, which ended with the 1998 Daytona 500:

We can't catch a break. Nothing but bad luck seems to follow us these days.[4]

You struggle at times through your career. That doesn't mean you can't come back strong when you get everything working right. Some people maybe gave up on me a little too quick.

Or maybe they were just hoping I was done.

On winning the Daytona 500:

I woke up this morning, and I still don't believe I won the Daytona 500.

On being judged as a driver:

I'm racing for the wins and racing up front and finishing in the top ten. It's puzzling to me how you can judge a driver on that.

On winning:

You've got to be closer to the edge than ever to win. That means sometimes you go over the edge—and I don't mean driving, either.

Earnhardt's 2000 season, with two victories and second place in points, showed some people that he was back:

Hell, in my mind, I had never left. I never went anywhere. I have always been here. I'll be here until I'm gone. After this deal with Richard Childress is over, I'll probably look at retirement. I'm not going to make any bones about it or set a time deal on it.[5]

Before Talladega qualifying in the spring of 2000, he relaxed:

I went turkey hunting with the Realtree guys this morning. I had a good time. I got soaking wet, but I got a nice turkey.[6]

After breaking Davey Allison's record with his ninth Cup victory at Talladega:

It always is an honor to set a record, but it was a bigger honor to have known and raced against Davey.[7]

On quitting school in junior high:

I wanted to race; that's all I ever wanted to do. I didn't care about work or school or anything; all I wanted to do was to

The Earnhardts—Dale Jr., Dale, and Kerry—had the opportunity to race together in 2000 at Michigan.

INTERNATIONAL MOTORSPORTS HALL OF FAME

work on race cars and then drive race cars. It was always my dream, and I was just fortunate enough to be able to live out that dream.

I tried the ninth grade twice and quit. Couldn't hang, man. Couldn't hang.

He (Ralph Earnhardt) was against me dropping out of school to go racing. But he was the biggest influence in my life.

<hr />

Earnhardt remembered racing against his father, Ralph, in the early seventies at Metrolina Speedway in Charlotte, North Carolina:

I did race against my dad at Charlotte in the dirt one time, but I never really did it in a Sportsman car like he had. The one thing I probably would have liked to have done that I didn't get to do was drive for my dad. The year he died, he was talking with Mom about putting me in the car the next year rather than having other people drive for him.

I didn't find it out until after he passed away and my mom and Uncle Bud was telling me about it. That would have been great. I would have gotten my ass chewed out a lot, but that would have been great. I think that would have been a lot of fun.[8]

<hr />

On borrowing money from the bank on a Friday to go racing that weekend (he'd have to repay the loan from money earned that weekend):

If Dad had been around then and knew that was the way I was financing my racing, he'd have whipped my butt in a minute. And let me tell you something: If he'd have wanted to, he could have done it, no matter how old I was. He was that tough. It wouldn't have mattered to him if I was bigger than him or not![9]

After finishing second to Jeff Gordon in 1999 at Martinsville:

I got to him too late. I'm feeling pretty bad. I've got the flu bug, but we'll be at Dale Earnhardt Chevrolet tomorrow signing autographs.[10]

On racing:

Finishing races is important, but racing is *more* important.

On racing in the season finale at Atlanta and running second to Gordon for the 1995 Winston Cup title:

I knew he had the thing won and that we weren't going to get our eighth championship this time. It made me mad. I wanted to get this season over and get started with next year.

I knew I could pass him fifty times and it wouldn't make any difference. He knew he had the championship locked up.[11]

On winning his sixth championship, in 1993:

Every single championship is precious to me. But this one means a whole lot. We came off a kind of bad year last year and had a great year this year.[12]

On introspection:

I don't analyze things. I go out and make 'em happen.

On his longtime car owner:

You can't say enough about Richard Childress and this whole crew. They have given me the cars and support to win races and championships. All I do is drive 'em.

Over the years, I've driven for Childress. I've been offered bigger deals, but I'm with Richard because I want to race, I want to win, I want to be with somebody who wants to win as badly as I want to.

On tying Richard Petty's seven championships:

I'm proud and honored to be in the same group with him. But he got us here and will always be "the King." Nothing will ever take that away from him.

On running for championships:

You've got to use every resource you have to win today, as competitive as it is. You intimidate another guy when you drive up beside him, and you can go in the corner a little deeper than he does.

It's harder and harder to intimidate, though, because of the quality race cars out there and because of the quality of people running them. You think you can intimidate Rusty Wallace? No way.

More on championships:

You're focused on winning the championship. If you don't, you're disappointed. You don't achieve your goal.

—✦—

Still more on championships:

All of them have been hard. Winning your first championship is hard. Winning the one after that is hard. Ask anybody—Jarrett, Elliott, Wallace—you don't go out and just do it again. Terry Labonte and Rusty Wallace have never won the Daytona 500. Have you asked them about that? Winning (the eighth championship) is the next one. It's our next goal. That's our next focus.[13]

—✦—

On winning:

I don't weigh if I want to win this race or put this race against that race or this championship against that championship. I've really enjoyed them all. Again, I'm so damn fortunate to grow up in a family that raced. To get into it and accomplish what I have in my life, it's pretty awesome. I'm excited about what I do. I'm not content with not winning. If somebody tells you I'm riding my years out, they're not paying attention.[14]

—✦—

On winning championships and the business side of racing:

It (winning an eighth championship) would mean a lot. It's something no one else has done. It's our opportunity right now. We have that opportunity and we really want to focus in on it, not just getting this championship but racing for another one or two. We feel that good about things, Childress and I and the team.

It's really a tough business. A tough business to stay competitive. A tough business in negotiations with sponsors and souvenirs and deals with car owners. The pressure you have on you to make the budget and make things work, to give the teams what they need. Me being a car owner, I've seen that more and more.

It's not easy for a Richard Childress or a Rick Hendrick or a Roush or an Earnhardt to make things happen like they need to happen with the competitiveness of it. People are changing all the time, and prices of things are going up all the time. NASCAR and the tracks really need to focus and make sure the car owners are taken care of to be able to perform.[15]

After winning the 2000 spring race at Atlanta, in which he edged Bobby Labonte by inches, Earnhardt was asked about being focused late in his career:

I never had any problem being determined. I work hard trying to stay focused on the job at hand. Richard (Childress) and everybody in the garage will tell you there's a lot more going on than there was in the eighties. There's a lot of things happening in that garage area now that used to not happen that a driver has to contend with. Life itself. I have a lot of things going on outside this race team, and Richard does, too. How do you focus on all of it and keep it going in the right direction? You've just got to have good people, and you've got to also keep your eye on what got you there. That black 3 car got me there. That's the ball as far as I'm concerned, and I'm going to keep my eye on it.[16]

On edging Labonte at Atlanta in his next-to-last victory:

I held him off. It sort of seemed he was waiting, biding his time. Sure enough, he made his run there on the last lap and got close to beating us. It definitely wasn't a boring race.

I felt like I did beat him. When we were getting close to the line, I looked over and his car wasn't really side by side with me as far as looking into the driver's door, the right door, so I felt pretty good about what our chances were that we beat him out by a nose.

I was racing for all I could get and for all it would do. I was just driving the car as hard as I could go and giving it everything I had. It was just that time of day. It wasn't time to take it easy.[17]

Explaining his last victory, in the fall of 2000 at Talladega, when he was eighteenth with five laps to go:

I was very lucky. I kept working the outside, and it didn't work. It got three-wide, and it didn't work, so I started working the middle. I knew I had to pass those guys on the inside. I kept working the middle and kept working the middle, and finally it started moving. And then Kenny Wallace got behind us, and when he got behind us we started to the front. We finally got it to the front, and Kenny hung on. He was going to try to make a move down the back straightaway, but I kept moving and he really couldn't make a run on me. It worked out, and he stuck with me through (turns) three and four and back to the line.[18]

After winning the Coca-Cola 600, Earnhardt talked about his childhood dreams:

I have always wanted to win the 600. I used to come over here to the Charlotte track when I was a boy and watched the races from the infield, while standing on my dad's truck. Then I would go home and stay awake at night, dream(ing) about winning the race.[19]

In 2000, on losing his abilities:

Your reflexes and health or whatever is going to tell on you. I don't see it happening in the next three years.

More on his health, in 2000:

I may have been hurt for the last two years and working with pain and stuff and didn't realize it until it got worse and worse. I had to have something to do about it. That's all in the past. It's over. We're healthy. The team is healthy. Everything is there.

On aggressive racing:

Ain't no place for sissies here.

I've heard people say that we're going too fast. Maybe we do, maybe we don't. (But) do you want to race, or don't you?[20]

I want to give more than 100 percent every race, and if that's aggressive, then I reckon I am.[21]

It's not a sport for the faint of heart.

In 2000 Adam Petty and Kenny Irwin both died in crashes during practice at New Hampshire International Speedway

*in Loudon, New Hampshire. Earnhardt later talked about
risks in racing:*

Mistakes get people hurt and get people killed, and big mistakes happened up there (in New Hampshire). There's an element of danger in any form of motorsports. I take that risk. This is Winston Cup racing, an elite sport. It's not Late Model Stock racing.

---

*He talked about intimidating Bill Elliott after a 125-mile
qualifying race in 1987 at Daytona:*

I guess I scared the hell out of Bill in that qualifying race, and I don't think he will forget it, either. I didn't hit him. I just got up there and got the air off his spoiler and his car got loose.

But that is how you have to race him on the superspeedways. Bill would be tickled to death to jump out on everyone and just ride. We can't let him do that. You've got to move him. Scare him. You know, mess with his head.[22]

On getting in "the zone":

It's pretty hard to get that combination, but when it's there, it's there, and the confidence level's high and nobody (on the team) makes mistakes.

---

*Jeff Gordon turned twenty-three the year he won the inaugural
Brickyard 400 in 1994. The next year, Earnhardt won the
race, which has become the second-biggest race on the circuit,
following the Daytona 500. While doing a late-night TV
show, Earnhardt took a jibe at Gordon's youth:*

I'm the first man to win the Brickyard 400.

Earnhardt, who had nicknamed Gordon "Wonder Boy,"
also kidded Gordon about drinking milk at the Cup banquet
instead of champagne. At the banquet, Gordon raised his
glass of milk and toasted Dale, who responded with champagne.
Earnhardt later decided to change his nickname for Gordon
to "Wonder Man":

Jeff turns twenty-nine today. He's finally become a man.[23]

On being injured at Talladega one week, then coming back to
race at Indy the next race:

I don't want to take a chance and do something to injure
myself or endanger somebody else's life. There's a lot of
guys out there with me that I've got to think about.[24]

On passing Cale Yarborough in 1996 to set the Atlanta
victory record:

I like Atlanta Motor Speedway. I hope Cale is not mad at me
for breaking his record.[25]

On his eighth victory at Atlanta:

That's a proud mark. I broke the record on the same track
that the old guys ran. It means a lot.[26]

On car ownership and his son winning a race:

You're so proud of your kid. That's a given. You're proud of your kid. You see that (win) happen, and you're proud of your kid, but when you win a race as a driver, that's pretty damn exciting. That's what I'm driven to do. That's what I get up in the morning to go do—race. Yeah, I'm proud of him (Dale Jr.) winning. I'm excited about it. I'm excited about it for our (No. 8) team. I'll probably get more excited as I become a full-time owner.

In 2000, on his family:

Look at all my kids. I'm pretty proud of all of them. All of them did the right thing in life. Kerry raised his two kids and got married again and is doing well. Dale Jr. is doing well with keeping his head on straight and going forward. Kelley is getting ready to give me a granddaughter in another month. She's got a great job. She's making more money than I would pay her. Then Taylor Nicole is growing into running the show back home.

I didn't make Dale Jr. go be a racer. The kid wanted to be a racer. I'd just as soon him be a doctor, a preacher, or whatever. I'm not sure I'd want him to be a lawyer. Again, that's another subject.

I'm as happy as I can be. I'm like Dale Jr. This is fun, you know. It's fun to get in the race car and go race now.

After Dale Jr. tore up his car at Daytona in his first of two
Busch Grand National championship seasons:

I guess I picked the wrong time to go be a car owner. He's tearing up my equipment. But seriously, I made a lot of mistakes early on in my career, and I'm sure he's going to make a few, too. It's all part of the process. But I also see a lot of success for him down the road. Maybe in a couple of years after he gets seasoned in the Busch Series . . . well, we'll see what happens.

On his third wife, Teresa:

From the first time we met, Teresa and I have been friends. But it was several years after I met her that we began dating and then got married. That was the best business decision I have ever made, too. She has been good for me in business, and was good for me as a friend.

She was there when I didn't have anything, and she has stuck in there with me. She was there through the bad times until we finally got something. She came right in and was mother to my kids from the previous marriage, and she has got a good business head on her shoulders and makes smart business decisions.[27]

More on Teresa and family in general:

I'm proud of what we have accomplished, Teresa and myself and all the folks that supported us and worked with us. I'm proud of my family and the way they have grown up. They may not be the brightest kids, but they are good kids. They have done well.

Teresa helped me. I have the common street sense, and she has the book smarts. We are fortunate. She has a great family and mom and dad. Her dad is the type of guy who can take chicken shit and turn it into chicken salad. He is good at making ends meet and making things happen. He takes things and turns them around.

My dad was like that. He was an innovator. He'd take a little of nothing and make a good race car out of it and win races. We both came from a hard-luck background where we take what we have and make the best of it.

People always talk about us not having a lot. Shoot, I thought we were rich. I never thought we didn't have a lot. I thought we were always rich. I never wanted for anything. Teresa and myself grew up that way, and I think we've been fortunate, very fortunate.[28]

On his last crew chief, Kevin Hamlin:

Kevin Hamlin is more my type and style of crew chief. He's constantly thinking. He never quits on making it better. He's not the kind of guy who blows it off and kicks and screams. He's the kind of guy who sits down in here, listens to what I say, talks about what we're doing, and tries to make improvements.

He's so much like Kirk (Shelmerdine). When I say something, he's already thinking it, and that's the way Kirk was. We're thinking a lot to the same note. It's been that way. I'm so happy Richard Childress made that change (switching Larry McReynolds to Mike Skinner's team and giving Earnhardt Hamlin). I haven't regretted it one bit. I love Larry McReynolds to death as a person. We won the Daytona 500 together, but day in and day out, I work well with Kevin.[29]

Darrell Waltrip started out as Earnhardt's nemesis. Late in his career, he drove Earnhardt's No. 1 as a replacement for injured Steve Park. Finally, Waltrip retired after the 2000 season, and Earnhardt commented:

Darrell and I have had some great races and some excitement between us through the years. To see him retire, I'm proud to see him race through his career and enjoy it and then retire. He's going to TV, and he's got a lot of things to be excited about. It is going to be sad to see him retire and not be around. As you go through your career and racing changes for you, it becomes time at some point to retire. Darrell was quite a statesman. He was a good leader and champion when he was champion. I think he's been good for the sport.[30]

On the possibility of his own retirement:

I'll probably know when it's time to retire when I'm racing for thirty-first instead of first in points. The last twelve years, I've been in the top ten in points. When you're racing in the top ten in points, I don't think that's getting less competitive. I'm still winning a race or two and still racing competitively. Why would you retire? Why would you even think about retiring? Why would people think you'd be ready to retire? Why would people think you're over the hill when you can still race these guys and race up front? We've had bad races like last week at Homestead. We finished twentieth. That was a bad day, but still we finished twentieth. We didn't finish fortieth.[31]

More on being competitive:

If I was thirtieth in points and not making races and not being competitive in races, I could understand them saying I'm over the hill or I'm ready to quit or whatever.

On racing:

It's my job to drive that black No. 3.

On winning:

Second place is just the first-place loser.

On night racing:

The atmosphere seems to change once the sun goes down, and the race fans get to watch a good show.

On people saying that he could "see" the air roiling around him in the draft:

As far as seeing air, I know it's there. I've just got to play hunches right and hope it's there when I need it.

On Jeremy Mayfield bumping his way past Dale in 2000 at Pocono:

You race with guys and you feel like you know how far to go with them or how far they'll go with you—just like Mayfield. I felt like we'd go in the corner and he would try to race under me and we'd race off that corner. Instead, he got into the back end of the car and pushed me out. It was just a little experience. I gained a little experience, and I'll know how to race him next time.[32]

On competition:

To come in and win three races already this year and maybe set a record by winning four is pretty unique. But guys like

Mark Martin, Rusty Wallace and these guys are not wanting that to happen.

On being a natural racer:

It's just a natural thing for me to race. I'm so at ease driving a race car in competition. It's really ridiculous to think

INTERNATIONAL MOTORSPORTS HALL OF FAME

Earnhardt finally broke down and showed the extent of his love for his younger son, Dale Jr.

about. I'm more tense sitting here talking to press guys and
to go out with the fans than I am driving a race car.

When I'm in that car, I'm a pretty relaxed character. My
heart rate is probably about eighty right now talking to you
guys. When I'm in that car, it's probably about sixty. That's
what I enjoy doing. It seems like I was put here to do that.[33]

On racing and hunting:

Two of my favorite things are my steering wheel and my
Remington rifle.

More on racing and hunting:

When he was young, I told Dale Jr. that hunting and racing
are a lot alike. Holding that steering wheel and holding that
rifle both mean you better be responsible.

On pressure:

I think I've been a good driver the whole time. I enjoy the
pressure. I thrive on it.[34]

On his reputation:

Being mean and intimidating? I've never tried to be. I've
never meant to be.

The Angel in Black

"He just did it because he wanted to do it."

— Eli Gold

The stories have gotten out that Dale Earnhardt wasn't a monster, just a free-spirited guy with a lot of talent, intensity, and compassion.

Earnhardt helped Motor Racing Outreach, the Special Olympics, the Cody Unser Foundation, various racetracks and, as we learn below, the Kannapolis Education Foundation. He was always quick to help out with charities and other causes. And he loved children.

One race at Charlotte Motor Speedway in the nineties, someone pushed a boy in a wheelchair over to Earnhardt, and Dale was going to take the boy into the Cup garage and the 3 hauler. I prepared to go with them because I could see a good story. Earnhardt got up close to me and said, "Come on, man, don't tell nobody. Please. Please." I was disappointed, but I nodded. Then he wheeled the happy boy, wearing his Earnhardt cap and T-shirt, toward his hauler.

I didn't tell nobody, Dale. Until now.

Here, we learn that the Intimidator was a teddy bear disguised as a grizzly.

Former racer **Dave Marcis**, *on Earnhardt's good side in business:*

I went to him one day at Darlington—this was after Dale had the Chevy dealership. I told him that I needed some money for the next race, at North Wilkesboro. He said, "What do you gotta have?" I told him, "I need $2,500." The next race was at North Wilkesboro. He called on Monday and said, "I'm sending you a copy of how we want the decals to look at Wilkesboro." So he overnighted the decals to me, and we qualified side by side for that race. He sent me a check for $5,000, double what I asked for. That's what kinda guy he was.

Former Cup racer **Jerry Nadeau:**

I thought he was a great guy. I got personable with him my rookie year at Sears Point when I qualified (on the) outside pole. I got a picture with me, Jimmy Spencer, and Earnhardt.

Jerry Punch, *a longtime racing announcer for ESPN and a former emergency-room doctor, was friends with Earnhardt. Here, he tells a story that shows Earnhardt's compassion, and, yes, his vanity. This happened just before the 2000 season:*

In December, right after he'd had his neck surgery, his fusion, he had to wear a neck collar. Earnhardt wearing a neck collar is not the vision of the Intimidator that everyone has, so he didn't want anyone to see him with that collar on. So he stayed pretty much close to the farm, and I don't think many of his employees at DEI saw him with that collar. He just didn't want people to know.

I was contacted by a group in a small town in the mountains of North Carolina about a little boy who was critically ill with a debilitating disease. The father was a farmer, and the little boy is getting weaker and weaker. The father goes to the little boy and says, "Whatever I can do for you, I will do." The little boy says, "Daddy, all I want is to meet Dale Earnhardt." And the little boy's laying there, and the father breaks down. He said he'd sell everything he's got, his farm, his tractors, his livestock, if he could make it happen, but that's something he can't buy.

The people in the little community found out about this and they said, "If we can somehow make it happen, but millions of people want to physically meet Earnhardt, and he just can't meet everybody." It so happened that some nurses and doctors volunteered, and an ambulance company volunteered to take him to Mooresville to meet Earnhardt.

I made a few phone calls; I called Don Hawk, talked to Earnhardt. He wasn't making personal appearances, traveling nowhere. No one outside the family was seeing him. He said, "I can't travel because of my surgery, but if they'll get him here, I'll do whatever I can." So we set it up, and I think it took them four hours to make a trip that should have lasted an hour and a half in an ambulance. They had to stop and reposition the young man, and I think they had to suction him out.

So they were late getting to Earnhardt, and he basically sat in the front seat of a pickup truck in the parking lot of

DEI with his collar on, waiting for the ambulance to pull in. They were a couple of hours late. He met the little boy, they went in a back entrance, took him inside, the little boy, his medical attendants, and his parents. They took a picture of Dale Earnhardt and the little boy, and the little boy had a collar on, too, and other support devices for his head.

Earnhardt knelt down and said, "This is the only picture of me with this collar on, and it'll be taken with you." Dale hugged him, gave him a kiss, talked to his parents. This was like three days before Christmas. It was special for the little boy, but for those parents, that was the best Christmas present anyone could have given them. They got to see the little boy smile, probably for one of the final times.

That was one of those things Dale Earnhardt didn't want publicity for, didn't want anyone to know about. It was one of many, many examples of random acts of kindness that he did for people that no one ever knew. They saw the crusty, cantankerous Intimidator image at the racetrack, but people rarely saw that side of Dale Earnhardt, the soft and tender side. And I don't think anyone else knows that story. (They do now.)

Larry McReynolds, Earnhardt's crew chief in 1997 and '98, talks about typical Dale:

Michael Waltrip and Buffy (Michael's wife), they'd go to the Bahamas a lot on Dale's boat; they were best friends. Michael hit the nail on the head. He said, "When you hang out with Dale, you need to take your brain out of your head and lay it down, because you're not going to use it anymore. He's going to think for you."

I'd go over there to his motor home. The track was closed. Him and Teresa would be over there, and I'd have dinner with them. And, mentally, I'd be absolutely drained when I finished dinner. It'd be, "Here, eat some of this, eat some more of that, put some more of that on his plate." It would be nonstop. And I'd get back to my motor coach after having dinner with him and just sit in the quiet, trying to get myself mentally composed again.

The thing I'll always treasure is saying that I did work with him two years. I was very disappointed that we didn't have the success that anyone thought we'd have together. But every day I can walk by the trophy in my office, I can grin because we were able to get him into Victory Lane in the (Daytona) 500. Even though Richard (Childress) swapped us (the teams) around and put me with (driver Mike) Skinner in '99 and 2000, we were still great friends. The thing about Dale, once he was your friend, he was your friend. You weren't his friend or he wasn't your friend because you were working with him. You were his friend, and you stayed his friend.

Max Helton remembers Earnhardt as a generous, giving man:

There's a lot stories that could be told. He was just a generous person, and he helped other people out a lot. When Phil Parsons lost his ride in the No. 4 Kodak car back in the early nineties, the next day when Phil went out on his porch, he found a bouquet of balloons from Dale Earnhardt to let him know that he was thinking about him. That was the type of thing that he'd often do.

I remember one Christmas day in the mid-nineties—I don't remember what year—a friend of mine and I went over to Dale's to install a computer program for his little daughter, Taylor. My friend is a computer expert, and Dale called and wanted him to do it. So I went up with him.

While my friend, Teresa, and Taylor were putting together the computer program, Dale took me on a tour of his farm, and it was quite an experience, driving back through the woods, around his lake, and I had a tour of his house. *Here,* I thought to myself, *is this man on Christmas Day, and he's reaching out to me and helping me understand him more.* He was taking me into his life for the day. Wow, it's really something for a man of his stature to open up, to share, to talk, to invite me into his home, particularly on a holiday such as Christmas Day.

But Dale Earnhardt was that type of person, very kind and generous, very open, even though he was a very tough competitor on the racetrack. But, away from the track, he was just like a different person. He was unbelievable in his generosity.

Helton, the founder of Motor Racing Outreach, on whether Earnhardt was a religious man:

He seemed to be, although he did not talk about that a lot. He was private in that aspect, but if you were around him enough, you could certainly see that he was. I spent some time with him back in December, about an hour and a half, just me and him. We talked about that, and he was very much a man of faith.

He was a very generous man as well, a very kind-hearted man, contrary to his image.

Dr. Joe Mattioli, chairman of the board and CEO of Pocono Raceway, says his wife, Rose, was intimidated until Earnhardt showed his good side:

The one story that sticks out in my mind, and we always

laugh about it: Over the years we've been here a long time, and Earnhardt came up here and raced a lot. We knew him, and we would see him from time to time at different affairs. And one day, he braced my wife—in other words, he stood in front of her and asked her a question, put her on the spot. He talked to her and looked her in the eye, he said, "How come you see other drivers and you hug and kiss them, but you don't give *me* a hug and a kiss?" My wife looked up at him—he was a big guy and she's small—and she says, "You scare me." He started laughing, and said, "Why?" "I don't know; you just scare me." He grabs ahold of her and gives her a big hug and a kiss, and he says, "From now on, I'm not going to scare you; I'm just going to kiss you." He did.

From then on, whenever they met, he'd come over and give her a big hug and a kiss. My wife was really intimidated by him. All of the other drivers, from Richard Petty, Cale Yarborough, (David) Pearson, Darrell Waltrip, she new them, and she'd give them a hug or a kiss or something. But Earnhardt she stayed away from (until Earnhardt braced her).

This may not be an Angel in Black *story, but it goes well with the anecdote above.* **Mattioli** *says Earnhardt had intimidated him, too, and there were two other intimidators:*

We've known A. J. Foyt—he's been coming here since 1971, and I would never go near his garage. I'd go *by* his garage, and if our eyes met and he'd call out, I'd go over. Otherwise, I'd keep on going, because he was a real pistol. Paul Newman was the same way when he came up here. When they're racing, they don't want any talk, they don't want any bullshit. My wife (Rose) and I always respected that with those two people. And Earnhardt was the other.

Those three guys stick out. When they're focused, they're focused; there's nothing else they can even look at. You could drop an atom bomb next to him, and he wouldn't even know it went off.

Mattioli *recalls how Earnhardt helped maneuver him into buying a painting for charity, and this involves Bruton Smith, the owner of what was then called Charlotte Motor Speedway, and Humpy Wheeler, president of the Charlotte track:*

Oh, this was a long time ago. This was when Bruton Smith and Humpy Wheeler were starting that children's charity team (Speedway Children's Charities), affairs to raise and they invited my wife and I to Charlotte to a banquet or ball for an auction to raise money. Bruton had us sit at his table with Humpy and Dale Earnhardt and his wife. We were sitting at this table, and of course I was set up. We had this nice dinner, and we were shooting the bull. They were going to auction off an original Sam Bass oil painting of Dale Earnhardt. Here, I'm sitting right next to him, right? The bidding starts, and I'm sitting there like a horse's ass—and I thought, "I can't not bid. I'd better bid."

To make a long story short, it cost me $6,000, and this was in something like 1985 or '88, and $6,000 was quite a bit of money then. I was hooked for it, and I got the painting, and we still have it here. I said to Humpy and Bruton, "You really sucked me in on that deal, didn't you?" But that was a sort of cute little thing, and every time, of course, Earnhardt would come up to me and say, "You still got that picture?" Of course we still have it. It was an original, and I think they made copies from it.

---

*Longtime racer **Morgan Shepherd** didn't see Mr. Nice Guy. Morgan was asked if he saw Earnhardt's good side, and that reminded Shepherd of Earnhardt's aversion to signing autographs:*

I didn't ever really see the good side of Earnhardt. In this business, some people feel they get above race fans and other fans, whether they're in Hollywood or whatever, and feel like they don't have to sign autographs or do this or that. That's always bothered me quite a bit, because it's the race fan who's paying the bills. Of course, you can't do every one; that's the reason Richard Petty was so popular, because he'd take the time to sign autographs, even when he was in a hurry. Even when he had to go somewhere, he'd try to do what he could. I didn't ever see that kind of respect out of Earnhardt; I've seen him tell people off. I don't like that part of anybody in the entertainment business, when they think they're above others, where they don't owe anything back.

***Tom Dayvault** grew up in Kannapolis, North Carolina, but he and Dale went to different elementary schools, and he didn't get to know Earnhardt until they were adults. "If you weren't looking at Ralph Earnhardt's crankcase, you didn't know Dale," he says. Dayvault later became president of the Cabarrus Regional Chamber of Commerce, located on Dale Earnhardt Boulevard:*

On the fifth of October in 1993, Kannapolis had Dale Earnhardt Appreciation Day. I was president of the Kannapolis Chamber of Commerce at that time, and we headed up that event. In meeting with Dale to set up the efforts there, he was excited about it and a little bit anxious. Excited in that, right off the bat, he asked, "Can the proceeds go to help education in Kannapolis city schools?" and we said, "Absolutely." Immediately, the results of that day were earmarked for education at his request. So the Kannapolis Education Foundation was the beneficiary of the Dale Earnhardt Day. There was absolutely no hesitation. It was the first thing out of his mouth.

That was at the early stages of Brooks & Dunn. We were talking to Dale out at the Kannapolis Country Club where every year Dale had an appreciation day for kids. All the kids came out, and he signed autographs, and he talked about whatever was on his mind. He never missed one.

On this day Brooks & Dunn were going to be a part of Dale Earnhardt Appreciation Day. Not being a huge country music fan, I thought Dale was talking about his law firm. When I inquired about bringing attorneys into the event, he quickly called the two of them in. On the spot, they said, "Yes, we'd love to sing the national anthem for your day." Quickly, I went from a little bit of anxiety on my part to "What a treat!" I went right out and bought the first of many Brooks & Dunn albums. I have since become a country music fan. But then, I'd never heard of that law firm before.

The event itself turned out to be a wonderful day, and now we look at the video and realize that there was some discussion about maybe we should wait until he retires to have the day. But it was a wonderful, happy day to celebrate how proud we are of him. We had tens of thousands that came from all over. So I was thankful we did that. And when I go back and look at it, I realize what a tribute it was for him.

That day, a couple of things really stand out. They named Dale Earnhardt Boulevard that day. The state of North Carolina did that, and, of course, our new Chamber of Commerce is located on Dale Earnhardt Boulevard. Naming the boulevard happened long before we merged the Kannapolis and Cabarrus County chapters, which happened in '98. At that time, it was a little country road; there was no interchange to I-85.

In his comments, Dale said he went rabbit hunting and running cars on that road growing up. The mayor of Kannapolis at that time said that, "Well, today it may look like Watkins Glen, but before it's through, it'll look like Daytona." Right now, they're finishing up the five lanes to be the connector to downtown Kannapolis.

That night we had a black-tie affair, and the emcee of that event was Neil Bonnett. One of the guests that night was a young kid named Jeff Gordon, (whom) nobody knew. It was a magic night, a special night. I'm just so thankful we were able to honor him and his family and let him know he was our favorite son. We were able give the education foundation $30,000 off of that day because of him.

For us in Kannapolis, we were so proud of him. He never tried to be anything but what he was. He never forgot to say thank-you or to remember the people who helped him along the way before he was Dale Earnhardt Inc. And we always knew of the giving spirit that was there.

⁂

Bobby Allison and Earnhardt were strong rivals on the track, but Allison remembers Dale's wanting to be liked by the other drivers:

He always came on as a 100 percent, dedicated competitor, and everybody around him knew that. I think just about everybody at the racetrack, every competitor—whether it was a driver competitor or team competitor—liked him. He just had that personality that was so positive and so enjoyable that people wanted to be his friend, regardless.

I really don't think I met anyone else like him. His friendly personality while being competitive in racing was very similar to Red Farmer. Red Farmer wanted everybody to be his friend, and Red wanted to beat everybody every time he got in a car. I'd seen that, I'd seen a successful competitor have that attitude. I'd seen Red Farmer win hundreds of feature events on the short-track stuff. I just really admired that about him (Earnhardt).

Chris Browning, now president of Darlington Raceway, was the executive vice president and general manager of North Carolina Speedway in Rockingham when Earnhardt died. Before that, he did publicity at Michigan Speedway and at Nazareth Speedway in Pennsylvania, two Roger Penske tracks:

We had an IROC event at Nazareth, and we had a media day planned. It was going to be the first IROC race at Nazareth. In the process of planning for the media day, we found out about a young man who was seriously ill. He was a huge Dale Earnhardt fan, and Dale just happened to be our driver for the media day. We arranged for him to come over, and he met Dale, and Dale was just absolutely fantastic with this young man. He just took all the time in the world. He was very kind with him, answered all his questions, and signed his jacket and hat.

We were going to give some rides for media members in one of the cars, and we put this guy in the car and buckled him in, and I remember Dale looking at him and grinning really big. He said to the little boy, "Look, I'm not going to go real fast, but if I go too fast for you, you just reach over and hit me on the leg right here." He just nodded at him. I think the young man was just in awe, speechless, to be honest with you.

They went around the track two or three laps and came back in, and I remember you could not get the smile off the boy's face. Dale was just raving about how he didn't have to tap his leg at all. He went around the track and didn't tell him to slow down at all. And that made that young man's day.

Dave Marcis was a longtime Cup racer—he was second to Richard Petty in career starts until Ricky Rudd passed him —and he was Earnhardt's hunting and fishing buddy. Did you see the Mr. Nice Guy, Dave?

Oh, Christ, yeah. He was such a different person hunting and fishing than he was at the racetrack. People don't realize. I think some of the drivers get a bad rap for being maybe grouchy or not good with the public. But when you're at the racetrack, you have a job to do. You're concentrating on springs and shocks. Dale was a hands-on guy, and that makes matters worse.

Some of the guys today don't have to set up the cars themselves or worry about shocks and springs; they've got engineers to do that. But in my day, when I was at the racetrack, my mind never stopped. Because I built my own shocks and gears and changed my own springs, and I done so much stuff that I was always thinking, concentrating on that. If someone came up to me at the track and wanted to talk, you really weren't pushing them aside, but you really didn't have time to talk. Practice sessions were short, and you had to get a lot done right away. I considered myself a friendly guy, but at the racetrack your brain is working. You're constantly thinking, so it's hard to stand around and talk.

---

*Motor Racing Outreach's **Max Helton** said that Earnhardt shocked him once:*

All of the drivers had some relationship with MRO. Taylor (Earnhardt's daughter) was very involved, and Dale was very supportive, both vocally and financially. I was really surprised when he was interviewed on one of the talk shows a year or so ago—he made the statement that his hero was Max Helton. I was shocked when he said that. A year later someone asked him about that in my presence, and he said, "Yes, the men I admire most are preachers. I admire them because of what they have to go through, dealing with life, tough situations, and counseling people."

Russell Branham, the former publicist for Darlington Raceway, says Earnhardt always came through when they needed publicity or help:

There was more to him than being behind the wheel, and I'll say this: Anything we did from a charity standpoint, he helped. I have seen him on so many occasions, so *many* occasions, talk to a handicapped child. And it would just totally bring that person such joy, you would not believe it. He'd take him up in the truck, give him signed postcards, give him a signed car. He would always do that, always accommodate. There used to be some photos at the track of him doing that.

For different charitable events that the track would host, he'd send sheet metal or an autographed car, and he sometimes came to the event itself. I can remember one event we had, we had a large group of people there, and he got up on stage.

We had a one-twenty-fourth-scale car of his that we were going to sell. Benny Parsons was the master of ceremonies, and Dale said, "Let me get up on stage." He said, "Whoever buys it, I'll autograph it personally to them." This is a $15 car, and it sold for nearly $1,000, simply because of his presence and the fact he was going to personally autograph it.

But he had a soft side, particularly with handicapped children.

Jim Hunter is now chief publicist for NASCAR, but he was president of Darlington Raceway in the 1990s. Years earlier, he covered racing for newspapers, and he got to see Earnhardt grow up from a mill-town boy to a legendary driver:

I knew Earnhardt at an early age. But when someone gets as busy as he was—I certainly considered him a friend. But a lot of people considered Dale their friend. I don't think I was a confidante or anything. He and I had a mutual friend, Joe Whitlock. Joe was a writer, worked in Columbia (South Carolina), and he later worked for Earnhardt. Let's put it this way, I knew his dad and covered his dad's racing career, so I met Earnhardt when he was pretty young. I say Earnhardt was a friend, but he was always as irascible as he could be. I never saw that, and I think that was more his love for Darlington than his friendship for Jim Hunter.

You know, I think he just loved that racetrack, and very obviously he was very successful at it. But he'd do things for us, helping us sell tickets, so that other people at times were asking, "How'd you get Earnhardt to do that?" Then he liked Russell; Russell was his friend. And Earnhardt had a tremendous amount of respect for David Pearson, who is another driver who loved Darlington.

Chris Powell, now the boss of Las Vegas Motor Speedway, was a publicist for Winston when he took a charity photo to

Earnhardt for his autograph. Dale loved charities, but he also was a practical businessman:

We made a poster; I don't know if you've seen it. The top half is Earnhardt, sunglasses, arms folded, straight-on shot. Great shot, and the bottom half of the poster has the car going across it. But the picture of him . . . it was just a great picture. So I had one done up, about four feet tall by three feet across, and I was going to get him to autograph it. We were going to auction it off at Speedway Children's Charities auction that night.

I just loved this picture so much, and I thought he's going to say, "I want a copy of that." So I took it by his trailer. "Dale, I got something you need to sign." He turned around, looked at it, and he never batted an eye. He said, "Who's it going to?" I told him we'd auction it for charity. He said, "Just make sure there's only one of them." He didn't want us out there selling this picture of him. I was kinda deflated after that. I thought he was going to love this picture; it was a great shot.

Ed Clark, president and general manager at Atlanta Motor Speedway, was working at Charlotte Motor Speedway several years ago when one of those heartwarming Earnhardt stories unfolded:

We've all heard so many things since he's passed away about the things he's done for other people, but he never wanted you to know it. When I worked in Charlotte about twelve years ago, we were contacted by someone who had a child who was pretty sick. This little boy was about eight or nine years old, and one of his dreams was to meet Dale Earnhardt. So I talked to Dale, and I think it was on a Friday when the Winston Cup cars weren't practicing. Dale said,

"Bring him down, and I'll talk to him." His mother and I drove this little boy inside the track.

Dale saw us coming and walked over and put his arms around the boy's shoulders, and he said to us, "Y'all come back in a few minutes. We'll be okay. Y'all just leave us alone." We went outside the garage gate and stood there and watched. Dale sat the boy on the back of the truck, gave him a hat and postcards, put him in his car in the driver's seat, put his helmet on him, raised the hood to show him the engine, and he talked to the kid about ten or fifteen minutes.

You could tell the kid was beside himself with happiness, and the mother was crying. It was really very touching. Finally, we walked back up to the truck, and I thanked him and said, "You're my hero." And he said, "Don't you ever tell anybody about that."

He liked being the Intimidator; that was his, I guess, brand. But there were two sides to him: the Dale Earnhardt on the track and the Dale Earnhardt off the track.

Retired racer **Ernie Irvan**, *before Earnhardt's death:*

Dale will go out of his way to help people, and I know he's really helped me out. He's really a nice guy—he just doesn't want people to think that.[1]

Eddie Gossage, *then the publicist at Charlotte Motor Speedway, learned that Earnhardt had time for a friend in pain:*

You probably remember a little bit of this: It was the '94 media tour, and we chartered an airplane and took everybody down to Daytona for testing. We get down there, and everybody was really good; all of the drivers there testing were good about spending time with the media. But Earnhardt wouldn't talk to anybody. So I go over there and ask, "What's the deal here?" He kind of chewed on me, "We're here to work and test, and you bring all these reporters who get in our way. We've got things to do." I told him my two-cents' worth, and we went at it for a second. And I walked off on him, just walked off on him.

Later that night, my mother died. Dale apparently read about it in the paper. So I had to return to Tennessee for the services. On Monday morning, after being out of the office for several days, I thought, *I'll go early and try to catch up a bit.* The office is dark, but my office is open and my light is on. I rounded the corner, and there's Earnhardt sitting behind my desk.

I had a collection of helmets, and he'd been telling me for a long time that he wanted to give me a helmet. So he pulls a helmet out from under the desk and says, "I brought this to you. I'm sorry we had an argument, and I want to talk to you about your mother." We shut the door and spent forty-five minutes talking about my mother . . . and his dad. It just really was touching that this big-time superstar still had time to put his arm around a friend and empathize with him some.

So that's the Intimidator for you. He was a good guy; he was a good guy.

---

*Car owner **Larry McClure**, who has fielded No. 4 Cup Chevrolets in NASCAR's top series:*

My father died in a tragic accident two years ago of the same head injuries that Earnhardt died of. When he heard of my devastating loss, he consoled me by talking of his own pain for the loss of his dad. Earnhardt's advice was to carry on and make my dad proud, as if he were still present.

I use this advice every day in my life. It gives me a tremendous desire to succeed, and it helps ease the pain.[2]

⌇

Ed Clark got help from Earnhardt when he left Nashville Speedway to take a job with Charlotte Motor Speedway. He also saw Dale take a few lumps:

When I moved to Charlotte in '81, Dale and Richard Petty both talked to me at Daytona, while I was making a decision to change jobs. I was at Nashville, the general manager there. Humpy Wheeler had offered me a job, and I guess Richard and Dale had both heard about it. They both sat me down and told me, "You've got a great deal where you are, but Charlotte will advance your career in so many ways, so that's what you need to do." So after I took the job, I called Dale and told him about it. I didn't have anywhere to live. I drove a Ryder truck eight hours from Nashville to Charlotte, and Dale offered to let me stay at his house until I found someplace to live.

I'll never forget it. That was the weekend that Dale Inman had switched from working with the Pettys and had gone over to work for Dale. And when I got there, I rang the doorbell. I didn't have a radio in that truck, so I didn't know what had happened in the race. I went in the kitchen, and Earnhardt's sitting there with his shirt off, and he's got bruise marks on both shoulders. He'd been in a wreck with both Pettys, which is kind of ironic. I said, "What in the world happened to you?" and he said, "They got me."

Back in those days, I spent more time with him. I was the PR director at Bristol when he won his first race, so I got to know him a little bit from that. And he came in and did the winner's circle stuff for us that fall. I spent the day with him, and we just became friends. We never did spend a bunch of time together, and I guess everybody in the garage will tell you that they were Dale Earnhardt's friend. I wasn't one of his best friends, but when we did have time to get together, we always did enjoy that.

———※———

Charlie Powell, the longtime promoter at short tracks in South Carolina, used to have a special Race of Champions event featuring eight big-time drivers. Naturally, the most memorable driver was Earnhardt:

What stands out in my mind, he came to Summerville (Speedway) on three or four occasions in the eighties to run in our Race of Champions. It was Dale, Dale Jarrett, Michael Waltrip, Rusty Wallace; eight of them in all, but Dale Earnhardt was the highlighter. There was always a big line for autographs, and some of the other drivers were wanting to get on with the program, but there was still a line, and Earnhardt said he wasn't going nowhere until everybody got autographs. So he stayed there, and he signed until he was done, even after the race.

There was a child who was handicapped—I don't know if she had cancer—but the child was an invalid. After the race was over, Dale took a few minutes to hold the child, to have pictures taken with her, to talk to her. People were always saying he didn't take time, but he did take time.

———※———

Dick Thompson, who worked as a publicist for Martinsville Speedway for thirty-five years, on Earnhardt the man vs. his image:

The thing about Dale was that he was Intimidator, with a stare that could melt steel, but inside he was really a teddy bear. He would work with kids and fans, and he did so many nice things for people. But if you tried to write about it, he'd say, "Don't you do it." He didn't want you to mention the good things. I don't know if it was against his image, or if he didn't want to appear so nice.

Charlie Powell says Earnhardt would always find time for Powell and his sons:

I knew him over the years, even before he had won everything, and a lot of people criticized him and said he was not personable. It's just that he was a reserved-type guy. He was not an outgoing person. If he didn't know you, you might think he was sarcastic.

I didn't get to see him often, but he always took time for me. When my son Robert ran the Busch Series at Charlotte and Darlington, Dale took some time for him and helped him. At Richmond one time, Robert was driving Dale Jarrett's Busch car, and we were late to the racetrack for the rookie drivers' meeting. NASCAR was upset, and they said, "You've got to go see Earnhardt and talk to him before you can get on the track." So Robert goes over, and Earnhardt was still driving Busch then. He asked how Robert was doing, and Robert said, "They say I gotta talk to you before I can get on the track." And Dale said, "I don't need to talk to you; get in your damned race car."

When I saw Dale at Daytona or Charlotte, he always took a moment or two to speak to me. He'd ask, "How's Little Charlie?" That's what he called my son Charles. Of the thousands of people he knew, if he would see somebody every once a while, he'd remember you. For us, that was quite a happening.

Eli Gold, longtime announcer for Motor Racing Network and various television broadcasts, recalls another instance in which Earnhardt took the time to brighten someone's day:

About eight or nine years ago, I got a call from the Make-A-Wish Foundation for children who are suffering from terminal illnesses. There was a boy who all he wanted to do was to meet or talk to Dale Earnhardt. He didn't want to go to a race; he wasn't in the physical condition to do so.

I called Earnhardt and told him about this boy. I said, "I don't know the young man, but this was legit; this was for the Make-A-Wish Foundation. He'd like to meet you or speak to you. Could you make the time to call him?" I gave Dale the phone number. I learned subsequently that a few moments after we hung up, Dale called the boy in Alabama, and they spoke for over thirty minutes. Then Earnhardt called his people, and they put together a box of souvenirs—shirts, caps, collectible car, and such—and they Federal Expressed the package to the boy and the family in Alabama.

The father called me after Dale had called him, and he was ecstatic. Then he called again the next day and he had gotten the overnight package from Earnhardt with the goodies. I went up to Dale the next race weekend, and I thanked him profusely for calling. He said, "Aw, I was glad to do it. But do me a favor, don't say anything about it," meaning he didn't want me to say anything on air.

It was a nice thing to do. And he didn't do it for publicity; he just did it because he wanted to do it.

Gold remembers Earnhardt as a generous guy:

I didn't allow myself to be a big personal fan of any driver. You try to like them all, respect them all, but we're fans of the sport, not fans of the driver. My wife, Claudette, was a big Dale Earnhardt fan. On race weekends when I'm out of town, although I didn't like her to do it, she'd have a big Earnhardt flag flying outside our house. She just loved Dale, and Dale was cordial to her.

We were somewhere making an appearance umpteen years ago, and I was the master of ceremonies. Dale was involved, and he came in wearing a good-looking Goodwrench jacket. My wife commented on it about how beautiful the jacket was, and, "Is it going be for sale?" He didn't know. As the appearance concluded, we were walking out to go back to our respective hotels. Dale took that jacket off and threw it to my wife. He said, "Here, I'll find myself another one." Just gave her this jacket. He did it just because he was a nice guy.

Dick Thompson of Martinsville Speedway says Earnhardt always pushed education:

We had him at Martinsville High School one time, and he was talking to the kids about education. The kids were on the edge of their seats listening to him. He had the ability to relate to all kinds of people, especially kids. He told them that his wife did a lot of his business deals and that, if he had gotten an education, it would have helped him a lot.

In this story, Jerry Punch's daughter got a walking lesson from Earnhardt:

We were on his boat in Daytona Beach—my wife (Joni) and I and our daughter Jessica, who was a toddler then. She was just crawling, actually. I went topside to look at something on the back of the boat, and I came back down to the

With seven Winston Cup titles under his belt, or cummerbund, Earnhardt showed off plenty of tuxedos over the years at the annual Winston Cup banquet in New York.

main salon. And there's my wife, Joni, and there's Teresa sitting there, and he's got my daughter Jessica by the top of her coveralls. He's holding her by the two shoulder straps between his legs and getting her to put one foot down and the other foot down and the other foot down.

Here's this seven-time Winston Cup champion . . . and I said, "What are you doing?" He looked up at me with that big smile from ear to ear and said, "I'm teaching your daughter to walk." And we all started laughing. And I said, "You can teach her to walk; just don't teach her to drive." And we all had a big laugh.

That's one of my fonder memories, because that was a special side of him where he would do so much for people randomly. I've seen him offer to help families, have checks sent to families who have had misfortunes, get on airplanes and sign autographs.

Eddie Gossage, who later became president of Texas Motor Speedway, had some run-ins with Earnhardt, and Dale kept making up with him:

In '97 he comes to test at Texas for the first time. He gets here, and it's raining, so he sits in his truck. The next thing I know, all the reporters come running up to me, and they say, "Earnhardt said the track is too narrow, and the transitions off the corners are not right; it's just a terrible racetrack." So, knowing Dale as well as I do, I think, *He's just creating headlines, so I'll just play along.* I tell them, "I guess that, if that's the way he feels, Dale can load that car back on the trailer and take it back to North Carolina. We'll still race without him." So, of course, they go running back over to his truck.

The next morning there are big banner headlines in the paper. So Dale comes stomping into my office, plops down on a chair, and he's got the newspaper. He holds it up in front of his face and says, "Did you say, 'If he doesn't like it, he can load that car back up and go back to North Carolina'?" He kinda folded the paper so all I can see are his eyes, and I said, "Yeah, I sure did." He pulls the paper down, and he's grinning ear-to-ear, and he says, "Great line! I hoped you knew what I was doing."

And I did. We were doing the pro wrestling thing, making headlines. He said, "I'm sorry if I've said things about the track. I haven't been around it enough to know what it's like." And he felt bad about it.

At ten-thirty or eleven o'clock, he comes in carrying a fender from his car. He says, "I brought this for you. I'm sorry I said anything bad, and I want you to have this." I say, "Well, Dale, I can give it to charity and they can auction it off. I don't need a fender from your car." So he says, "Okay," and goes out the door. About one-thirty, he comes bopping in the door and says, "Here, I brought you this," and he throws me a uniform. He says, "I brought you this. It's the uniform I wore when I made my first laps around your racetrack. I want you to have it." I say, "Dale, I appreciate that. You don't need to do that. That's very kind of you." He goes out the door.

About five o'clock, he comes running back in the door with a brown grocery bag. He throws it on my desk and says, "Here, I don't like them. They pinch. There's only two of these in the world. I'm going back home." He goes out the door. I open the bag, and inside was a pair of the Nike racing shoes. At the time, he was the only one they made them for, and they only made him two pair. Later, he told me they were the ones he wore when he flipped down the backstretch at Daytona, and he didn't wear them again because he felt they were bad luck.

So it dawned on me when he died that I've got a helmet, uniform, and shoes of his. He just didn't want me mad at him. He didn't want what he said to hurt my feelings, so he tried to make it up to me. He didn't have to make it up to me, but he tried. I was never mad at him. I was never mad about anything. He was very concerned what people thought about him. If you ever wanted something from Dale, if you'd be mad at him first, he'd come up to you and want to know what he could do for you. Then you could write your own ticket.

He never wanted you mad at him, and I was never mad at him. I think Dale Earnhardt was the kind of guy that every guy ought to be like. He was just "what you see is what you get." He was just a solid guy. He was one of the great guys. I'm not talking about race-car drivers; I'm just talking about one of the great people.

8

SPEED SHIFTS

"Compared to Earnhardt, we're babies."
— JEFF BURTON

J eff and Ward Burton were rookies in 1994. At the last race of the season, at Atlanta, I asked them if they felt like veterans after racing a full season. **Jeff Burton** answered:

"It's crazy to run one year in Winston Cup and pull your (yellow) stripe off your car and think you know everything. Compared to Earnhardt, we're babies. We may think we know everything, but we don't."

———

*Two-time Busch Series champion **Randy LaJoie**, on the loss of Earnhardt:*

We lost a personality, that's for sure. He was the black-hat guy. He had his swagger, his demeanor, and his *gimmick* on the racetrack, that he was the Intimidator. He wore that black hat and wore it well, even though, under that black hat, he was one of the nicest guys you could ever be around.

———❧———

*NASCAR publicist **Jim Hunter**, on Earnhardt's mechanical ability:*

Unlike many of the drivers of today, Earnhardt could work on a car. He knew cars inside out. He could take a motor apart. When he was racing those dirt tracks, he had to do it all.

———❧———

***Hunter**, on Earnhardt the man:*

He was mischievous. He loved to pick on somebody. You've heard countless people say how he'd come up and grab them around the head, around the neck, in a headlock. And I got to see him with Neil Bonnett; Neil was a good friend of mine also. He and Neil became really good friends. They loved to hunt and fish, and they loved to race.

———❧———

*When Earnhardt was about to tie **Richard Petty's** record of seven titles in 1994, Petty was asked to compare their feats. Naturally, Richard defended his turf:*

More power to him, but I did my thing in my time, and he's doing his thing in his time. But it's a different deal now.

We didn't run for the championship; we ran races, and, at the end of the season, whoever had won the championship, won it. I didn't try to win more championships than anybody else or try to win a certain number.

Now, they run for the championship because of the

money. There wasn't any money back then. We just ran races. It was a different deal.

---

*Even when he was a Winston Cup rookie, **Tony Stewart** said he was starstruck with Earnhardt:*

I don't feel like I can approach him. I still see him as an idol instead of a competitor.[1]

***Stewart** talked more about his relationship with Earnhardt:*

He's been good to me. It's been kind of fun with him. Even in some practice, he has kind of raced me harder than he did in the races. He's never laid a bumper or fender to me and he has raced me clean all year. He's been the most fun guy to race this year. I can remember the first race we pitted side by side, and I was nervous thinking this guy was going to growl and snarl and give me dirty looks.

One time I was climbing in my car, and he'd pull out. One time I was leaning on my toolbox, and he'd kick my legs out, just joking around. He was always a guy I looked up to when I watched Winston Cup on TV, and it's been neat to interact with him.[2]

---

*Years ago, **Benny Parsons** was asked if Earnhardt would change with the times:*

I don't think so. He's Earnhardt.

***Parsons** once talked about Earnhardt's driving for Wrangler. This was back when Dale was shy and not much of a talker:*

When he signed with Wrangler in the eighties. I thought, *Dale Earnhardt does not have the communication skills to carry this off.* But Wrangler got around the fact that Dale wasn't a good talker then; they called him "one tough customer, just like our jeans." It's something I'd not expected, and it was probably the best marketing job anyone's done, ever.

Now he communicates as well as anybody else.

Clay Campbell, president of Martinsville Speedway:

He never played tricks on me, but he was always jovial, I guess you might say. Every time I saw him, he was that way.

Short-track promoter Charlie Powell was a racer in the sixties and seventies:

Mostly, when we raced together, I saw him when he passed me. I went up to Concord to race one time, and Earnhardt started in the rear. He won the race; he got by me and everybody else, too.

Buddy Baker:

Once in a driver's meeting, I heard Earnhardt tell Bobby Allison, "Bobby, you taught me everything I know." And Bobby said, "Yeah, but I didn't teach you everything *I* know."

Baker, on a driver's ability to go through traffic:

You get in a zone as a driver, and the ones who have been there understand that. You get in a zone where you know every inch of where that car's at; you know the momentum. I knew how long my car was within inches, and I've watched Earnhardt do the same thing. He knew exactly where he was at all times. I've seen Pearson do the same thing, and Cale (Yarborough) was a master of that, too. He knew exactly how long his car was, and he didn't have to ask anybody when he was clear.

Bobby Allison, on flying airplanes:

He rode in my Aerostar before he ever had a plane, and I thought it was pretty neat that he saw the value of an airplane. When he got to that point, he bought one pretty quick.

Jim Freeman, who ran the International Motorsports Hall of Fame in Talladega, Alabama, at the time of Earnhardt's death, said people had suggested that Earnhardt should have gone into the Hall of Fame in '01, rather than waiting the requisite five years:

We got some suggestions by Earnhardt fans, e-mails and letters encouraging us to put him right into the hall. Ironically, by a fluke of scheduling, our board met the day after the Daytona 500 for our regularly scheduled meeting. The suggestion came up that people would put pressure on us to put Dale in. He's certainly deserving, but we decided that Dale Earnhardt wasn't greater than the whole.

We already have eighty inductees, and every one waited to get in, including Ayrton Senna (who died in the early 1990s in a Formula One crash). Senna waited, Richard Petty, A. J. Foyt, Mario Andretti . . . I realize it was a different situation, but they all waited. If you had to put the dozen top guys on a plateau, Earnhardt would be one, but those guys would be there, too.

Jeff Gordon, after Earnhardt won the 1998 Daytona 500:

He did what he does here every year, except he kept doing it all the way to the end. We all would have loved to have been in Victory Lane, but we're all real happy for Dale. If we couldn't be there, we all loved for him to be. He's earned it, man. He deserves it.[3]

Gordon, after he beat Earnhardt to win the 1999 Daytona 500:

To me, winning this race is much sweeter and more meaningful because I was battling the guy I learned from. But that was the longest ten laps of my life.

When a driver comes down with an injury or sickness, a team often will find a relief driver to take his place. And then the real problems begin, as driver Mike Wallace learned:

Drivers have a hard time getting out of a car, even if they are uncomfortable. A few years ago Earnhardt had a broken shoulder or something at Bristol. His team knew he could not make it the entire race at such a physically demanding track, so they called me in for standby. Once they radioed Earnhardt and told him I was there as a relief driver, he would not get out of the car for anything. He hit the wall a few times and was all over the place, but he would not get out of that car. We cannot imagine how much pain he must have been experiencing.[4]

Humpy Wheeler figures one record is safe now:

One of the by-products of Earnhardt's death is that Richard Petty's seven championships and the same for Earnhardt likely will never be broken now, and that's one thing Earnhardt certainly wanted to do. Last year (2000) he realized how close he came to it. He never said it, but when Earnhardt didn't win his eighth championship last year, I think he mentally said, *It ain't going to happen.* I'm sure he never actually said it, but I just felt that way.

Wheeler talks about Earnhardt's ability in the draft:

Nobody drafts better than Dale Earnhardt. He knows how to play the air. He's learned that black magic. The hardest thing for a stock-car driver is to run the high-bank speedways in multi-car situation, how they work strategy. It's a blessing and a curse. What makes Earnhardt do it so well is that he's unpredictable. He'll use you when he wants and discard you when he wants to.

Wheeler says Earnhardt was unusually gentlemanly during the 2000 championship chase:

Bobby Labonte did a great job in 2000; he never folded one time. But Earnhardt was not Dale Earnhardt with Bobby Labonte. If that had been ten years ago, it would have been a whole different ballgame. There's a whole lot of intimidation by that second- or third-place person when you're trying to hold onto that championship run. And Earnhardt pretty well stayed down the middle of the road on that one. He could have needled him, thrown out a lot of intimidation. We've seen people get stirred up in that situation, and we've seen championships lost that way.

Buddy Baker, one of Earnhardt's former-racer friends, said the grin was his favorite memory of Dale:

It was like he was saying, "I got something on you."

Grant Lynch, former president of Talladega Superspeedway, in 2001:

I remember that impish grin he had; he had a lot of trickster in him. He enjoyed pulling something over on his fellow competitors as well as on us track owners. He got so good with my maintenance department that when he needed some extra gravel around his coach, he would just call them himself. And then he'd laugh, because he thought he was cutting out the middleman—which was me.[5]

Buddy Baker, on Earnhardt's greatness as a driver:

He wrecked at Daytona giving 100 percent. That's what he always was to the race fan. He never gave less than 100 percent. I don't know anybody else who gave 100 percent in every race.

Baker:

One thing about Earnhardt was that he went out on top. You'll never read about him as an old man; you'll read about him as a champion. Everybody said this was his year for his eighth championship. He was right there, in typical form.

Hall of Fame driver/car owner **Junior Johnson**:

I've never seen anybody that could manipulate traffic like he could. It was just a knack he had. He'd gamble on getting in a hole not big enough to get into. Then he was through the hole. He just anticipated a lot of things. With ten laps to go and he was in contention, he'd beat you if you were not mighty careful.

Johnson:

He made the sport more exciting than any other driver.

Richard Petty:

When I talk about champions of NASCAR, then I want to have somebody who is a winner. Dale Earnhardt races to win races, so you ain't got nobody backing into nothing. He's got one speed, and that is wide open—and that is the way the champion ought to be.[6]

Driver **Mike Wallace**:

He was "The Man." That sounds kind of silly to say, and a lot of people use it superficially, but it just fits him. He was The Man.

---

*Driver **Kyle Petty**:*

When he was at the top of his game, he was amazing. He could do things with a race car that you didn't think anybody could do. There was a time when you could see a twenty-car pileup, and if just one car made it through, it was the one Earnhardt was driving.

---

*After Earnhardt's death, **Jeremy Mayfield** was still talking in present tense:*

The guy is a master. He's been doing this for years, and he's been doing it better than anybody.

---

*Driver **Dale Jarrett**, who beat Earnhardt twice in the Daytona 500:*

Dale is the best pure racer I've ever seen. He's the only driver I've ever watched who I feel was actually born a race-car driver.[7]

---

*Three-time Cup champion **Darrell Waltrip**:*

I've driven against Richard Petty, and I've driven against Dale Earnhardt, and let me tell you that Dale is far and away the best purebred stock-car driver I ever saw. He can do more with a race car than anyone I ever raced against.[8]

***Bobby Labonte**, who beat Earnhardt for the 2000 Cup title:*

When the Intimidator is that happy, it isn't real good for the rest of us. He's a tremendous driver, and he still knows more about these cars than a lot of people.

After winning the May 5, 2001, night race at Richmond, **Tony Stewart** *gave Earnhardt credit:*

Dale Earnhardt taught me a lot about this place. I followed him a lot of laps here, and he would just flat wear you out. You would think you were going to beat him and pass him and go on, and the next thing you would know he would run back on you. So you learned how to save your tires, you learned how to not abuse your equipment around here. I learned a lot from him here.[9]

Hall of Fame driver **Jack Ingram** *compared Ralph and Dale Earnhardt:*

They were theoretically the same on the racetrack. (Off the track) Ralph was really, really quiet, a lot like Dale Jr. is, or maybe a little more quieter. But that was the only difference that I could see. Dale was a little bigger.

Max Helton *of Motor Racing Outreach:*

He was always pulling stuff. He was a big jokester. He just had a tremendous attitude about him, and he'd often grab the back of my neck and pull me inside the car. He'd say, "Max, let's pray a bit." So I'd pray and thank the Lord for his victory, and that was it. But he was always doing little stuff like that.

Mike Skinner, Earnhardt's teammate at Richard Childress Racing, compared his own drafting ability with Earnhardt's:

He's just got a talent in air that seems to be superior over anybody's. I watch him and I try to learn. Every time I watch him, I'm paying attention.

I'd say, for the rest of us, you're really not much in control of your own destiny. You get shuffled back, and if the right car will go with you, you can go to the front and take that car with you. The problem is, with five or six laps to go, everybody is looking for the same thing and nobody wants to work with you. It's really tough.

<hr>

Skinner, on subbing for Earnhardt in the 1996 Brickyard 400:

I wasn't that nervous before the race. The nervousness that I had was for wrecking Dale's car. I did *not* want to wreck Dale's car.[10]

<hr>

*It was estimated that Earnhardt's memorabilia accounted for 40 percent of all Cup memorabilia sold, doubling the total for second-place Jeff Gordon. Racing historian **Bob Latford** tried to explain the reason Earnhardt, as well as other well-to-do people, would be driven to make money:*

I remember hearing Dolly Parton one time . . . they asked why she worked so hard when she'd made so much writing songs (and making) records, appearances. She said, "If you've really been poor, there's never enough money."

<hr>

Tom Higgins *recalls Earnhardt almost glowing after catching* *a twenty-five-pound striper on six-pound test line. Another time, in 1984, Earnhardt killed a wild turkey on land he and some friends had leased in Chester, South Carolina:*

He didn't get many chances to go huntin' because racing season conflicted with turkey season. But he'd gotten to go one time, and he'd learned just enough to call a turkey in. At that time, he said it was the most exciting thing he'd ever done.

—✦—

Longtime television announcer **Ken Squier**, *on the last time he saw Earnhardt:*

When I first got to Daytona this year, I went to get my (media) credentials, and I heard this horn honk on a mustard Corvette. And it was him. He got out, and we talked for a while. I said, "You must have had a great time in the Twenty-four Hours (endurance race)." He said, "I really got to do that again." He really seemed to enjoy it, and it was a different, far more relaxed Earnhardt than I remember.

This last year, he was a different person. He was a far more confident person. He was more confident in everything. He exuded confidence in himself, in his family, in his business ability.

—✦—

Driver **Derrike Cope**, *on people's feelings about Dale:*

I think everybody felt they had a tie to Earnhardt. Whether you loved him or hated him, you had to love what he did on the track. Even newspaper reporters feel a tie with him. They have interviewed him, they've touched him, and they feel they've taken away a part of him. And that's one reason this sport is so unique; people have access, they actually feel they get a piece of you. He gave so much for so long to so many; that's why his death meant so much and people were so hard hit.

Clay Campbell, president of Martinsville Speedway, and **Dick Thompson**, the track's longtime publicist, both remember the same incident. On September 29, 1980, Earnhardt was leading the Cup points while leading the Old Dominion 500 at Martinsville. He and Dave Marcis banged fenders twice, and Earnhardt spun out. He kept going and passed Cale Yarborough for the lead with thirteen laps left, and that victory helped him beat Cale by nineteen points for Earnhardt's first championship. Here are Campbell's and Thompson's recollections:

Campbell: I can't remember what year it was, but Dale came off turn four, he spun and did a 360, and kept on going. I don't know who spun him, but I think it was whoever was driving the 28 car at the time (actually, it was the 71). He did a complete 360, never missed a beat.

Thompson: Dale got spun out one time coming off of the fourth turn. He did a 360 right on the track, didn't hit a thing, and he almost maintained his race speed. Now that's driving! I think he won the race, to tell you the truth.

Bobby Allison lost two sons in accidents; Clifford, in a racing crash similar to Earnhardt's, and Davey, in a helicopter crash. He said the Earnhardt crash made him think of Clifford's August 1992 wreck at Michigan Speedway:

It brought back memories of Clifford, for sure. Clifford's death was so similar to that one. Clifford died even more instantly than Earnhardt did. He didn't even bleed. He had a cut on his forehead that didn't bleed. No, I went to the car with Clifford, and it was certainly the most horrible feeling and sight, although Clifford wasn't disfigured. Just seeing this absolutely still person was just incredibly painful, mentally and physically painful.

For that car (Earnhardt's) to hit the wall like that and for it to be all over with, that certainly made me think of Clifford.

———————

Max Helton, a Presbyterian minister and founder of Motor Racing Outreach, says he and Earnhardt held hands through Dale's window the day of the Daytona 500 on February 18, 2001:

He says, "Just pray that I'll be wise in putting the car at the right place at the right time . . . and be able to drive with wisdom." And we did pray about that. And we did pray for safety.[11]

———————

*Former Richard Childress Racing crew chief **Kirk Shelmerdine**, on first realizing Earnhardt might be dead:*

I was at home watching it, and it surprised me how alarmed Darrell (Waltrip) was. He was very concerned. He was standing at the window watching his brother win the race, but he had commented three or four times about how bad a wreck it was that Dale had just had. And Darrell's angle of view was a lot different than the camera angle we got on TV. But the broadcast went off pretty quick after that, and they weren't saying anything more, which puts a question mark in your mind.

And when I saw (Ken) Schrader's face as they were interviewing him, I started panicking right then. I tried to call Sammy Johns (Schrader's crew chief), because he's a friend of mine, but I couldn't get his cell phone to answer. So I was feeling pretty helpless there. I couldn't get anybody on the phone. And I didn't know who to ask . . .

It was about six o'clock when (longtime Childress employee) Will Lind called the house. As soon as I knew it was him, he didn't have to say anything else.[12]

Tom Dayvault, *then the president of the Cabarrus Regional Chamber of Commerce in Kannapolis, North Carolina:*

I got a letter after Dale's memorial service from a family in Enola, Pennsylvania. It was a nice letter about what Dale had meant to them and how much they appreciated the memorial service that we did. But, in there, it stated that a funeral home in their hometown had opened for three hours for people to pay tribute to Dale Earnhardt, and 2,000 people came. I wonder if that was happening all over America. It let me know the impact he had worldwide. We (in Kannapolis) were too close to him; I don't believe we realized that.

Clay Campbell, *president of Martinsville Speedway:*

There was definitely something missing from our recent race. I think we'll all feel that way for a pretty good while. You can't have a Winston Cup race and not see the black No. 3 out there. It's just different without him.

Dick Thompson:

It was strange. I kept looking down on the track for the No. 3.

I used to like to watch him right at the start of the race. He'd come up through the pack like a snake.

It was touching when the third lap came and 86,000 people stood up and held up three fingers. You had to choke back tears, really. It's been like that over the years. The drivers, while they're here, they're kinda your heroes, but they're also your friends. And when you lose someone like Curtis Turner, Joe Weatherly, or Davey Allison, it hurts. It's like losing your next-door neighbor.

And you don't expect it, especially with Dale. I always thought the last thing to happen would be for him to be killed on the racetrack. He was so much at home on the racetrack; it was almost second nature for him to drive a race car. But it happens. I remember back to what Turner once said. He said, "People get killed racing; nobody said it was safe."

Buddy Baker, in 2001:

Every time I walk in the gate at a track anymore, I expect to see Earnhardt walking around in there. It really hasn't sunk in yet.

Junior Johnson:

This is just a shock beyond belief. A guy like him, you never expect anything to happen. He'd wrecked many times and was not hurt. How he'd walk away, you don't know how. Then, boom, he's dead, and it's hard to accept. I don't think I'll ever accept it. You move on, but you still don't accept it. You know it happened, and you need to move on and forget it, but I won't, and I don't think anyone else will, either.

Bobby Allison, on his feelings when Earnhardt died:

Disbelief, really. You know, he is the one person I never thought would die in a race car. Somehow he just seemed stronger than that, less vulnerable, more able to deal with anything that went on. I saw him crash a few times and get broken up a little bit a time or two. It was just an incredible disbelief.

Humpy Wheeler:

He was a good friend, and I'm still in shock. This is a terrible, terrible loss, and for me, it ranks right up there with the death of JFK. Dale was the Michael Jordan of our sport.

We always thought of Dale as being invincible, so when he didn't climb out of that car after the wreck I knew it was bad. I talked to him the morning before the race and he was poised to challenge for an unprecedented eighth championship and was really looking forward to a fantastic season.

I knew Dale's father, Ralph, and I've known Dale since he was a little boy. He had things pretty tough when his father passed away when he was young, and I was so proud of the way he turned out and the way he represented our sport.

Behind that macho facade was a real sensitive individual who did a lot of things for a lot of people and didn't want any publicity in return. He was part of a very loving family and was truly an extraordinary human being. To think he is not around anymore is incomprehensible.

Right now, we've got to do what we can do to help his family get through this terrible time. Our thoughts and prayers are with his mother, Martha, his wife, Teresa, and his children—Kerry, Dale Jr., Kelley, and Taylor Nicole.

We will never fill the void left by the loss of Dale Earnhardt.[13]

———※———

Bruton Smith, who owns several racetracks, including the one at Charlotte, spoke at Dale's funeral and compared Earnhardt to Elvis Presley:

The sport has lost great drivers before, but I think this has brought attention to our sport in a way that is unbelievable. If you're not an avid race fan, you've heard about our sport now—and maybe it is an awakening. Maybe, even in death, Dale Earnhardt is going to continue to build our sport. That's the way I look at it.

We've exposed our sport internationally now, maybe in a way that we never could have. I guess the only way I can put it is that this reminds me a great deal of when Elvis died. And you saw what occurred there. It makes me wonder if Dale Earnhardt will have the same impact on his world that Elvis did on his world. That could happen easily. I didn't realize how many millions of people knew, or thought they knew, Dale Earnhardt.

———※———

*During the eulogy for Earnhardt at the Calvary Church in Charlotte, North Carolina, Motor Racing Outreach chaplain **Dale Beaver** recalled going to see Earnhardt to get a permission slip so that Dale's daughter Taylor Nicole could attend a youth camping trip in the Poconos:*

I half expected to find a man eating a bear, tearing it apart with his bare hands. I thought, *He's eating bear, and I'm going to be dessert.*

(Instead) I saw a man eating an orange, who with a very warm demeanor welcomed me into his presence. I didn't come into the presence of a racing icon or an intimidating figure. I came into the presence of a dad, a father who was concerned about his daughter.

Jeff Austin of the Kannapolis Country Club talks about the loss of the town's most famous son:

No one even pondered when other drivers were dying from injury . . . it just couldn't happen to Dale Earnhardt. You assumed that he'd drive a couple more years, win his eighth championship, retire, and let Dale Jr. follow in his footsteps. . . . The stage he set was the last lap of the biggest race with his two cars in front of him—that's how you'd expect him to go out, if that was the case. It wasn't a practice crash at Martinsville; he had the largest audience.

It's still an impact for us. I still feel like the phone could ring, and it could be him asking about something. I've lost family members before, but if there's such a thing as a shock, this certainly was it.

Larry McClure, owner of the Morgan-McClure Cup team:

Dale Earnhardt's death is a tremendous loss to our NASCAR family and to the entire nation. Whether you liked him or not, he stood as a hero. Many looked up to Dale as a man who stuck to his convictions. Earnhardt set the stage in Winston Cup. What he did, everyone followed. He was a fierce competitor, one that we did battle with many times.

He lived a life that was full. As a father, a husband, and a businessman, Dale experienced success. He showed people that they can follow their dreams and reach their goals. Dale accomplished more in his life than most of us ever

could. It is unfortunate. All of us in the NASCAR community live on the edge. The drivers are on the edge all of the
time, every weekend.

This seems more of a shock to people, because the
wreck did not look that bad. When someone so talented is
involved in such a deal, it is unbelievable. I know we will all
go into the garage at Rockingham next weekend and expect
to see that sly grin that Earnhardt patented.

It is going to be tough on NASCAR fans and Dale Earnhardt fans. For those of us who saw him and talked to him
every weekend, it will take a long time to deal with this horrible loss.

Cherish the memories of Dale. Realize we were lucky to
be able to share his life with him. Finally, believe. If you
believe in Christ, the pain will be easier to handle.[14]

Jeff Austin, on the Kannapolis reaction to Earnhardt's death:

We were concerned about all of the media that came in and
the memorial that was created in front of Dale Earnhardt
Inc. for days and weeks following his death. People were
trying to liken it to Princess Di or Elvis Presley. It was just
overwhelming.

We had a radio station, WRAL from Raleigh, come in to
cover the tragedy. They set up shop in front of the memorial at Dale Earnhardt Inc. During the off time during the
day, they'd go out and hunt stories, and their producers
were calling them and saying, "Don't come back. We need
continuation. We need more." People just weren't satisfied
with information. And it just didn't go away.

And, still, it continues with the controversies over the
safety issues, what's transpired. You can pick up any magazine or newspaper, and Dale Earnhardt is still at the fore-
front of the industry. And I think he will be for a while. He

was the sport. He was the reason people cheered for Jeff Gordon and booed him.

Family probably was the only thing that meant as much to Dale Earnhardt as racing. Here he poses with wife Teresa and daughter Taylor Nicole.

*Driver **Sterling Marlin's** reaction:*

Dale Earnhardt *was* NASCAR. He had a tremendous amount of fans everywhere. I think the shock of it . . . it shocked me. We didn't know it was that bad. (Team manager) Tony Glover told me about the time we were getting ready to leave the racetrack in Daytona that it didn't look good for Earnhardt. I said, "Well, what do you mean?" He said, "He's hurt pretty bad."

By the time we got to the airport, they came and told us. I was in total shock. I've seen him hit and flip and tumble, and me and him have been in some at Talladega, upside down. I couldn't believe it. It made you just want to throw up . . . just sick to your stomach. You couldn't believe it could happen.[15]

---

*Short-track operator **Charlie Powell** knew Earnhardt pretty well:*

The memories I have of Dale are dear to me, and I couldn't believe he was dead. It's still hard to believe he's gone. I was thinking last night—have you ever thought about a person in death and you could see that person in a casket? It's hard to see Dale Earnhardt lying in a casket. To me, it was like he didn't belong there. Most people have stories of Dale. For most people who knew him, he was The Man.

They interviewed me on a television station the week after he died, and they said, "What do you think will happen? Who will replace Earnhardt?" And I said, "Replace Earnhardt? That word don't exist. You can't replace him." I don't believe there's anybody now in the same category. He was the last of the real race-car drivers.

9

THE FANS

"What would I do if that was ever taken from me?"
— RON GLANCY

In 2000 Beckett Books published my coffee-table book, *Racing Families: A Tribute to Racing's Fastest Dynasties.* A friend of mine brought his young son, a big Earnhardt fan, to a book-signing party. I don't remember exactly what I signed for the boy, but it was something like "To Dale Earnhardt's biggest fan." I did it partly because Earnhardt and Dale Jr. were featured on the cover, and, too, this boy was more an Earnhardt fan than a racing fan.

The smile on his face was huge. "Look what he wrote!" the boy said excitedly to his dad, showing off the inside-front cover of the book. That's still my highlight from that book.

Earnhardt had the biggest contingent of followers as well as the largest group of haters (Anybody But Earnhardt). Dale Jarrett, the 1999 Cup champion, talked about the loss of Earnhardt, for him and for fans. This was right after the 2001 race at Las Vegas:

I can honestly say there is not a day and there are very few hours in my day that something doesn't come up that I think about Dale—something that he did for me or helped me or just something he did for the sport, that he did for the fans—just what he really meant to us," Jarrett said. "It's gonna take a long time, but it is important. We've had two good races as far as the competition goes and, hopefully, that will continue.

This fan base that Dale drew for us—these millions of fans that we have across the country—we have to find a way to keep them excited about NASCAR racing even though we have all lost our hero. We have to find a way, and I think good racing will help do that.

At the 2001 spring race at Martinsville Speedway in Virginia, the black-and-silver-clad Earnhardt fans were out in force. Often, you'd see a parent or an aunt or uncle wearing a Dale Earnhardt cap and shirt, and the accompanying youngster would be decked out in Dale Jr.'s red cap and T-shirt.

The Earnhardt shirts boasted everything from "One Smooth Ride: Dale Earnhardt" to "Man of Steel" to "But the Man Remains the Same." Clearly, some of those shirts had been washed many, many times.

Since Earnhardt's death, fans have searched for ways to say their good-byes. Many put up items in the Earnhardt "shrine" in front of Dale Earnhardt Inc. in Mooresville. And at the Martinsville race, one of the Earnhardt trailers was covered with fans' sentiments, and the authors were from places like Fort Worth, Texas; Omaha, Nebraska; Gretna, Virginia; Claremont, Minnesota; Las Vegas; Marlow, Oklahoma; Conyers and Elberta in Georgia; and Lake Arrowhead and Taft in California.

One said: "Forever a Champion. To the Best Friend I Never Met!" There was "Kannapolis Loves You, Big E!" and "Kannapolis Loves You. Thanks. Cathy." Many said, "Dale, Thanks for the Memories." A Larry Smith wrote "1 Last Good-bye to a Real American Hero. U Will Be Missed."

One fan from Pineville, North Carolina, wrote, "Race on, Brother," and a group of fans added collectively, "Dale, Vegas loves U. God bless."

There was more: "Sadly Missed. Fondly remembered"; "Dale Was NASCAR. Miss You Always. Eric"; "Dale, Thanks for Showing Us How a Brave Man Lives and How to Be a Man!"; "Dale There Will Be Only One Man in Black"; "Champions Never Die. NASCAR fans"; "Winner of 7—a Hero—a Legend"; "You Were the Best #3. Donald."

Here's one of the most elaborate sentiments: "Chasing No. 8 Made Him Great, with Victories in 7, He's Still Smiling from Heaven."

Other fans found other ways to express their loss.

John Murley, a fireman from Memphis, Tennessee, has added to the fans' writings on the Earnhardt trailer. More importantly, he wrote a Dale Earnhardt song that has been published online at www.mp3.com/jmurley/. And his fellow fans have responded:

"NUMBER 3"

Verse one:

Every Sunday we'd sit down,
And turn on our TVs
We'd watch the boys go racin'
And we'd root for Number 3.
Even if you weren't a fan,
I think you'd agree
That he amazed you with his moves,
And dazzled you with speed.

Chorus:

He was a father to four,
Husband to one,
A hero to millions,
He was NASCAR's shining son.
We loved him and we'll miss him,
And to us he'll always be,
Number one in our hearts that drove
The Number 3.

Verse two:

Sundays just won't be
The same without him here
But I know he's in Heaven
Runnin' races way up there.
I bet he just qualified
And he's sittin' on the pole,
Ready to take the checkered flag
On the speedway of gold.

Repeat chorus . . .

Yea, we loved you and we'll miss you
And, Dale, you'll always be . . .
The number one INTIMIDATOR,
You drove the hell outta
NUMBER 3.

John Murley:

I've been a fan of his for about seven years. There was a lieutenant who worked at the fire station, who had followed NASCAR, and Earnhardt had been his favorite driver since he first came on the Winston Cup scene. When I was started working with him, he was always watching races at the fire station, and he got me hooked. I started following Earnhardt, because that's all he'd talk about, and that got me started. I became an Earnhardt fan from then on out.

By the time he died, I was a big fan. I was in shock just like any fan of his, like everybody else who couldn't believe he'd died in the crash. I write songs quite often anyway, play the guitar and sing. So, about two days later, I got this tune in my head and some words. I got home and wrote the song. It didn't take long; forty-five minutes or so.

The first line that came into my head was, "We love you and we'll miss you; and to us, you'll always be number one in our hearts that drove the No. 3." That's what was initially going through my head. So when I got home, I wrote it. Really, it's amazed me. I went to the fire station the next day after I wrote it, and I played it for some guys at the fire station, one of them being that lieutenant that got me started. They really liked it a lot, and they were saying, "You really need to record that song." I said, "I don't have any plans of doing that. It would cost a quite a bit of money, if you're going to do it right, with the studio time, paying the musicians."

So this other lieutenant at the station offered to pay for it. He believed in that song; he thought that everybody ought to hear it. So the next thing I knew, a few days later we werc up in Nashville and recorded that song. At Razzy Bailey's studio up there. He's a songwriter who's actually had some albums out. Back in the seventies and eighties, he had a few hits.

We submitted it to the mp3.com, a music site on the Internet, because we felt that was a good place for people to hear it. After six or seven days, it started getting some attention. It's been number one on their new country charts for about a month, and they rank the songs every day. I guess we've had twenty-some thousand people download the song and listen to it.

It's unbelievable the people who have sent me e-mails about the song. I've got e-mail from Germany and Canada; I wasn't aware that NASCAR was so broad, so popular, in other countries. Apparently, NASCAR is real big in Canada.

After I recorded it, I wanted all of the Earnhardt fans to hear it. But there are so many Earnhardt fans that that may never happen.

---

*But he's hit a bunch of them. **Murley** says several newspapers, wire services, and radio stations have interviewed him, including rock stations in Baltimore and Fort Myers, Florida. For the Fort Myers station, he actually sang and played the song over the phone during the interview. The mp3.com Web site called him, and a publicist interviewed him for a press release. The song has the thirty-three-year-old Murley thinking of pursuing a singing/songwriting career:*

Razzy Bailey, whose studio I did it in, has his own independent record label, and he wants me to do some more songs in the studio and work on an album. For a long time I've thought of a music career, but then I haven't pursued it. I've played around Memphis in clubs, but the club scene ain't what I want to do every night of the week. I enjoy songwriting and playing for people. What I'd really like to do is sing at a race for a bunch of fans, Earnhardt fans. That may or may not happen.

*But **Murley** swears he didn't think of cashing in on Earnhardt's death:*

I'm not greedy. I didn't write the song to attempt to make money. I wrote it as a way of coping with his death.

***Murley**'s mission, he said, is to honor Earnhardt:*

I want as many people to hear (the song) as possible, Earnhardt fans or just NASCAR fans, a Jeff Gordon fan or a Terry Labonte fan. I didn't want to focus on just the race-car driver. From what I've seen, read, heard, and from people I've talked to who had encounters with him, family was important to him.

***Murley**'s first live race was the October 1999 race at Talladega. That was the year Earnhardt won both races there, and Murley and his friends, all Intimidator fans, partied. In the off-season before the 2001 season, he bought tickets for the spring race at Talladega, figuring Earnhardt had a chance to win again. Then came the 2001 Daytona 500:*

I couldn't wait to see him run this year, but it wasn't meant to be. Dale Jr. ran good. He led quite a while Sunday, and I was hoping he'd do something. After the race, I bought some Earnhardt stuff for myself, my boy, and my wife. I signed the (memorabilia) trailer, and I've had quite a few people respond (on the Internet). I get 100 to 200 e-mails a day from people. A lot e-mailed me after I'd come back from the race.

They said how much they miss seeing Earnhardt run.

Just as Murley expressed missing Earnhardt in his song.

Ron Glancy *was a lucky race fan in the early nineties. He was the manager of the Hampton Inn in Florence, South Carolina, and his hotel hosted a few race teams and many media members for the races at Darlington Raceway:*

You were constantly seeing racing people there. I walked in the hotel one day and the person in front of me was Teresa Earnhardt, with Taylor Nicole in her arm. Later that night, we saw a couple of Atlanta Braves, Earnhardt's favorite team, walking through the parking lot. In fact, shortstop Jeff Blauser, whom I'd met at the track earlier that day, waved.

I was visiting Ron on the Saturday night before the 1993 TranSouth 500, and he told me that he rooted for two drivers who stayed at his inn, Alan Kulwicki and Dale Earnhardt. Ron asked me if I'd like to see his display, so we went into his office and he showed off his Alan and Dale collections. He was proud, since they'd won the last three Cup championships, including Kulwicki's title in 1992. In fact, Earnhardt would make it five in a row by adding titles in '93 and '94.

The next morning, I went to the continental breakfast, and Kulwicki was sitting in the corner. As was his way, he ignored me. Alan was in no mood to talk, especially to a sportswriter.

That afternoon, Kulwicki ran in his last race. Later that week, he died in a plane crash while flying into Bristol, Tennessee, for a race.

I didn't know Alan well, so I called Ron Glancy. He was nearly hysterical, and we talked for more than an hour. He even talked about going up to Tennessee to visit the site of Alan's crash. One of us, I don't remember which, said that at least Ron could root for Earnhardt forever (note the irony here). At the end, he thanked me. He said the chat made him feel better.

The next week, he called me back. He'd read my column in the Charleston, South Carolina paper, and he didn't realize I was interviewing him for publication! That's how out of it he was. But he seemed to love the column, and he had it framed.

That leads us to 2001. Glancy, by that time, had become manager of a hotel in Sumter, South Carolina. He was a bigger Earnhardt fan than ever. He'd go to races and almost become part of the action. Because Earnhardt knew him, he'd let him stay up close and take photos, and he got several photos autographed. At one race, he got to sit on car owner Richard Childress's hauler. He was in stock-car heaven.

Then Dale died in the 2001 Daytona 500. I was hurt and shocked, and several people I knew were wailing about Dale's death. I told someone that at least he wasn't Ron Glancy. His heroes both were gone—Alan Kulwicki and Earnhardt.

Then it hit me. *Duh . . . Why not call Ron again?* I hadn't talked to him in a few years, so I had to look him up. I found his number in Sumter, called, and left a message. A few minutes later, he called back. He was both enthusiastic and sad. It was great to hear his voice, but I knew Ron. This time, I made sure that he realized that he was being interviewed for a book. And in typical **Ron Glancy** fashion, he poured out his heart:

It's been a rough spring (2001), to be honest with you. It's been hard, man. That's all I can say. For some reason, I always thought that, with Dale, everything seemed so perfect. But, for some reason, I always had premonitions. You know what I'm saying? What would I do if that was ever taken from me? What would I do if I didn't have him to pull for on Sunday? When the three guys (Adam Petty, Kenny Irwin, and Tony Roper) died last year, something just told me that NASCAR's going to have to learn a lesson, or something. And it was going to take somebody like Dale. You know what I'm saying? I just had a feeling it was going to happen to me.

Notice that **Ron's** taking this personally. If it happened to Earnhardt, it happened to him, too:

If you've got children, you worry, "I hope my children don't go before me. Because it would be too painful a memory." That's kinda what it's been like with this Earnhardt thing. It really has been that horrible.

Glancy said that, about a week after Earnhardt died, he had panic attacks and had to go to the hospital:

In researching panic attacks, I realized that some of the things that can cause them is the death of a loved one. When some people had their wife die or their mother die or someone very close to them, they have these panic attacks. I feel that literally happened to me. I was suffering that bad in such a painful way that it was hurting me.

Glancy was working February 18 but watched the race on TV:

I felt concerned when I saw the wreck, the way everyone was acting, the way Ken Schrader was acting. I was thinking, *You know, he may be hurt. He may not be able to race next week. This might mess up his chance for that eighth championship.* Never in my mind did I think it's serious enough that he'd die. I went online immediately and was trying to find any information from NASCAR or from anywhere. About ten or fifteen minutes before it showed up on TV, the NASCAR Web site popped up something that said "Earnhardt killed in Daytona crash," or something like that.

They talk about the different stages of grief that a parent or somebody goes through when somebody dies unexpectedly. I guess they go through anger, denial, and these other stages. I remember being in the back just kicking things, throwing things, just being so mad. I didn't believe it could happen. I still have denial. I'm thinking maybe it really didn't happen. Maybe Earnhardt didn't feel like messing with NASCAR anymore. He wanted to take it easy. But I'm thinking, *No, it really happened.*

I haven't done much smiling, to be honest with you. It's been hard. Some things I see hurt me, and I break down. Some other things I see, and I take pride in them. If I see a 3 on the back of a truck, it kinda makes me feel good. The people who have 3s on their flags, their trucks, and their cars are trying to give a tribute to Earnhardt. You know?

Here's just how bad it's been for **Glancy**: When Earnhardt died, Ron had a poster by artist Garry Hill in the frame shop, so he decided to get it back and put it up as part of an Earnhardt display. He'd have a shot of The Winston all-star race in 1987, with Earnhardt's "Pass in the Grass," plus a shot from The Winston in 1990, which Earnhardt also won, and he'd top the display with the Daytona 500 win.

Then he started thinking: He figured that Earnhardt got the first print, that Chevrolet or General Motors got the second print, and that car owner Richard Childress would get the third print, since Childress owned car No. 3. Glancy had gotten print number 218 out of 500.

I thought, *What significance would there be to 218?* I was thinking, *Did he win a race that day?*

Then, to his horror, Ron realized that Earnhardt died on 2/18—February 18.

When I saw I had that number, I broke down. I just lost it. It's almost like I should have known something. It was almost unbearable.

Jerry Punch, the longtime auto racing announcer for ESPN, talks about Earnhardt's passion for his fans:

I also remember when he won his seventh title; it was like a few weeks before we'd go to New York for the banquet. We did a sit-down with him at his home or his shop, because he was going to go hunting. Talk about his year, et cetera, et cetera, talk about things he still wanted to do. He wanted to win the Daytona 500. He'd just tied Richard Petty for seven championships; he'd like to win eight.

So, at the end of the interview, we talked a little bit, and I said, "You are leading in the voting for Most Popular Driver. You could win." I said, "Since you're going to go hunting tomorrow and you're not going to be back until the banquet, why don't we go ahead and ask you what it would mean to win?" He said, "I can't answer that. Bill Elliott's won it several years." I said, "There's only a few days left in the voting, and you very easily could win this." He said, "I'll tell you what, you and I have been friends a long time; what I'll do is answer the question. But you've got to promise me that you'll take this tape and bury it if I don't win it." I said, "Sure, sure."

So I asked him the question about winning the award, and he was incredible. He showed so much emotion about what being voted most popular by the fans meant to him, and how much winning races on the track means. But when the fans say you're the best, how special that is. And I was just flabbergasted.

Corky Corcoran, the cameraman who has worked with me for most of my years at ESPN, he was the cameraman. He was one of the few cameramen that Dale Earnhardt trusted. And Corky and I were just overcome from seeing him answering questions. . . . With the exception of him talking about his father, Ralph Earnhardt, I don't think I'd ever heard him speak with that much passion. It was special to him.

As we all know, a massive avalanche of votes come in, and Earnhardt finished second. So we went to the banquet, and he said, "Did you put that tape away?" And I said, "It's gone." He said, "Thank you." But that moment, knowing how much that meant to him, that was really special.

Part of the Earnhardt legend is his fan following and his collectibles sales. Beckett Racing Monthly *editor* **Mark Zeske** *talks about the special collectibles that Earnhardt did, which included his "7&7" promotion with Richard Petty and all of the special paint schemes that spawned collectible car sales:*

He was practically the market by himself. He lapped the field, so to speak. He was the leader not only in terms of popularity in the fact he had his own strong supporters, but just about everybody who collected felt they had to have Dale's pieces. People who weren't huge Dale fans found themselves buying his stuff because they thought that, one day, they'd be the most collectible.

But, besides all of that, he was the leader on the business side of racing. He was the innovator behind all of the special paint schemes, which turned out to be a big part of the NASCAR circuit. He was the guy who made that possible. He was the guy who boosted licensing sales. He's the reason that NASCAR has a lot of the licensing partners that they do, because he did a lot of the hard work himself.

He owned several of his own companies and was always about business. He was always willing to push things to the next level. I think he very much mentored Jeff Gordon in that part of the business. I'm not sure they talked that much about racing, but they sure talked about business. They pretty much started Chase Authentics together, and they owned land near Lowe's Motor Speedway. They had plans to build stuff there. He was just ahead of his time.

They obviously worked together. I think Jeff frequently went to Dale with questions. And Dale obviously led him to Action (Performance), which was obviously one of Dale's strongest partners. Dale obviously hooked up with good people his whole career, starting with Wrangler, with Chevrolet.

Some of the collectible stuff he has done is amazing. He was the first Winston Cup driver on a Wheaties box, and that came from the orange car that they race in The Winston. I loved the Olympic car they did in '96 in Atlanta. That was General Motors, which was a big sponsor of the Olympics. That was a beautiful car. The silver car was in '95, in '96 he did the red-white-and-blue Olympic car, in

'97 he did the car for Wheaties. In '97, Gordon did the first *Jurassic Park* car, and now everybody looks to change things (paint schemes) now and then.

There was the Tazmanian Devil, the Olympics, Wheaties. Those things are icons in their own right, and they hooked up to be with Earnhardt, just adding to his legend and helping him become an icon unto himself.

Tom Dayvault, president of the Cabarrus Regional Chamber of Commerce, was about to go to the memorial service. Then a family of fans called:

I got a call, and they said, "We got a song for the memorial service that my brother did." And I thought, *Oh, man, I should have let the phone ring.* They said, "Can I play it for you?" It was a magnificent song, which they did over the telephone, and I went, "How can I get that?" They met me at the Chamber office, and it had never been published. It was professional quality. It was a handshake, and I grabbed it, and took it to the memorial service.

Afterward, a young man came up to me and said, "That's my song. All I ever wanted was for Dale Earnhardt to hear that song." And I said, "I think he heard it today." I said, "I want to get a copy of it," and he said, "You can have that one." Well, it's gone. I have no idea what the guy's name is. He's from China Grove (North Carolina), and I'll track it down eventually.

Bill Limer, a pipe fitter from Charleston, West Virginia, figures Earnhardt was his type of racer:

I don't know, he was just the type racer that good ol' hard-working boys like to see race. He was that type person. He caught my eye, and I've been rooting for him since the early eighties. That No. 3 blue-and-yellow Wrangler car just fit him, but the black car added to it. He was just my type of person. All the people I know are blue-collar workers, and all are Earnhardt fans.

I was watching racing before he came along. But after he died, it didn't seem the same, it wasn't the same. I'll pull for the Dale Earnhardt Inc. drivers: Junior, Michael Waltrip, and Steve Park, all of the drivers racing under the Dale Earnhardt name. Of course, Kevin Harvick, you've gotta pull for him, since he's in Earnhardt's car.

Limer, on getting over the loss:

I talk about it with other people sometimes, and you think you're getting over it. But I don't think I can. For the Bristol race, I went to qualifying, and then went to the Busch race on Saturday. Everything was all right. Then on Sunday, they played the national anthem, and a man got up and asked for a few minutes of quiet time for Earnhardt. You could hear a pin drop; it was deathly quiet.

I started thinking about some races he'd been in; I had some flashbacks. Three cannons went off in turns three and four, and they shook the track. There were three big smoke rings. People who were walking stopped, and a guy beside me was crying his eyes out. He's going to be hard to get over.

Limer, on Earnhardt's importance to racing:

It seems that 70 percent of the people there at the track are rooting for him, and 100 percent are there to watch him or watch him wreck or see somebody beat him. He was a drawing card. At Bristol when him and Terry got together (in 1999), that was the talk of the town, them bumping on the last lap. Darlington the next weekend, they weren't sold out, but they said they sold 3,000 or 4,000 extra tickets, and those people were going to watch him race.

If he was anywhere near a car and ready to make a pass, everybody would stand up. If he'd get the lead, they'd be on their feet till he'd lose the lead.

Limer:

This is the biggest thing I've ever seen in sports or anything that took such a toll on people, as far as a big-name person losing their life. It's unreal the things that went on. I didn't work the next day. I called my boss the next day. There was no way I could work.

---

*Fans remember meetings with Earnhardt. **Limer** does:*

Years ago we were at Bristol. I have pictures from that race, probably in '87 or '88. At one time at Bristol it was nowhere as crowded as it is now. They'd bring their Busch cars into the parking lot and load their trailers. It wasn't fenced off. I was walking by and saw Earnhardt's Busch car—No. 8, that's the number he ran in Busch then—and I thought, *My gosh.* I took a picture. Somebody hollered to watch the car. There stood Earnhardt in the trailer. I said, "My God, there's Earnhardt." He was talking to Teresa, and there was nobody around but the guys on the crew. I had a hat with me, so I said, "Man, is there a chance I can get an autograph?" He said, "Sure," and signed it. I was happy.

Joe Shepherd, a pipe fitter/welder from Mansfield, Ohio:

I've been a Dale Earnhardt fan since they started putting racing on television more in the early 1980s, and his name caught my eye. He has a racer's name. Since his death, I pull for Little E and Richard Childress.

I met Dale at an autograph thing in Akron. He ignored me, but he was awfully friendly with my wife. I got a kick out of that. Is she attractive? I think so. So did he.

Mike Bouissey of Cainhoy, South Carolina, is a Ford fan, but he admits that he misses Earnhardt. He says he enjoys the Ford-Chevrolet debate at the chemical plant where he works as a training coordinator:

He was one of greatest drivers to hit the track. I miss him, to be honest with you. I miss that black No. 3. All of the rivalries of the past are gone, the big showdowns with Rusty (Wallace) and Earnhardt at Talladega and Daytona, and even the tracks like Bristol. Both of those guys were short-track masters. It's like a piece of the competition has been taken away, and a lot of the excitement, too. You were waiting to see what he'd do on each weekend. Yeah, I miss him as much as the dedicated Chevy fans do.

I was ecstatic to see him win the Daytona 500, finally. It took him twenty years to get the big one, and I probably was as happy as he was that he finally won the Daytona 500. You saw the expression of joy that every pit crew member exhibited down there. He had all of them on pit road come out to shake hands and give their approval. When he cut those donuts in the middle of the Daytona 500 logo, there was only one person who could do that and get away with it, and he was it.

I was very happy for him. I was rooting for him, yeah, I

was. He was due. It would have been nicer to see a Ford out there, but if he and Rusty had been going head-to-head, that would have been a tough one to call. I'm glad it didn't happen that year.

Last year, he was sort of on the comeback, and I think everybody was anticipating some really exciting races this year. He sort of had the handle back on his car, and he was moving to the front every race. It was gearing up to be one heck of an exciting season, but, unfortunately, all of that excitement has been taken away. That was devastating. I'm not ashamed to tell you that the evening we found out that he had died, man, I cried as hard as everybody else. It was bad.

And even now, on the third lap of every race when they put out the No. 3 (in Earnhardt's honor), I get cold chills, I get teared up. Yeah, I miss the big guy out there. He brought a lot excitement to the profession.

Richard Cunningham, a commercial carpenter from Clinton, Maryland, wears an Earnhardt cap, while niece Alexa has a Dale Jr. cap:

I've been a fan since 1990. To tell you the truth, I was sitting watching with my folks, and, since everyone else was an Earnhardt fan, I didn't have a choice. I really didn't know what NASCAR was all about then.

I'm still a fan. I can't say how sad it was when he died. It was unbelievable, hard to put into words.

Cunningham showed off a photo of his Chevrolet 1500 Series truck that is painted black and covered with Earnhardt decals in memory of the No. 3 GM Goodwrench Plus Chevrolet:

I got that in '97, and I'll drive it until the wheels fall off.

Dale Jr.'s our main man now, and we certainly pull for Kevin Harvick. As for Dale Earnhardt Inc., I like them all. Anyone close to Dale is all right with me. He's gone, but the teams he built will be here a long time.

Douglas Hyatt, *a fan from Lynchburg, Virginia, also speaking for his wife,* **Cheryl**:

I've been an Earnhardt fan since '77. I met him and Richard Childress when they drag-raced at the Rockingham Spring Nationals, and my favorite memory of Dale was him winning the Daytona 500.

He was the best driver on the track, and no one can take his place. Kevin Harvick has done a good job, though. Earnhardt—hey, the man *was* NASCAR. But now, Dale Jr., Steve Park, Michael Waltrip, and Kevin Harvick are our men now.

When he died, both of us broke down crying. Then when Kevin Harvick won at Atlanta, it felt the same way it did when Dale won Daytona. But it's not the same. Our biggest upset is going to the track and not seeing the 3 car.

Joni Grant, *Virginia Beach, Virginia*:

My biggest problem is finding a new driver to root for. A friend of mine was a Darrell Waltrip fan, but he retired this year, and he has no one to root for. Dale Jr.'s not Dale Earnhardt, and Michael Waltrip isn't Darrell. It's not the same.

When those fourteen cars wrecked at Daytona, a lot of people said, "Thank God that Earnhardt wasn't involved." I guess they need to be careful what they wish for.

10

HOMETOWN BOY

"Yeah, I took the belt to him many times."

— MARTHA EARNHARDT

D ale Earnhardt became world famous, but he remained a guy from a mill town in North Carolina. Just one of the boys.

A week after he died in the 2001 Daytona 500, the town of Kannapolis held a tribute in Fieldcrest Cannon Stadium. The site was fitting, for Earnhardt had recently bought into the local minor-league baseball team, and it had been renamed from the Piedmont Bollweevils to the Kannapolis Intimidators in Dale's honor.

More than 4,500 people—locals as well as folks from as far away as Canada—attended, and many had lined up at 4:00 p.m. to attend the 7:30 p.m. event.

Ray Moss, then Kannapolis's mayor, was among those to speak that day. "Dale Earnhardt learned to drive on the streets of Kannapolis," Moss said. "He's a family member.

He's more than a NASCAR driver to us. He's one of our boys."[1]

***

Drive through a major portion of Kannapolis, North Carolina, nowadays, and there's an Earnhardt theme. Dale Earnhardt Boulevard starts off Exit 60 from Interstate 85 and is one of the major thoroughfares of the town. Dale Earnhardt Boulevard is on NC 3, which was changed from NC 136 on October 22, 2002.

And all along through there, you'll encounter the Dale Trail.

Judy Root, communications director of the Cabarrus County Convention & Visitors Bureau, says that they came up with the Dale Trail because there was an almost constant flow into the visitors center of tourists wanting to find Car Town or Ralph Earnhardt's grave or Dale Earnhardt Inc. So the visitors bureau identified nearly twenty places and came up with the name the Dale Trail.

The bureau designed a brochure with a stylized map that includes information and stories about Earnhardt.

"It was more in response to tourists coming to the visitors bureau, and many of them were just hungry for a connection with Dale and his community," said Root, who never met Earnhardt. She moved to Kannapolis in November of 2001, about nine months after Earnhardt died. "(They were) looking for Ralph's grave, wanting to see the statue in downtown, wanting to know how to get to Dale Earnhardt Inc. Those were the things that were drawing them here, where fans were asking directions. Also wanting to know where he grew up, the house where his family lived. We don't give exact directions to that, because his mom still lives there. It's still in Car Town.

"But we thought, instead of giving fans individually the directions how to get to these places, we would sort of connect the dots with some stories that related to his grow-ing-up years here in Kannapolis."

Dale Earnhardt Boulevard and NC 3 are prominent on the Dale Trail, as is Old Earnhardt Road, which was long ago named for an Earnhardt not in Dale's immediate family. According to the brochure, the teenage Dale drove his '56 Chevy—usually sideways—around Earnhardt Road's 90-degree turns. No. 7 on the map is Main Street/Midway, where Main Street and the Dale Trail intersect. When Dale was a teenager, there was a slot-car emporium—D&D Model Raceway—and Dale won trophies there. Idiot Circle is where teenagers would cruise one side of West Avenue from Vance Street to First Street and then back on the other

An Earnhardt family get-together, circa the early seventies. From left: sister Kay, Dale, mother Martha, brothers Danny and Randy, and sister Cathy.

side of the traffic circle created by pull-in parking down the center. According to the brochure, Martha Earnhardt said that her son may have logged more miles around Idiot Circle than he did around racetracks.

Some places on the Dale Trail—like Lowe's Motor Speedway, Sam Bass Gallery and the Richard Childress Racing—are not in Kannapolis. The speedway and the gallery are in Concord, maybe eight miles away, and RCR is about forty miles away in Welcome, North Carolina.

Bass's art, by the way, is prominent in the Dale Earnhardt Tribute Center on the corner of West Avenue and West B Street. The Tribute Center is No. 11 on the map.

And the brochure talks about places that aren't there anymore. Eddleman's Garage, for instance, is where Ralph Earnhardt perfected his mechanical skills while working on moonshiners' cars, and, yes, Junior Johnson was one of Ralph's customers. You learn about the Flying Mile, another place that has no landmark; apparently this is where moonshiners "hit the ground running" to test out their souped-up cars.

There's Car Town, the area where the Earnhardts lived, and Martha Earnhardt, Dale's mother, still lives there. You can find Car Town because of the street names—V8, Chrysler, Dodge, Plymouth, Ford, Chevrolet, and Cadillac. The Dale Trail includes Cannon Village/Cannon Mills, where Ralph Earnhardt first met Martha. The mill buildings are being torn down to make room for the North Carolina Research Campus, a biotechnology center. One of the most prominent features of the Dale Trail is Ralph Earnhardt's grave site at the Center Grove Lutheran Cemetery. The brochure explains that Ralph Earnhardt, known as "Mr. Dirt Track," amassed more than 350 racing victories over a twenty-three-year career.

Dale Earnhardt Plaza has a nine-foot, 900-pound statue of Earnhardt smiling and folding his arms, plus a granite monument that was contributed by fans from New York and Vermont.

Also on the tour are Curb Motorsports, since Mike Curb owned cars for Earnhardt, and Kannapolis Intimidators Stadium, as the Piedmont Bollweevils of the South Atlantic League were re-named for Earnhardt. And there's even the Punchy's Diner, No. 12 on the map, where they sell Dale's Favorite Sandwich—a tomato sandwich. Punchy's replaced the Junction Cafe & Grill, where Earnhardt got his sandwiches. The brochure even explains that Martha said she'd make Dale a tomato sandwich at home, with sliced tomato, sometimes lettuce, and Miracle Whip on white bread.

Perfect for a growing boy in a mill town.

Bob Misenheimer, now Kannapolis' mayor, recalls talking to Earnhardt fans looking for the past. They were seeking the Junction Cafe & Grill; it's been replaced by Punchy's Diner, which now serves up Dale's favorite tomato sandwich:

I remember walking up through town one cold Saturday afternoon, and there was a man and his family in a van. He asked me, did I know where the Junction was uptown? There was nothing there. It's gone. This was part of the Dale Trail. It's where (Dale would) go in and get tomato sandwiches. The uptown has had a rough time, and the Junction was one of them (businesses that closed).

Misenheimer, on his favorite driver:

I shouldn't tell you this, but in the late forties, I was in high school and going to various and sundry places to watch races. Speedy Thompson was my favorite driver until the speedway (Charlotte Motor Speedway) started (in 1960). David Pearson was my favorite then; then it was Dale until he got killed. (And now it's Dale Jr.?) Yeah, I'm going to continue to pull for him; my family feels the same way. I have tickets for Daytona (in February 2008), and I'm looking forward to going to SpeedWeeks. I'm looking forward to see what the 88 (Earnhardt Jr.'s car next year at Hendrick Motorsports) looks like.

<hr/>

Jeff Austin took charge of the Kannapolis Country Club in 1990. He was a big Darrell Waltrip fan, and he was dealing with Darrell's rival, Earnhardt:

Growing up in this area, I'd been an avid race fan. In fact, I'd become a very good Darrell Waltrip fan. I'd met him a couple of times, but Darrell Waltrip would not have known me personally. I took the job here at Kannapolis Country Club, and one of the office staff said, "You'll probably be getting a call from Dale Earnhardt. We have a Kids Day that he comes and does for us. He normally brings Neil Bonnett with him, and they'll probably want to fish." I didn't realize it at the time, but part of my responsibility here was controlling access to the reservoir.

The day did come, and Dale Earnhardt called. I picked up the phone, and he was very cordial. He said, "Mr. Austin, this is Dale Earnhardt. I just want to introduce myself and let you know that Kids Day is coming up. Is it all right if Neil Bonnett and me come up and fish?" At that point in time, it was an accurate statement. I said, "Mr. Earnhardt, it's a pleasure to speak with you. I don't totally know the parameters of my responsibilities on that." I said, "I need to get you an answer on that. I don't want to make that decision at this point in time."

For a split second, it just popped out of my mouth, I

said, "If you'll do me a favor, if you run into Darrell Waltrip, have him call me, because I'd love to fish with him." He sat there quietly for a moment, and I burst out laughing. I said, "I'm just kidding." So he knew I was a Waltrip fan, and he had to win me over to an Earnhardt fan, which didn't take long. After spending a little time (with him), he was a charming guy.

Steve Ellsworth cut Earnhardt's hair for fifteen years. Sometimes Dale would go to Steve's shop; other times Ellsworth would go out to Earnhardt's house:

He was a real good guy. He was always real good to me and my son. A lot of times, he'd have me to come over to his place to cut his hair, and he'd let my son go back to his pond where he and Neil Bonnett would fish, and my son could fish in the pond.

Every time he came in wearing a hat, my son would get it. And he has tons of hats from him. But the one thing I'd like put out there is how he was with the children. If there was a child out front, he'd stop and take the time to talk to them, if they knew who he was. He'd shake their hand, sign an autograph if they asked for one.

One day, he had some pocket knives in here—he used to bring me one at Christmas sometimes. He also gave one to a child. He was great and loved the children. He always took the time for them. He might walk past the parents and go right to the child.

One day there was a child in here, and the little fellow got a crew cut. And Dale looked at him and said, "Hey, fellow," and he rubbed his hair. He said, "You think I'd look good with a haircut like that?" That got a good laugh. He always had something to say or do with the kids when they were in here.

For fourteen years, Earnhardt was involved in the Kannapolis
*Country Club Kids Day. Since 1990, **Jeff Austin** dealt with*
Dale, and he got to know the Intimidator as just a guy:

We couldn't advertise it as Dale Earnhardt Day, because
we'd have thousands of people showing up. There was no
admission; it was never an issue. It was for the kids of club
members, and they'd bring guests. So it was not just a
member function, but a guest had to be with a member to
attend.

We wanted to make the function large enough so Dale
would appreciate the attendees, but we didn't want to make
it so large as to be a burden to him. Traditionally, we
expected 175 to 250 to show up. We'd turn the club over to
the kids for a day. We'd have golf camps and tennis camps.
Our facility here includes a working farm and a lodge, so
we'd have fire-truck rides, dunking booths. The Kannapolis
Intimidators—in years past, they were the Bollweevils—
they'd send their mascot out. We'd have pool games in the
afternoon, fast-pitch machines and face-painting, and
everything was highlighted by a visit from Dale Earnhardt.
We always said "Special Guest," and our members all knew
who that was.

Each year, Dale would surprise us with some celebrity
guest that he'd drag along with him, and we'd never knew
who was going to be with him. For many years, his best
friend, Neil Bonnett, would accompany him, and they'd
mix in a little fishing on the lake. Our golf course is situ-
ated on Kannapolis Lake, which is an almost 300-acre lake
that is our city reservoir. The whole thing is privately
owned, and you cannot fish from the banks of a watershed,
which this was. Periodically, Dale would want to fish with
Neil, and they'd sneak in a little fishing. They would actually take out time from lunch to do Kids Day. That's how it

initially started. He and Neil would fish, then they'd come up and he'd sign autographs and spend several hours with the kids. We'd have a couple of show cars up here.

When Neil died in '94, from that point on, Dale didn't feel like fishing in the lake. He kinda felt like he'd lost his fishing buddy. They could get away, and nobody would bother them. It was a buddy-type thing. After that, he brought Jody Davis with him, formerly of the Braves and Cubs. He was a good friend of his. Davey Allison came with him prior to his death. Brooks & Dunn came, and they actually went fishing. They came a couple of times. They talked Dale into having a Dale Earnhardt Day for the community. That night was a wonderful event here, too. Neil hosted that event. We had T. Wayne Robertson (of Winston sports marketing, sponsor of NASCAR's top series) and Jeff Gordon prior to him ever winning a Winston Cup race, Humpy (Wheeler of Lowe's Motor Speedway), and a few of those guys.

Once he created Dale Earnhardt Inc., he would bring all of his drivers. That went through the Jeff Greens and the Steve Parks. Eventually, Dale Jr. came on board. Sam Bass, the artist, would come over and bring posters. We'd just have a nice autograph session. He'd sit at the tables with kids.

We'd host a golf tournament for the speedway in May, and Dale had dropped by in his helicopter one year to help us out, gave a little notoriety to the event. He didn't play. He said he retired in '78 after he broke a leg. He started playing again—he had started a relationship with Greg Norman when they starred in some truck commercials. Greg Norman had talked to the late Payne Stewart . . . if Dale was going to play golf, his ego wouldn't allow him to go out there and be a hacker. He was very competitive in that sense. He wanted to be competitive, so we had talked about some private lessons out at his farm.

He'd drop his helicopter in for the speedway event, but he wouldn't do that for the kids. He felt that was too dynamic. He'd drive up in his pickup truck, just as an ordinary guy. The kids loved that, and he'd stay and sign and sign. He never charged us a dime. And we tried to make sure we did our part by not commercializing it and not profiting from it. That was a day he'd give to the community. We certainly had more dealings than that, but that was something that, for fourteen consecutive years, he never missed a Kids Day. I'd meet him in May in his race trailer, and we'd hammer out the days that worked into his schedule.

Earnhardt even helped out when the kids weren't from Kannapolis, or even the United States, for that matter. **Austin** *explains:*

This happened (around 1999). Raleigh was hosting international Special Olympics finals. And these were teams of children from all over the world that congregated in Raleigh, North Carolina. The local towns in North Carolina each adopted a country, and Kannapolis had adopted Paraguay.

Kids Day was on a Tuesday, and it just so happens that our club hosts Rotary every Tuesday, which normally consists of about a hundred businessmen showing up at the club in their suits. It was just kind of a weekly event for Rotary. The Special Olympics team from Paraguay was to be the guests of Rotary. We had our parking lot blocked off, in almost a carnival atmosphere. People had to park in one of our off-site parking lots because of the speed pitches and the tents and the hayrides in preparation for the Kids Day.

It was typical Dale Earnhardt; he was always interested in the community, but he never wanted to steal the spotlight from anyone. He understood that, when he walked into a room, he'd draw the attention away from whatever the event was. He was very concerned about that. So we had an upstairs dining room where the autograph session was going on; we had Rotary going on in the main dining room. And I asked, "Dale, would you step into the Rotary?" He had several acquaintances in there. Someone was actually giving a speech, and he said, "I don't want to do that, because I don't want to take away from the speaker."

At the door, the activity bus was pulling up with the children from Paraguay, and he had no idea what was going on. He said, "What's this? This is more kids." I said, "These are the special guests of the Rotary Club; this is the Special Olympics team from Paraguay. We're their host city, and they are having lunch as guests of the Rotary." These kids ranged from severely mentally challenged to moderately challenged. Certainly, they didn't speak English.

And when the bus pulled up, I followed Dale, and he walked over to the door, popped up onto the bus, and one of the little kids stood up and pointed and said, "Dale Earnhardt." You could just hear the bus explode. I don't know how these kids knew of him. He kind of went down the bus, and everybody was high-fiving him. It was just a very spontaneous, unrehearsed . . . he obviously cared about kids. Everybody got a poster or photo signed. Many of them never knew who he was, but the fact that one of them did was really special. That brings back a lot of fond memories.

We would keep the media away. We wanted enough media here that he could do a little sponsor entertaining, make sure the sponsors knew he was doing something good for the kids, but it was just an act of kindness for the community.

He was always extremely interested in the local education system, and I think I was his liaison to our school superintendent when we did the Dale Earnhardt Day. That occurred in my office. He said, "I'll do it, but I want the proceeds to go to education." He was always concerned. When kids would sit on his lap, he'd say, "How you doing in school? Do you like school?" And he realized he was one of the fortunate few who didn't excel at education that did well.

On October 5, 1993, more than 20,000 people attended Dale Earnhardt Day in Kannapolis. The state Department of Transportation named a street Dale Earnhardt Boulevard, and street signs were painted for sale. **Austin** *describes the day and talks about Earnhardt's importance to the town:*

That particular day, Brooks & Dunn sang the national anthem. Tom Dayvault (of the Cabarrus Regional Chamber of Commerce) was involved with that, and I was co-chair along with David Hawkins. At that time, Brooks & Dunn were at the very top of the country charts. Earnhardt comes pulling up in his pickup, and instead of him and somebody else, there's three people in the cab. He crawls out of the truck, and here's Kix Brooks and Ronnie Dunn. They had brought some of their cards as well. Our kids, rather than getting just Dale Earnhardt's autograph, they also got Brooks & Dunn.

Normally, Dale and I would go into an office for thirty or forty-five minutes and talk about community affairs. What's going on? Where do we need help? There was the story—you may have heard it—of the local church that needed the parking lot paved, and they were doing a fund-raiser. Dale wrote a personal check, but if they told where it came from, he'd bring his backhoe over there and dig it up. He didn't want anybody to know that those kinds of things were going on.

For the ceremony downtown, the mayor gave him the keys to the city, and we had lots of show cars and vendors.

It was a celebration for the community. He always wanted to involve the community because of his roots there. He did not want to place himself above his fan base. He signed autographs for hours and hours; he signed almost a thousand autographs an hour. It was incredible to watch him sign. How he didn't develop carpal tunnel syndrome . . . but he signed tons of autographs.

Then he went home and ducked into a black-tie outfit, and we had a continuation of the day here. He didn't want to do a roast, and Neil Bonnett was extremely involved in putting this evening together. We had Dale's mother and his brothers and his sisters here, and we sold corporate tables to General Motors and other big companies that raised a lot of dollars that evening.

We'd bring a guest to a microphone, and we would have kept this guest hidden from Dale for the evening. And they'd say, "Dale, do you remember when you were working in the mill?" And he'd have to guess who it was. Ned Jarrett, who urged his son Dale to victory in the Daytona 500, he did that same speech at a hidden mike. He said, "Come on, Dale, don't let him get inside of you. Stay low." And he kind of coached his own son to win the Daytona 500. Obviously, Dale knew who it was. He said he came up to Dale in the garage and apologized, and he said Dale stuck his finger in his chest and said, "Don't apologize to me. You've got to realize I'm a father, also."

We had Jeff Gordon here that evening, and Jeff had never won a race yet. We got to hear the stories about how Dale couldn't afford a set of tires. People would pitch in. Maybe the guy at the bank or the guy at the hardware store would loan him money, or they'd get together and buy him tires.

The fact that his racing empire is located here—it's between Kannapolis and Mooresville, so everybody takes credit for it—but he could have moved to bigger and better places, but he was just comfortable here. But he was not someone you'd just see at the grocery store. In our particular area, it's not unknown for me to go to the local cafeteria for lunch and see Ken Schrader and his crew sitting in there. Dale and Teresa had a private life, just as you'd assume someone of that status would, but when he traveled around, it was in blue jeans and a pickup truck. But he felt more comfortable on his tractor or in a pickup than he did in a black tie at the Waldorf.

That night, we had Delbert McClinton, Brooks & Dunn, and Dale Earnhardt at the microphone singing. If somebody would have had film of that, that was just incredible. These are his buddies and his corporate people and his family. It was a bit out of character for him. Without Neil Bonnett's help, Dale would never have done that day. I don't think he could comprehend his celebrity status. What if his own community had stayed away? What if nobody showed up? It was hard to get him to see that people would give a damn. But, when you think of Latrobe, Pennsylvania, who do you think of? Arnold Palmer. Dale Earnhardt was identified with Kannapolis.

Naturally, when Dale Earnhardt Boulevard first got signs, people confiscated them as souvenirs. Later, they had to put up a concrete monument, something you couldn't grab and run.

*In the late 1990s the Kannapolis Country Club was ready to do its Kids Day. While Earnhardt drove the black No. 3 Chevrolets, he didn't own those cars. Richard Childress did. So Dale would send over cars from Dale Earnhardt Inc. But this time **Jeff Austin** found a problem:*

I called DEI to find out how many show cars they were going to send over. Normally, we'd have gotten a transporter, a Cup car, a Busch car. Most of the time, it would be the blue No. 3 Busch car and the No. 1 Pennzoil car, plus Ron Hornaday's truck. I called and said, "This is Jeff. I'd like to make arrangements so we can find a place to put the cars. How many cars do you have?" They said, "Our show cars are all committed. We have none available." I told Judy Queen, who worked for Dale, and she reminded him that we had no show cars.

The day of the event, we had a parade of DEI vehicles. They sent three race-ready cars, a speedway car, a short-track car, whatever. He just took his inventory of race cars and sent them. There was no way he was going to come and not bring cars for the kids. The kids crawled all through those cars, although we made sure they didn't touch anything important.

I just called back and pulled rank.

⊰✦⊱

A few months before he died, Earnhardt bought a share in the Class A minor-league team the Piedmont Bollweevils, and the Carolina League team was renamed the Kannapolis Intimidators. Sadly, he never saw them play. **Tom Dayvault** *talked a month or two after Earnhardt's death:*

I think everybody wants to make it a tribute to him now, the spirit of the new team, the enthusiasm they're playing with. I look out at these young professional athletes working hard at their dream, and so few of them are going to make it. And they're winning because they're absolutely scrapping, and I just can't help but think that part of that spirit has to be because of who they are and who they were named after.

⊰✦⊱

Todd Parnell, *the Intimidators' general manager in 2001, discusses his team's late co-owner:*

It got to the point where people who knew him a lot better than I would say, "Dale wants you to go on." I don't know if it was after the memorial service we had for Dale at the stadium, but we knew it was the right thing to do.

We've learned that Dale would want us to just go out and play hard and win. If we have a tribute, it will be a working tribute.[2]

Parnell said a beautiful night and a great Intimidators crowd will make them think of Earnhardt:

I know at some point, we'll say, "Man, he would've enjoyed this."[3]

Jeff Austin talks about the media crush right after the 2001 Daytona 500:

When it happened, the community was overwhelmed with media. They came from everywhere; it was *People* magazine, *Time* magazine, the *Miami Herald*, the *Washington Post*. So many media came into our area, and everybody was looking for an angle. And we understand how private Teresa is, and out of respect to our fallen hero, we wanted to make sure the stories were accurate. We would try not to do things that would present a negative image.

Charlotte (later Lowe's) Motor Speedway, Earnhardt's "home" track, was the site of lots of highlights and lowlights for Earnhardt. That's appropriate, since the mile-and-a-half track isn't far from Dale's hometown of Kannapolis.

He got his big break in a Sportsman race at Charlotte, as he and Dave Marcis ran cars for car owner Rod Osterlund.

Dale's first Cup race came at Charlotte, where he started thirty-third and finished twenty-second in Ed Negre's car in 1975. He earned $2,425 and finished one spot ahead of his future car owner, Richard Childress.

In the 1987 Coca-Cola 600, Earnhardt had to go into the garage for repairs. When it was announced that he'd returned to the race eighty-five laps down, reporters in the media center cheered.

One year, Earnhardt was sitting on pit road when Ernie Irvan and Alan Kulwicki got together. One of them hit a tire and bounced into Earnhardt's car. When Dale tried to return to the race, he lost a wheel leaving pit road. He sat there helplessly while his tire rounded turn one and headed for turn two.

Earnhardt's crew, the Flying Aces, raced down pit road afoot in hopes that they could beat the flatbed truck that NASCAR was sending to pick up the 3 car. It was a scene out of the Keystone Kops, and only the ABE fans (Anybody But Earnhardt) could enjoy it.

Another year, Earnhardt started at the back. Earnhardt haters and baiters crowed . . . until he roared through the field and finished second.

In the 1993 all-star race at Charlotte, Earnhardt jumped the restart late in the race. Mark Martin, who was leading, was a little nonplussed when NASCAR didn't send Earnhardt to the back of the field. Since it was The Winston, they restarted again with Earnhardt still second. Martin, perhaps still smarting from the first restart, bobbled a bit on the second restart. Earnhardt got a clean jump this time and went on to his record third all-star victory.

Earnhardt didn't get a lot of wins at Charlotte— although his five Cup victories there put him just behind Bobby Allison and Darrell Waltrip, who had six each—but he had a blast. And the "home" fans were typical race fans.

Most of them got a blast out of Earnhardt; others just blasted him.

———❦———

Humpy Wheeler, president/general manager of Lowe's Motor Speedway since the 1970s, says his favorite memory of Earnhardt at the track came in the early 1980s. Earnhardt wasn't too far removed from his 1980 championship, and the track was still Charlotte Motor Speedway:

My favorite memory of Earnhardt at the speedway was not in the race car. He'd had a bad wreck at Pocono, with a broken collarbone and a pretty good concussion on top of that. So I called him up there, because I was concerned. He said he was going to fly back the next day—this was like Tuesday or Wednesday.

At that time, I had a '37 Ford coupe with a flathead engine in it. I had it in the Unocal building, and it was just like something his father used to race. He had his car parked at the airport, so I said, "Come on by the track." I always thought that, after a race driver gets hurt, they need to go back to a track right away to get this out of their system. It's a difficult time for a race driver after he's hurt the first time, and I've seen a lot of people who did not make it back. Over a period of time, they don't amount to much.

So he came out here. It was a nice day, summertime, and we had nothing going on at the track. I left my office and showed him the car like the ones his dad drove. His dad was a tremendous influence, probably even more after he died than when he was alive. Dale didn't say much. I could tell he was in a lot of pain, since he didn't take painkillers. He said to me, "Don't worry about me; I'm going to be all right." Just the way he said it, I knew the first bad wreck didn't affect him that badly.

I think having that old car there, his home track, put things back into context. I thought, *This guy's going to make it.* He'd already won a championship—this was 1981. That was a very bad accident, and that's the thing I remember most of Earnhardt at the speedway.

---

*Naturally, Earnhardt figured in a lot of **Wheeler**'s memories at the speedway:*

At Charlotte, I remember Earnhardt for "the Pass in the Grass," plus the Geoff Bodine whack in the second turn in The Winston, but I remember him better for the first night (all-star) race in 1992. Earnhardt was leading, with Kyle Petty second and Davey Allison third coming off the third turn on the last lap. Kyle pinched Earnhardt into the wall in turn four. Usually, the reverse would happen when Earnhardt tangled with someone. Earnhardt got into the wall, and Davey and Kyle went on and Davey crashed at the start-finish line.

But what I remember was Earnhardt being such a good sport about it and laughing. He was not mad at Kyle at all. He just shook it off, and said, "That's racin'." He laughed, and I thought that showed a lot of maturity then.

---

*Longtime crew chief **Barry Dodson** thought of Dale before the Coca-Cola 600 on May 27, 2001:*

This is Charlotte, and he always seemed to be the fan favorite here. I still find myself thinking he's going to be at the racetrack no matter where we are. It doesn't have to be at his home track. It isn't just here at the home track for thirty race teams. I just keep thinking he's going to be there and the No. 3 car's going to be there. He's sorely missed, in my heart especially.

He was so good to my little boys. They spent a lot of time with him and with Dale Jr. Back when we didn't have the motor homes and stayed in motels, I'd knock on the door early in the morning. My boy would get in the bed with Dale Jr. We'd come back, and they'd be at the swimming pool. Teresa would watch them all day. We spent a lot of time at the lake house with them.[4]

---

*When **Jerry Gappens** took over the Charlotte Motor Speedway public relations department in January 1993, he got a shock:*

The May race was my first, and I was in the media center for qualifying night. There was a big commotion, and I was wondering what it was. A lot of fans were booing, and the rest were cheering, and I realized Earnhardt had just come out on the track. I had never heard that kind of response just for someone going onto the track. I guess Dale had won the championship the year before, so he really was in his prime.

---

*Just before his death in 1993, **Davey Allison** talked about seeing an Earnhardt fan up on the trioval fence at Charlotte. Allison was asked how he could tell he was an Earnhardt fan at nearly 200 miles an hour:*

He was wearing an Earnhardt T-shirt and cap. Hey, you don't wait until you get there, because it would be a blur. You look ahead.

Anyway, every time I'd come around the track, he'd throw me the bird, you know, the finger. It must have been about twenty laps, and I was getting tired of it. After a while, I got mad and threw him the bird back. He was so shocked, he fell off the fence.

Jerry Gappens recalls bringing Dale's mother, Martha Earnhardt, to the Charlotte track for a luncheon so she could talk about her son:

One of my favorite Earnhardt stories didn't involve Dale. This was when Dale Jr. was a rookie in Busch (in 1998), and we brought Martha Earnhardt, Dale's mother and Dale Jr.'s grandmother, in for a media luncheon. She was real nervous about talking in front of the media, but she came to the luncheon, and she relaxed. She had some great stories about Dale as a child and as a teenager.

What came across to us in attendance was this—we knew Dale as the Intimidator and the seven-time champion, but you tend to forget that he's a son, a husband, a father. He had the same relationships as most of us, and she told us what he was like as a human being. To her, he was her son, not the world-famous athlete and race-car driver. She had some good stories. She said the first time she thought of him as a celebrity was when she was in a grocery store and saw his likeness on Sundrop cans or a Wheaties box.

I was moderating the program, and I asked her, "Did you spank him?" She said, "Yeah, I took the belt to him many times." You don't think of anyone disciplining Earnhardt.

Morris Metcalfe, former chief scorer and timer for NASCAR, got an Earnhardt autograph by accident:

We were at Charlotte in 1998, and Dale had a habit of coming to the NASCAR trailer. He'd tell the officials, "As long as I'm over here, fans won't bug me for autographs, and the people over at my car can get something done." Well, I walked in, and he says, "Here's somebody who needs an autograph." So he jumped up, grabbed my hat, and he signed the white bill. I said, "You just ruined that hat." He said, "Hell, you can get twenty bucks for that hat."

***

Jerry Gappens says Earnhardt liked to help the track officials, even with media events:

We used to use him for press conferences, and Humpy (Wheeler) likes to pick the winner of The Winston. He was going to pick Earnhardt, so we asked Dale if he could come. Earnhardt cleared his schedule so he could make it. Humpy was going to do a magic trick, something to entertain the media. It got down to two choices, Dale Jarrett or Dale Earnhardt, and he said, "Dale's going to win it."

It was going to be Earnhardt, and Earnhardt wanted to hide from the media. He didn't want to be seen and ruin the magic trick. If they saw Earnhardt, they'd know he was the pick. He actually hid out in his pickup truck with tinted windows so nobody'd see him until Humpy got to the punch line of the magic trick. Then he emerged from the truck, went through the curtain onto the stage. So he liked that element of surprise. When he was vintage Earnhardt, he liked to entertain people. He understood the value of show and entertainment, even the value of a press conference.

Notes

Chapter 1: The Legend

1. *NASCAR Winston Cup 25th Anniversary.* Charlotte, N.C.: UMI Publications Inc., 1995, 43.

2. Vehorn, Frank, *The Intimidator.* Asheboro, N.C.: Down Home Press, 1991, 102.

3. *Sports Illustrated Special Commemorative Issue,* 74.

Chapter 2: Young Dale

1. Chevrolet advance notes, Martinsville, April 8, 2000.

2. Ibid.

Chapter 3: Tales of Dale

1. *Atlanta Journal-Constitution,* Feb. 20, 2001.

2. Ibid.

3. Ibid.

4. Associated Press, Jacksonville.com., Feb. 21, 2001.

5. *Winston-Salem Journal,* March 7, 2001.

6. Through Travis Tritt's publicist.

7. *Nashville Tennessean*, Feb. 22, 2001.

8. *Atlanta Journal-Constitution*, Feb. 20, 2001.

9. *Sports Illustrated Special Commemorative Issue*, 76.

Chapter 4: Devilish Dale

1. Dodge pit notes, Feb. 20, 2001.

2. Vehorn, Frank, *The Intimidator*. Asheboro, N.C.: Down Home Press, 1991, 336.

Chapter 5: Racing with the Man

1. Vehorn, Frank, *The Intimidator*. Asheboro, N.C.: Down Home Press, 1991, 68.

2. Chevrolet notes.

3. *Sports Illustrated Special Commemorative Issue*, 76.

4. Chevrolet pit notes, Martinsville, Oct. 3, 1999.

5. Ibid.

6. Chevrolet pit notes.

7. *Sports Illustrated Special Commemorative Issue*, 76.

8. Chevrolet pit notes, March 12, 2000.

9. Vehorn, (from Little Bud Moore's foreword).

10. Chevrolet pit notes, Martinsville, April 8, 2000.

Chapter 6: Dale's Turn

1. Chevrolet advance notes, Indianapolis, Aug. 4, 2000.

2. Tiedemann, George, *Trading Paint: Dale Earnhardt vs. Jeff Gordon*. Kingston, N.Y.: Total Sports Illustrated, 2001, 110.

3. Vehorn, Frank, *The Intimidator*. Asheboro, N.C.: Down Home Press, 1991, 331.

4. Tiedemann, 96.

5. *Stock Car Magazine*, June 2000, 24.

6. Chevrolet pit notes, Talladega, April 14, 2000.

7. Vehorn, 332.

8. *Stock Car Racing Magazine*, June 2000, 30.

9. *NASCAR Winston Cup Series 25th Anniversary*. Charlotte, N.C.: UMI Publications Inc., 1995, 41.

10. Chevrolet pit notes, Martinsville, Oct. 3, 1999.

11. Tiedemann, 60–61.

12. Ibid., 43.

13. Chevrolet advance notes, New Hampshire, July 3, 2000.

14. *Stock Car Racing Magazine*, November 2000, 21.

15. Chevrolet advance notes, Indianapolis, Aug. 4, 2000.

16. Chevrolet pit notes, Atlanta, March 12, 2000.

17. Ibid.

18. Chevrolet pit notes, Oct. 15, 2000.

19. Vehorn, 140.

20. *People* magazine, March 5, 2001, 106.

21. Ibid., 103.

22. Vehorn, 155.

23. Chevrolet advance notes, Indianapolis, Aug. 4, 2000.

24. Tiedemann, 81.

25. Ibid., 73.

26. Ibid., 76.

27. Vehorn, 67.

28. *Stock Car Magazine*, June 2000, 31.

29. *Stock Car Racing Magazine*, June 2000, 23.

30. Chevrolet advance notes, Atlanta, Nov. 18, 2000.

31. Chevrolet advance notes, Atlanta, Nov. 15, 2000.

32. Chevrolet advance notes, Indianapolis, Aug. 4, 2000.

33. Huff, Richard, *Stock Car Champions, Running with NASCAR's Best*. Chicago: Bonus Books, 2000, 108.

34. *Stock Car Racing Magazine*, November 2000, 22.

Chapter 7: The Angel in Black

1. Tiedemann, George, *Trading Paint: Dale Earnhardt vs. Jeff Gordon*. Kingston, N.Y.: Total Sports Illustrated, 55.

2. Team statement from Morgan-McClure Racing.

Chapter 8: Speed Shifts

1. *Charlotte Observer,* June 3, 1999.

2. Pontiac advance notes, Sept. 7, 1999.

3. Tiedemann, George, *Trading Paint: Dale Earnhardt vs. Jeff Gordon*. Kingston, N.Y.: Total Sports Illustrated, 70.

4. Morgan-McClure pit notes after Charlotte, May 21, 2001.

5. *Sports Illustrated Special Commemorative Issue,* 78.

6. Vehorn, Frank, *The Intimidator.* Asheboro, N.C.: Down Home Press, 1991, 344.

7. Tiedemann, 54.

8. Ibid.

9. Dodge pit notes, May 6, 2001.

10. Tiedemann, 82.

11. Associated Press, CBS SportsLine.com, Feb. 21, 2001.

12. *Winston-Salem Journal's Special Earnhardt Edition,* Feb. 23, 2001.

13. Track statement by Lowe's Motor Speedway, Feb. 18, 2001.

14. Team statement by Morgan-McClure Racing, Feb. 18, 2001.

15. Dodge pit notes after Daytona 500, Feb. 20, 2001.

Chapter 10: Hometown Boy

1. *Charlotte Observer,* Feb. 25, 2001.

2. *Salisbury Post,* April 4, 2001.

3. Ibid.

4. *Winston-Salem Journal,* May 25, 2001.

DALE EARNHARDT'S
76 CUP VICTORIES

1. April 1, 1979   Volunteer 500   Bristol
2. March 16, 1980   Atlanta 500   Atlanta
3. March 30, 1980   Valleydale Southeastern 500   Bristol
4. July 12, 1980   Busch Nashville 420   Nashville
5. Sept. 28, 1980   Old Dominion 500   Martinsville
6. Oct. 5, 1980   National 500   Charlotte
7. April 4, 1982   CRC Chemicals Rebel 500   Darlington
8. July 16, 1983   Busch Nashville 420   Nashville
9. July 31, 1983   Talladega 500   Talladega
10. July 29, 1984   Talladega 500   Talladega
11. Nov. 11, 1984   Atlanta Journal 500   Atlanta
12. Feb. 24, 1985   Miller High Life 400   Richmond
13. April 6, 1985   Valleydale 500   Bristol
14. Aug. 24, 1985   Busch 500   Bristol
15. Sept. 22, 1985   Goody's 500   Martinsville
16. April 13, 1986   TranSouth 500   Darlington
17. April 20, 1986   First Union 400   N. Wilkesboro
18. May 25, 1986   Coca-Cola 600   Charlotte
19. Oct. 5, 1986   Oakwood Homes 500   Charlotte
20. Nov. 2, 1986   Atlanta Journal 500   Atlanta

21.	March 1, 1987	Goodwrench 500	Rockingham
22.	March 8, 1987	Miller High Life 400	Richmond
23.	March 29, 1987	TranSouth 500	Darlington
24.	April 5, 1987	First Union 400	N. Wilkesboro
25.	April 12, 1987	Valleydale Meats 500	Bristol
26.	April 26, 1987	Sovran Bank 500	Martinsville
27.	June 28, 1987	Miller American 400	Michigan
28.	July 19, 1987	Summer 500	Pocono
29.	Aug. 22, 1987	Busch 500	Bristol
30.	Sept. 6, 1987	Southern 500	Darlington
31.	Sept. 13, 1987	Wrangler Jeans Indigo 400	Richmond
32.	April 24, 1988	Motorcraft Quality Parts 500	Atlanta
33.	May 1, 1988	Pannill Sweatshirts 500	Martinsville
34.	Aug. 27, 1988	Busch 500	Bristol
35.	April 16, 1989	First Union 400	N. Wilkesboro
36.	June 4, 1989	Budweiser 500	Dover
37.	Sept. 3, 1989	Heinz Southern 500	Darlington
38.	Sept. 17, 1989	Peak Performance 500	Dover
39.	Nov. 19, 1989	Atlanta Journal 500	Atlanta
40.	March 18, 1990	Motorcraft Quality Parts 500	Atlanta
41.	April 1, 1990	TranSouth 500	Darlington
42.	May 6, 1990	Winston 500	Talladega
43.	June 24, 1990	Miller Genuine Draft 400	Michigan
44.	July 7, 1990	Pepsi 400	Daytona
45.	July 28, 1990	DieHard 500	Talladega
46.	Sept. 2, 1990	Heinz Southern 500	Darlington
47.	Sept. 9, 1990	Miller Genuine Draft 400	Richmond
48.	Nov. 4, 1990	Checker 500	Phoenix

49.	Feb. 24, 1991	Pontiac Excitement 400	Richmond
50.	April 28, 1991	Hanes 500	Martinsville
51.	July 28, 1991	DieHard 500	Talladega
52.	Sept. 29, 1991	Tyson Holly Farms 400	N. Wilkesboro
53.	May 24, 1992	Coca-Cola 600	Charlotte
54.	March 28, 1993	TranSouth Financial 500	Darlington
55.	May 30, 1993	Coca-Cola 600	Charlotte
56.	June 6, 1993	Budweiser 500	Dover
57.	July 3, 1993	Pepsi 400	Daytona
58.	July 18, 1993	Miller Genuine Draft 500	Pocono
59.	July 25, 1993	DieHard 500	Talladega
60.	March 27, 1994	TranSouth 400	Darlington
61.	April 10, 1994	Food City 500	Bristol
62.	May 1, 1994	Winston Select 500	Talladega
63.	Oct. 23, 1994	AC-Delco 500	Rockingham
64.	April 9, 1995	First Union 400	N. Wilkesboro
65.	May 7, 1995	Save-Mart Supermarkets 300K	Sears Point
66.	Aug. 5, 1995	Brickyard 400	Indianapolis
67.	Sept. 24, 1995	Goody's 500	Martinsville
68.	Nov. 12, 1995	NAPA 500	Atlanta
69.	Feb. 25, 1996	Goodwrench Service 400	Rockingham
70.	March 10, 1996	Purolator 500	Atlanta
71.	Feb. 15, 1998	Daytona 500	Daytona
72.	April 25, 1999	DieHard 500	Talladega
73.	Aug. 28, 1999	Goody's Headache Powder 500	Bristol
74.	Oct. 17, 1999	Winston 500	Talladega
75.	March 12, 2000	Cracker Barrel 500	Atlanta
76.	Oct. 15, 2000	Winston 500	Talladega

INDEX